D0402919

THE **Art** OF THE **Steal**

ALSO BY FRANK W. ABAGNALE

Catch Me If You Can (with Stan Redding)

THE Art OF THE Steal

How to Protect Yourself and Your Business from Fraud—America's #1 Crime

Frank W. Abagnale

BROADWAY BOOKS
NEW YORK

BROADWAY

This book is designed to provide accurate and authoritative information on the subject of the prevention of fraud. It is sold with the understanding that neither the Author nor the Publisher is engaged in rendering legal, accounting, or other professional services by publishing this book. As each individual situation is unique, questions relevant to the prevention of fraud and specific to the individual should be addressed to an appropriate professional to ensure that the situation has been evaluated carefully and appropriately. The Authors and Publisher specifically disclaim any liability, loss, or risk which is incurred as a consequence, directly or indirectly, of the use and application of any of the contents of this work.

Broadway Books titles may be purchased for business or promotional use or for special sales. For information, please write to: Special Markets Department, Random House, Inc., 1540 Broadway, New York, NY 10036.

BROADWAY BOOKS and its logo, a letter B bisected on the diagonal, are trademarks of Broadway Books, a division of Random House, Inc.

Visit our website at www.broadwaybooks.com

Library of Congress Cataloging-in-Publication Data

Abagnale, Frank W., 1948–
    The art of the steal: how to protect yourself and your business from
fraud—America's #1 crime / by Frank W. Abagnale.—1st ed.
        p. cm.
        1. Fraud—United States. 2. Swindlers and swindling—United States.
    3. Consumer protection—United States. I. Title.
HV6695 .A23 2001
362.88—dc21   2001035607

FIRST EDITION

Designed by Lisa Sloane

ISBN 0-7679-0683-7

10   9   8   7   6   5   4   3   2   1

To my wife, Kelly,
and my three sons,
Scott, Chris, and Sean

CONTENTS

PROLOGUE

[WHAT DID SHE **WANT?**]

It began on a winter day with a seemingly ordinary message on an answering machine. It was from someone at the bank. Something about her new Dodge Ram pickup and the payment past due on the loan. Michelle Brown figured it was one more of those misdirected calls. Not only didn't she own a pickup, but anyone who knew her realized that there was no way she'd ever own a pickup. She had a penchant for sports cars, and she actually detested Dodges. Because her name was a common one, it was normal for her to get messages for some other Brown. In the past, she'd received calls for Mike Brown, a message looking for a Brown to pick up relatives from Hawaii who were waiting impatiently at the airport, and a call from some Uncle Brown about her horse she didn't have.

Michelle Brown was a single woman in her late twenties. She lived in southern California and worked as a credit analyst. She was cheerful and luminous, and people found her fun to be around. Friends were always telling her how she was too nice. She worked hard and was tidy with her finances. She owned fifteen credit cards, but had never been late on a single payment. Ever since she was seventeen, she had had perfect credit. It was a thing with her. She liked everything in her life to be perfect.

She returned the call. She told the bank officer that there must be a mistake; she hadn't bought a truck. The officer quickly agreed that he must have the wrong Michelle Brown. The phone numbers on the credit application weren't working, and he had gotten this number from directory assistance in the hope that it was the right person. And the application did have her address on it. To prove beyond a doubt that it was another Michelle Brown he was searching for, she told him her Social Security number. She was stunned—it was the same one that was on the application.

Alarmed, she called up the credit reporting agencies and told them that something fishy was going on. They put a fraud alert on her credit and promised to send out a report on her recent purchases. She checked with the Division of Motor Vehicles, and learned something astonishing: a duplicate driver's license had recently been issued to a Michelle Brown. Someone else was using her name, her address, her Social Security number, and her driver's license. It was as if someone was slowly erasing her identity.

When her credit report arrived, there were delinquent bills on it for thousands of dollars, including a sizable phone bill and even a bill for liposuction treatments. What was this? She'd heard about people who got crosswise with creditors, but never her. She became afraid to open her own mailbox, for fear of what new debt would be awaiting her. In time, she would learn that there was an arrest warrant out for Michelle Brown in Texas. The charge was conspiracy to sell marijuana. She had never broken a law, any law. How could she be wanted?

Someone had appropriated her identity, but who and how? She felt chained to some stranger without a face, but with her name. How dare someone steal her name! She thought chillingly about the movie *The Net*, in which the actress Sandra Bullock plays a computer software tester whose identity gets erased by criminals.

Her whole life was thrust into darkness. She had just started a new job, but found herself unable to concentrate on her work. She had no appetite for food. She slept fitfully, if at all. Her bright personality darkened; friends didn't recognize her. Her relationship with her boyfriend, a professional volleyball player, became strained and finally ended. He didn't understand the depth of her distress. She spent a lot of time crying.

She began to worry that the other Michelle Brown might break into her apartment in search of her passport or her checks, or who knew what else. Whenever she got home after dark, she carried a flashlight and meticulously searched through the rooms, including every closet. She was weary and angry. When she went to bed at night, she felt haunted and scared. If she heard the slightest noise, her first instinct was that the woman calling herself Michelle Brown was out there lurking in the dark, right beneath her window. She shook with fear. Who was this person who was stealing her identity? Why, of all the people in the world, did she pick her? And what did she want?

[PUTTING DOWN
A POSITIVE CON]

There's this thing they always say about con men: they live a chameleon existence. That was certainly true for me. I'd find myself in an unfamiliar situation and I'd quickly adapt. And that's just what I did when they sent me to prison. I adapted to the role of prisoner, and I lived a life dictated by my imagination. In so many ways, the role felt small and unreal, when in fact it was the only real role I had lived in a long time.

Being cooped up in a confined space didn't suit me, so I sort of half-lived, numbed to my existence, waiting patiently for a second chance. My battle plan was to always be on my best behavior, in the hope that this would enable me to get out early. The problem was, the better I behaved, the more convinced the prison officials were that I was up to no good. Twice I came up for parole and was refused. One of the members of the review committee actually said to me, "I see that your record is perfect, and that's a problem. That tells me you're still conning the prison and getting away with it." In other words, if I had gotten into some fist fights or mauled a guard, then I might have gotten parole.

Everything I did right was always assumed to have an ulterior motive. That's what happens when you have a reputation, and the reputation is that of a master con man.

I had been imprisoned for six months in France and another six months in Sweden, and now I was in my third year of a twelve-year sentence in the Federal Correctional Institution in Petersburg, Virginia. But I wasn't one of those inmates constantly prattling about his innocence. There was no doubt that I deserved to be behind bars.

LIVING LARGE

For five immature years, I had lived a life of illusion and tricks. I had enjoyed a misguided and regrettable run as one of the most successful con artists the world has ever known. A lengthy list of exploits had added to my iconography, all of them income-producing. I had masqueraded as a Pan Am airline pilot (don't worry, I never actually took the controls), a pediatrician (I let my interns do the medical work), an assistant district attorney (I passed the bar while skipping the law school part), a sociology professor, and a stockbroker, all between the ages of sixteen and twenty-one. I had never gone beyond the tenth grade, but I had a limitless talent for fantasy and I lived a million lives in those five years. Before the authorities discovered my true identity, I was known throughout the world as "The Skywayman." The *New York Times*, in its coverage, referred to me as "The Great Impostor."

What landed me in jail was my other bad habit, which was my enthusiasm for passing bad checks. The main reason I adopted those guises was to give me credibility when I cashed hot checks—and to satisfy my great taste for women. Hotel clerks and merchants didn't question pilots and doctors too closely. Through my various hustles, I passed something like $2.5 million worth of checks, a blizzard of paper that I scattered in earnest throughout all fifty states and twenty-six countries, all before I was legally allowed to drink. I was proficient enough at cashing fraudulent checks that I earned the distinction of becoming one of the most hunted criminals by the FBI.

All bad things come to an end, of course, and I was finally caught by the French police after a stewardess recognized me from a wanted poster when I was doing some shopping. I was twenty-one. Convicted of forgery, I spent six months in a French prison, was extradited to Sweden, where I was again convicted of forgery, and served another six months in the prison in Malmo. Then I was turned over to the authorities in the United States.

That transition, however, got mildly delayed. After my plane landed in New York and was taxiing toward the gate, where the law awaited me, I escaped through the toilet onto the runway and took off. Within weeks, I got caught at the Montreal Airport, and was sent to the Federal Detention Center in Atlanta, to await trial. But I escaped by conning guards into thinking that I was a prison inspector. That kept me on the lam a bit longer. Actually, all of one month longer.

By now, a lot of cops had memorized my face, and I could never go anywhere without looking over my shoulder. The funny thing is that I never resorted to disguises. I didn't dye my hair or grow a beard. The reason why I didn't was because I was really sensitive to retaining my true identity. Regardless of the various aliases I adopted, I'd always be Frank Adams or Frank Williams or Frank something. I wanted to keep at least part of my real name intact. And because I didn't take further precautions, I did realize that I was going to get caught, and probably sooner rather than later. Any criminal recognizes that the law sleeps, but it never dies.

Finally, one day I was walking past the Waldorf-Astoria Hotel in New York. Two plainclothes detectives were standing on the street corner, munching on hot dogs. One of them stared quizzically at me and yelled, "Hey Frank." I turned around, and they identified themselves as police officers and said that I was Frank Abagnale. I vigorously denied it, but they knew better and took me in. Within a couple of hours, I had been positively identified. The following day, I was put in the custody of the FBI.

THE END OF THE ROAD

It didn't take long for the crush of state and federal complaints to pour in: forgery, passing worthless checks, swindling, mail fraud, counterfeiting, and on and on. Prosecutors and U.S. attorneys from around the country competed to be the one who would bring me to trial, as if I were some sort of lottery prize. They all had strong cases. There was a lengthy list of witnesses willing and able to identify me and testify against me.

An arbitrary decision was made to bring me to trial in Atlanta. There were plenty of cities where I was not likely to be honored by the Chamber of Commerce, but I had done a lot of damage in Atlanta. I had spent a year there pretending to be a doctor, and I doubted that I was remembered fondly. And, of course, there was that little incident of escaping from a federal prison. Needless to say, it wouldn't have been my first choice as a trial site. I had a good lawyer, though, and he was able to broker a favorable deal. In April 1971, I appeared before a federal judge and pleaded guilty to all the crimes "known and unknown" that I had committed in the United States. There were hundreds of outstanding charges against me, but the judge collapsed them into eight counts. He sentenced me to ten years on each of seven counts of fraud, to run concurrently, and two years on the one count of escape, which were to be served consecutively. And he remanded me to prison in Virginia.

TWENTY CENTS AN HOUR

The Petersburg jail wasn't the worst place to do time. It was a far cry from the French jail that had shattered my soul and nearly killed me. But it wasn't a great place to be, either. The days merged into one continuous blur.

I kept to myself and did my work diligently. I was assigned as a clerk in this big tire factory that recapped tires for government vehicles. I earned all of twenty cents an hour, and I was definitely not allowed a checking account. On the weekends, they showed movies to the inmates, the same ones that they played in town. The prison used to pay the town projectionist to come in and run the projector. But then they decided to train an inmate to do it, and for some reason they chose me. You had to be licensed to do the job, and so I was trained and took a test and got a license. I was the only one who was taught how to run the projector, and even when I was sick, I had to drag myself out of my cell on the weekends and show the movies.

When we had idle time, we'd sit around and compare war stories. I was constantly bemused by the dumb acts that landed some of the other inmates in jail. There were these two teenagers from Long Island. They were smoking dope one night when they encountered this Jamaican guy who introduced himself only as "Mustard." After hanging out with them, Mustard asked if they wanted to rob a bank. They had never stolen anything, but he made it sound like a rollicking adventure. The plans were a little ragged. Mustard waited for them a few blocks away from the bank. He gave them guns. They drove a car one of them had borrowed from his father and parked it right in front of the branch, where surveillance cameras were whirring. They wore no disguises. They entered, marched up to a teller, and collected five thousand dollars, all while the cameras taped them. They drove the two blocks to their rendezvous with Mustard. He took the five thousand dollars, let them keep the guns, and said he'd meet them that evening. After they drove a few more blocks, the cops had them surrounded. The police said they'd let them off if they gave up the mastermind. All they knew, they said, was his name was Mustard. And he had the money. In court, the judge said they were so stupid that he was giving them each five years.

Another guy from New York had never done anything wrong, either, but one day, badly in need of money, he decided to rob a bank. Almost randomly, he selected a branch on Lexington Avenue. He went up to a teller and made his demands. She said, "You better turn around." Everyone behind him had a gun trained on him. The branch was beneath what was then the New York City headquarters of the FBI, and all the customers were agents cashing their paychecks.

When the others learned why I was there—for passing $2.5 million of bum checks—they were practically drooling. At least I was put away for being clever.

But I didn't make any friends in prison. I felt no connection to the other inmates. No one I met felt like a defeated soul, a loser, but merely a winner waiting out a temporary setback. They were in a dangerous state of denial. Of all the inmates I met, none was remorseful about the crimes he had committed, and that genuinely bothered me. No one ever said to me, "Gee, I really screwed up my life. I'm going to set things straight." It was very demoralizing to me that in all the time I was in prison, not one of the six hundred inmates ever said that he was going to change. Instead, everyone was planning the next scam. And they were all trying to learn from me. Among inmates, con men are always looked up to as the upper echelon of criminals. Fellow inmates were always pressing me for applicable tips on getting fake IDs and ways to counterfeit checks.

LETTING TIME SERVE ME

I wasn't thinking that way anymore. I had crossed a crucial threshold. Crime no longer seemed romantic or noble, or in any way appealing to me. I had lived a life of incredible intensity. I knew I had made tragic mistakes and I wanted to make amends. So I'd refuse to offer them any advice that would merely perpetuate the treadmill they were on. I'd just brush them off by saying, "Do you just want to come back to the joint again? You know you'll get caught."

Don't misunderstand me, I don't believe prison rehabilitated me, or in any way fostered my moral and spiritual reform. A bright light didn't appear and God didn't speak to me. I simply grew up. I was a teenager when I was forging checks. As I got older, my conscience began to bother me. When I went into a bank at sixteen and wrote a bad check, I'd think, they've got millions of dollars, they won't miss a few hundred or a few thousand. A couple of years later, I would worry that the teller might lose her job. I started to look at things more rationally and as a more mature person. I had tired of a life where everyone you meet believes you to be someone you're not. It's pretty hard to have a serious relationship with a woman when you're lying and using a phony name.

And so, with my changed outlook, I never sat around thinking of my next scam. I had no idea what I would do when I got out, but whether I ended up roping cattle or selling kitchen appliances, the one thing I was certain about was that I would never pull another scam.

There's this whole thing about going to prison and serving time, or going to prison and have time serve you. I wanted time to serve me. I managed to get my GED, and I took some college courses to advance my limited education. Above all else, I dearly wanted to get out and rejoin society while I still had the time to construct a new life. I didn't know what that new life could be, but I was itching to start it.

As a con man, though, I was always given a hard time. My father died, and like all inmates, I expected to be allowed a funeral visit home. But I was denied this routine privilege, because the Bureau of Prisons was afraid that I would escape and embarrass it. All these murderers and violent criminals were allowed funeral visits, but not me.

With my parole rejections, I began to believe that I was going to have to serve every last day of my sentence. I was disturbed and baffled, but in prison you have no rights. Finally, on my third try, after having served three years of my sentence, I was granted parole. When I was asked what city I would like to be paroled in, I said that I didn't really care. I only asked that it not be New York. My mother and brothers were there, and I didn't think that I could handle the family situation just yet. I also thought New York offered far too many enticements for someone just embarking on a legitimate life.

I ended up being paroled to Houston, Texas. My instructions were to report to a United States parole officer within seventy-two hours of my arrival. And I was told that it would very much behoove me to find a job within those three days.

WELCOME BACK TO THE REAL WORLD

The real world was beckoning again, but I couldn't be sure I was ready for it. People who have never been in jail don't understand what happens to a person. Even if you're serving a short sentence, when you're in prison, you become institutionalized. You get up in the morning, and breakfast has been prepared for you. They take care of your medical needs. Your clothes are cleaned and pressed for you. You get lunch. You get dinner. You become dependent. Then, all of a sudden, the government says, you're free. You're on the train to Houston. You have no money. You don't know a soul. Even for an intelligent, resourceful person like myself, it was very difficult. Nobody likes an ex-con, and nobody likes an ex-con less than an employer, whether it's a bank officer or a bowling alley manager.

Even those who were ostensibly there to help me weren't that helpful. The supervisor at the parole office was both cold and defensive. He made it clear that, to him, any ex-con was repellent. "I don't want you here, Abagnale," he told me. "You were forced on me. I don't like con men, and I want you to know that before we even start our relationship. I don't think you'll last a month before you're headed back to the joint. Whatever, you had better understand this. Don't make a wrong move with me. I want to see you every week, and when you get a job, I'll be out to see you regularly. Mess up, and I'm sure you will, and I'll personally escort you back to prison."

I didn't waste my time with talk. This guy was not going to be any help. I was on my own.

My first job was at a pizza parlor. I was a combination waiter, cook, and managerial trainee. I didn't bother to tell my boss that I was an ex-convict, and I wasn't asked. I was an early believer in don't ask, don't tell. The work was about as tedious as you might imagine. I liked eating pizza well enough, but I didn't much care for serving it. On the side, to make ends meet, I drove a bus from the airport to downtown.

No matter how menial the job, I was a good worker. I was even entrusted with depositing the cash receipts at the pizza parlor, and every dollar got to the bank. But after about six months on the job, officials of the chain that operated the place took a closer look into my background in anticipation of naming me a manager of one of their shops. Discovering that I was a federal prison parolee, they fired me.

So I moved on. Within a week, I was hired as a stockboy in a supermarket, assigned to the night shift. Again, when applying for the job, I didn't point out my dark past. The job wasn't much, but one day I noticed a customer, a fetching young woman who was in graduate school. We started dating and we really clicked. I didn't reveal my past for several months, and when I did, while we were sitting on a park bench, she at first found it difficult to accept. But she realized that I was just a naïve kid when I committed the crimes, and that I was a changed man.

Her parents had a harder time warming to the notion of their daughter's ex-con suitor. She really worked on them, especially her father. She pleaded with him to go talk to my parole officer, for she knew he would tell him how I had changed. That pessimistic parole supervisor had assigned me to a highly supportive and unbiased parole officer who did all he could to elevate my spirits. He was a truly decent man, a born-again Christian with a generous humor who was always bringing up God in our discussions. We had a great relationship.

Finally, to appease her, my girlfriend's father did call my parole officer. He gave me a good build-up. He said, "I don't think Frank will ever go back to prison. He went down the wrong road, and he's smart enough to know the right road now." But then he had to insert a final thought: "I must tell you, though, I have five daughters, and I wouldn't let one of them get within six miles of Frank." That set me back months.

But finally they did accept me, and my girlfriend and I got married soon afterward.

After nine months in the supermarket, the district manager buttonholed me one day and said that they were opening a new store in the suburbs, which would be their first store to stay open twenty-four hours. He told me he wanted me to be the night manager. I was flattered. I liked that job, and I did it well. As always, I had made a point of being presentable and personable, and was dedicated to what I was doing. Then came the familiar story. A security check turned up my checkered past, and once again I was brusquely shown the door.

The truth is, I had felt extremely comfortable being a supermarket manager. I liked overseeing people and making the decisions that had to be made. There were enough complications to the work to intellectually challenge me and satisfy my ego. Had I not been fired, I honestly think that today I would still be running a supermarket, making decisions about canned peas and corn flakes.

The cycle continued for me. Nobody cared about my performance on the job, only my illicit past. Nobody was willing to believe that I was a different person. Once a con man, in their view, always a con man. It's a terrible feeling to want to reconstruct your life, and yet find yourself blocked at every turn. This made for a lot of tension.

A hopelessness sank in. This was not the routine hopelessness of a bad day or a bad week, but a deep despair and a recognition that nothing could go right again. Even though I knew the dire consequences, I seriously began to think of reverting to my past criminal behavior. There seemed to be no other way to get anywhere. I was angry at the establishment for refusing to give me that second chance that I knew I would make good on.

In my latest incarnation, I was working at night as a movie projectionist—that projectionist's license I acquired in prison had come in handy after all. In this case, I had told the manager about my past, and he didn't really care. I was upstairs locked in this booth for eight hours; what harm could I do? The job paid pretty well, but it was hardly thought-provoking work. I thought to myself that I was smarter than this, that I was wasting genuine talents that I possessed. What had made me so good as a con artist was my photographic memory that enabled me to acquire the knowledge and pose as someone else in an astonishingly short span of time. I could focus on things with an extraordinary intensity. And I was extremely observant, always noticing the small things that others didn't. These traits gave me an extra edge that I milked for all they were worth. But they didn't go very far in the cramped milieu of a projectionist's booth.

WHEN WRONGS CAN MAKE A RIGHT

Something had to change and change fast. Luckily, it did. One day my parole officer said to me, "You know so much about false documents and check kiting, have you ever given thought to going out and giving talks to law enforcement agencies about these things?"

"Well, no," I said.

"Well, the government has approached me about this," he said. "There would be no pay. And, of course, nobody could force you to do it."

"How would it work?" I asked.

"You'd just talk to law enforcement agents about cons and counterfeit documents and how to recognize them," he said. "Give them tips on how con artists work, so they could get better at catching them."

"I guess I could do that," I said. "I wouldn't have a problem with it."

So I began to go around locally and talk in front of members of the sheriff's office and the constable's office. I'd lecture to local FBI agents and postal inspectors. I didn't have any prepared remarks or slides or anything. I just told them what I did and how I did it, how I'd get false IDs and how I would open bank accounts and then withdraw money that wasn't really there. The agents asked me questions, and I found that I never had to say that I didn't know the answer.

The next thing I knew, the head of security for Target stores approached me and asked if I could come and talk to some of their store managers. I saw no reason not to, and so I did that, too. I got a warm and interested reception. They didn't pay me, either.

I was still working as a projectionist but these gigs forced me to take a long hard look at myself and my prospects. I still had vision and a dreamer's idealism. I was enjoying these little security presentations, and they ignited a new excitement in me. A plan slowly formed in my mind, one that I thought would allow me to use my expertise in a redemptive way and permit me to engage in a more satisfying life than the one I had in the projectionist's booth. I went to my new parole officer and told him what I had in mind.

I said that, in doing these little talks, I realized that I had as much knowledge as any man alive concerning the mechanics of forgery, check swindling, counterfeiting, and other similar crimes. I'd now realized that if I directed this knowledge into the right channels, I could help people. For instance, every time I went to the store and wrote a check, I would see two or three mistakes made on the part of the clerk or cashier, mistakes that a flimflam artist would take advantage of. I had concluded that it was simply a lack of training.

I was always looking at systems and realizing how simple it was to beat them. For example, if I was going to mail a letter and I didn't have a stamp, I knew I could take that letter and put the address of the person I was sending it to in the upper left-hand corner, and put my name in the middle of the envelope. The post office would then return it back to that person. So I would have sent it without a stamp. If I needed to get on a flight and it was fully booked, I knew that I could go to a phone, call the airline, and say, "Hi, do you have the manifest for flight 462? I'm Mr. Smith and I'm afraid I need to cancel my reservation." There's almost always a Smith or a Jones on just about any flight. Then I would call right back, ask if it were possible to get onto flight 462, and I'd be told, "Oh you're in luck, we just had a cancellation."

If I needed to make a long distance phone call and couldn't pay for it, I knew a way to do it. You'd look around for the first available corporate building and get their main number. Say it was 999-2000. You'd dial 999-2020, figuring that it had to be someone's extension. You get Bill Kenner in human resources. You'd say, "I'm sorry, I must have the wrong extension, could you put me back to the switchboard?" When the operator came on, you'd say, "This is Kenner in human resources, I need to make a long-distance call, could you give me an outside line?" And then you'd make your call.

It was obvious to me that every system had loopholes in it. I guess I thought in loopholes. And so I realized that I could teach people who handled checks and other legal documents how to protect themselves against fraud and theft. And I wanted to charge them.

"Well, if they'll do it, go right ahead," my parole officer said. "It's up to you. But not the law enforcement people. That's got to be free."

I approached a suburban bank director and outlined what I had in mind. I was upfront in relating my sordid background as a chronic bilker of banks. I told him that I wanted to spend an hour one day after the bank closed to give a lecture to his employees. I told him that consumer fraud is committed today in the blink of an eye, and you needed to be prepared. If he felt the talk was worthless, I said, he didn't owe me anything. If he found it beneficial, then he had to pay me five hundred dollars and make a few calls to colleagues at other banks and recommend that I come in and tutor their employees. I told him that if what I taught his people stopped just one bad check from crossing a teller's window, then he would have more than made his five hundred dollars back. He told me to come on by.

The ways of the world are truly unpredictable. He liked my presentation, and I got both the pay and the referrals. This first paid appearance as a "white-collar crime specialist" led to another lecture at another bank, and another and another. Banks heard about me in Dallas. Then I got calls from El Paso. Before long, I was in demand not only by banks, but also by hotels, airlines, and other businesses. In retrospect, it was a godsend that I was paroled to Houston, because Houston was booming and that allowed me to get off to a very good start.

Twenty-five years have passed. I talk to all sorts of businesses today, and I've increased my fee. But to this day, I never take a dime from any law enforcement agency. I do a lot of lecturing to new agents at the FBI

Academy, but I won't accept any remuneration, not even my expenses. Part of it is, I'm just grateful to be where I am. And another part of it is that I feel this is one way I can make amends for my past.

ONCE A CON ARTIST . . .

And so I had turned things on their head. I had converted something negative into something positive. I had found a way to meld my expertise with social good. I still had all the needs that had made me a criminal. I had simply found a legal and socially acceptable way to fulfill those needs.

In a certain sense, I'm still a con artist. I'm just putting down a positive con these days, as opposed to the negative con I used in the past. I've merely redirected the talents I've always possessed. I've applied the same relentless attention to working on stopping fraud that I once applied to perpetuating fraud.

Living this way is much better than life the wrong way. I feel I've been handed a rare and precious gift. Clearly, I'm in a flourishing industry. For so many people, fraud has become the tactic of maximal gain. Fraud has grown so enormous throughout the world that it touches everyone. To be honest, it will never go away. If I lived to be four hundred years old, I'd still have a good job.

One of the nice things about my new life is that I'm making more money trying to prevent fraud than I ever did by committing fraud. Going straight does pay.

Estimates are that businesses lose an unprecedented $400 billion a year from fraud of one sort or another. I'm not talking about armed robbery, burglary, or narcotics, but fraud. It's a staggering sum, equal to twice the budget of the U.S. military. If we were able to do away with fraud for just two years, we'd erase the national debt. We'd pay off Social Security for the next one hundred years.

Today bank tellers and salespeople are asked to accept so many different forms of payment, not just cash and checks but traveler's checks, credit cards, debit cards, money orders, NOW accounts, and credit union share drafts. Each and every one of them is susceptible to fraud. And it's not only embezzlement of money that's a problem. It's also embezzle-

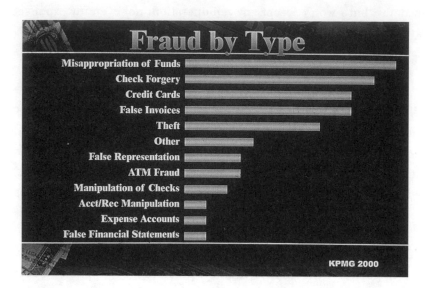

ment of information. Because information has become extremely valuable. And so far as restitution is concerned? Unheard of.

About a third of that $400 billion is from embezzlement, employees stealing from their employer. Out of embarrassment, the vast majority of companies never report these thefts to the police. They merely fire the employee, then tell human resources that if they receive a call about this person, say that they worked here but no longer work here. Consequently, the person goes on to steal from somebody else.

One of the things that always amuses me is that back when I was on the other side of the law, it was harder to commit fraud than it is now. You'd think it would be the opposite. And five years from now, it will be easier than it is today. And that's because of one word—technology. Technology breeds crime and it always has. Thirty-five years ago, if I had to make a check, I literally had to print the check, and so I had to be a skilled printer. I had to know how to do color separations, make negatives, and make plates. It was very time-consuming and tedious. Today, sitting at home in an apartment with a PC, a scanner, a color printer, and a color copier, you can reproduce just about any type of document, including hard cash.

So when people ask me, if I were a con artist today, what would be different? I tell them, "Instead of making $2.5 million, I'd make $20 million. It's that much easier."

And we look on white-collar crime a lot differently. China, many years ago, printed a warning on its currency that whoever forged counterfeit money would be beheaded. Until the early 1800s, forgery in England qualified as a hanging offense. Justice got a bit more civilized, but thirty-five years ago you at least got sent to prison. Today, I'd probably get probation or community service, and maybe have to make some restitution. That's not deterrence, that's encouragement.

It's a dark, morally ambiguous world today, but one problem we have in our society is that people don't really care if some big company was embezzled for $100,000. They figure that's the company's problem; they've got billions. Instead, people want to know what law enforcement is doing to clear the streets of murderers, rapists, drug dealers, and other violent criminals. People want them off the street, because they pose a physical threat. If you ask them about some guy selling counterfeit Gucci bags for twenty bucks down by the supermarket, their reaction is, "Well, I don't care about that. If the purse looks good, I'll buy one myself." In addition to the cost of fraud, counterfeit goods are responsible for $350 billion in losses in the United States every year, but people don't care

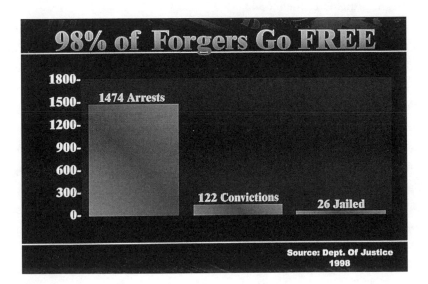

about the problem because they think it doesn't really affect them. What they don't understand is that ultimately, it does affect them. It means we all pay higher fees for goods and services.

The police are frustrated. They complain that if they go out and arrest a check writer, then the district attorney doesn't want to fool with the guy because it's not a high profile case. The guy just wrote some bad checks. If they do prosecute him, the judge says the prison is full. He can't put this check writer behind bars; he needs the cells for murderers and rapists, the really scary guys. Thus, something like 98 percent of forgers go free. Prosecutors have a benchmark. Rarely will they prosecute a fraud of less than five thousand dollars. So criminals know that if they stay under the benchmarks, they're safe.

There's no reason to rob a bank the old-fashioned way, with a mask, a gun, and a prayer. Why go and stick a gun in someone's face? You're talking about armed robbery, ten to twenty years. You could end up shooting someone. Someone could shoot you. And for what? The average bank robbery in 1998 and 1999 netted less than one thousand five hundred dollars. You're a lot better off doing your robbing with the point of a pen. Why not walk in and cash a fraudulent check for twenty thousand dollars? Maybe you'd get six months in the county jail, if they caught you, if they prosecuted you, if they sent you to jail. And so the machinery of fraud functions almost untouched.

Another big difference is, thirty-five years ago you had to be a con man with a con man's idiosyncratic personality. You had to be facile. You had to be persuasive, with good improvisational skills, and you needed icy self-control. You were taking something and replicating it, not perfectly, and you had to make someone believe it was the real thing, make them believe it sufficiently that they would cash it. Today, criminals can make a traveler's check or counterfeit bill that is so good that it doesn't take any acting skills to walk up to a teller and pass it off as the real thing. Someone who truly looks like a crook can get away with it.

Bear in mind, the person accepting counterfeit bills and forged checks these days is far less trained than in the past. Years ago, bank tellers were professional employees with months of training. Banks don't want to pay benefits anymore, and so they don't bother with full-time employees. They hire part-time help, and they don't give them any more than the most superficial training. If a bank teller can't tell the difference between a good hundred-dollar bill and a phony one, what hope is there for a hotel clerk or a sales clerk at the Gap?

Wherever I go, I find that security is pretty dreadful. Four years ago, I went to the Las Vegas Airport United Airlines ticket counter and was asked to show my driver's license in order to pick up my ticket. In my haste to catch my plane, the ticket clerk forgot to return the license. When I got back to the Midwest, where I live, I went to the Driver's License Bureau, told them that I had lost my license, and they issued me a new one on the spot. A week later, an envelope arrived from United with my license. Now I had two. Since I travel a lot, I kept the old one in my briefcase so it would be handy to display at airports. Soon, the old license expired, but, as an experiment, I kept offering it for identification to see if anyone would notice that it was no longer valid. For four years— at airports, banks, and stores hundreds of salespeople and clerks have looked at that license. Not one has noticed that it was invalid. I've decided that as soon as just one person says to me, "This is no good, the license has expired," I'll throw it away. But no one has. Is there any wonder we have this mad frenzy of fraud?

KIDS TODAY

What bothers me a lot is, it used to be just the hardened criminal you had to worry about. Today it could be anyone. I'm not being politically correct, but I'm convinced that the main reason we have so much fraud today is because we live in an extremely unethical society. There's been a sharp slippage in ethics that has inspired a culture of fraud. And so what you're up against today is people who you'd consider trustworthy who have no ethics.

There are all these computer-savvy kids, many of whom are making twenty-dollar bills on their computers at home. They're scanning them in and printing them on their ink jet printers and taking them to the convenience store or the school cafeteria and spending them. This happens all the time because they think it's okay to do it.

We live in a society that doesn't teach ethics at home. We live in a society that doesn't teach ethics in school, because teachers would be ac-

cused of teaching morality. We live in a society where you can't even find a four-year college course on ethics, and if you could find one, they'd be talking about ethics three hundred years ago that have no relevance to ethics in the business world today.

I don't know anything that shows it better than *Who's Who Among American High School Students.* For more than thirty years, the organization has gone out and selected sixteen thousand high school students to be honored each year in their publication. In order to be accepted, a student had to have maintained a 4.0 average through the tenth, eleventh, and twelfth grade. Once accepted, a student has to fill out a form and answer five questions. I've always been interested in question No. 3, and I've followed the results for twenty years, because they've changed dramatically. The question asks, During the last three years of high school, did you steal, cheat, lie, copy, or plagiarize? In the latest survey, more than 80 percent of the students said that they did. Like it was okay.

I believe we should be teaching ethics as early as maybe fifth grade, but we're not doing it. Not long ago, I visited two major pharmaceutical companies. Abbott Laboratories and Glaxo Wellcome, and both of them told me that they had brought ethics training in house. They established their own ethical standards, and they require their employees to go through training. They've had to create their own code of conduct, because it's not being done at home.

When I talk to people about con artists, they always ask me, well, is there a certain type of person to beware of? It's been my experience, on both sides of the law, that there is no profile of who's a con artist or forger. I've seen men who were eighty years old and women in their teens commit the same types of fraud. There may be a profile for bombers or serial killers, but not for the confidence man. Most of the time, it's the people you least expect who steal from you. Of all the calls I get from corporate managers lamenting that an employee stole from them, it's never, "Well, I had this person and six months later I found out he was embezzling from me." Instead, it's always, "This man worked for me for twenty years. He was a saint. I trusted him like my brother. I can't believe he stole from me." It's far more often the long-term employee than the newly-hired one who steals from you. In the world of the con, the unexpected becomes the expected.

AN OUNCE OF PREVENTION

As easy as these crimes are to commit, I firmly believe that most of them are easily prevented. Banks and companies simply have to learn to secure their systems as best they can. And you have to be a very smart consumer today.

I travel all over the world talking about fraud, and one of the interesting things is that in Europe or Australia, even in Canada, the societies are very proactive. Americans are very reactive. A guy in Britain, for instance, will say, "This check? We could use this check, but then somebody might do this or might do that, so let's fix it so he can't do that." In the U.S., the attitude is, "We'll use this. If we have a problem, we'll fix it." They worry about it later on. In fact, 90 percent of those who hire me to design secure documents, they've only hired me because somebody counterfeited their documents. No company has ever called me in to design their check ahead of a problem. It's always, "Somebody really got to us for a ton of money, and we don't want that to happen again."

It's much better to avoid becoming a victim than trying to figure out how to get your money back once you become a victim. Once you're a victim, you won't get your money back. Everyone has to start being proactive. You have to ask yourself every time you go on the Internet, which is probably every day, what information am I putting out there, and how could someone use that information? The crime of the future is identity theft, when some stranger acquires enough of the basic information about you that, when it comes to buying things on credit and making withdrawals from the bank, he in effect becomes you. It's already the fastest-growing crime in America, as criminals assume other people's identity in disturbing numbers. That's what happened to Michelle Brown, whose ordeal I'll return to in the final chapter.

In the following chapters, I plan to take you into the world of the confidence man. I'm going to tell you about some of the most ingenious scams that I've encountered during my twenty-five years as a fraud specialist. I'll tell you how to spot a bogus check and how to recognize a counterfeit bill. I'll tell you why a piece of Scotch tape can make a check worth a lot more, and why you shouldn't write your grocery list on a deposit slip. I'll tell you about how a man made a considerable amount of money off supposedly broken windows, and why criminals iron credit cards. I'll tell you about the mustard squirter and the rock in the box, about the Vickers Gang and their long-running refund scam, about how to earn $100,000 from a demolished car, and why a thief brings glue with him to the ATM. This is all for the purpose of teaching you how to avoid becoming a victim of fraud. For I strongly believe that punishment for fraud and recovery of stolen funds is so rare today that prevention is the only viable course of action.

Above all, the thing to remember is that nothing is foolproof. Every form of payment has an inherent risk in it. Every system has a flaw. Every system has been designed by a man or woman, and that means a man or woman can defeat it. Sherlock Holmes said it best: "What one invents, one will discover." And, you can be sure a man or woman will defeat it. I can only laugh when someone says to me that this electronic system is foolproof, you can't beat it. That's a ridiculous statement. Someone had to create it, so obviously someone can defeat it.

I do recognize that by revealing how scams work, I run a risk. During my career, I have never conducted seminars open to the general public, but always under the sponsorship of an association, a company, or a financial institution. I hope, when you read this book, you see it as a useful educational tool for a business person or a consumer. I, with a criminal mind, know that some will see it as a bible and a great instructional book for the amateur forger. In order to educate the masses, though, I feel it's worth taking that risk. Why should only the criminals know the tricks?

Fraud goes on every day, in every city, all over the world. Practiced today by increasingly wily criminals, fraud is incredibly complex, and full of nuance and creativity. Businesses and consumers have never been more vulnerable. To more and more people, fraud is no longer an abstraction but an act with a face and a name. The most effective strategy to prevent it is to make things difficult and complicated enough to raise a murmur of distress from the crook. That way he'll decide it's not worth the effort to try and take advantage of you.

A criminal always looks for the easiest path to riches. At my house, I have a security camera and security system, and after dark the place lights up like Yankee Stadium. A burglar takes one look at my house and heads to the next block. It's the same thing with a forger or a con artist. He'll search for the easy mark. So let's learn how to keep it from being you.

❷

[LOOKING FOR
MR. GOODCHECK]

A few years ago, a man double-parked his rental car in Miami and was given a parking ticket. He was from Argentina, visiting on vacation. He stuck the parking ticket in his briefcase and it went back with him to Argentina. While he was unpacking his luggage, he came across the ticket. The fine was twenty dollars. He searched around in his pockets and found that he still had some leftover U.S. currency. He stuffed a twenty-dollar bill and two singles in the envelope along with the ticket, sealed it, and mailed it to the Miami city clerk.

When the city clerk opened the envelope, he noted that the man had overpaid by $2.00. Instead of sending him the $2.00 back, the city mailed him a check for $2.00. When the man opened the envelope and found the check, he thought it was too good to be true. He took that check, scanned it into his computer and changed the amount to what he deemed was a more appreciative refund—$1.45 million. He printed out the corrected check and deposited it in a bank in Argentina. The city of Miami dispenses many checks for more than $1 million, and so it was paid without question. Because we don't have extradition rights with Argentina, the man got away with it. He became a millionaire from a twenty-dollar parking ticket.

Since he was never caught, I can only speculate on the actual mindset of the Argentinian. But I happen to think the guy was doing this little caper as a lark, just to see if he could get away with it. Obviously, since he knew the mechanics of how to forge a check, he had to be at least a little bit crooked. But I sort of doubt that he ever imagined he could succeed at something so outrageous; he just couldn't believe that forgery had become so easy.

Oh, but it has.

THE TRULY NOTEWORTHY NEWS

Despite the fact that we read a lot of stories in the newspapers about someone downloading credit card numbers from a website, or manufacturing phony Visa cards in some warehouse in Queens, the truth is, check fraud is much more prevalent. And although the average value of a fraudulent check is less than one thousand dollars, the Office of the Comptroller of the Currency estimates that total check fraud losses exceed $19 billion a year (and if we start giving out more parking tickets it might get a lot worse). Visa and MasterCard losses are less than 10 percent of that. And bank robbers, by contrast, got away with a relatively paltry $68 million in 1999.

Payment by check is far and away the most popular form of payment in the United States, easily exceeding payments by cash and credit card combined. Americans wrote 69 billion checks in 1999, and every year they write a billion more. No one knows that better than criminals. That's why worthless checks are one of the most serious white-collar crimes affecting businesses today. Every day, American banks, savings banks, and credit unions return 1.3 million worthless checks. That's $27 million of bad checks, every single day.

But only about 2 percent of bad check passers are arrested, and only about 62 percent of all bad checks are ever collected. And the conviction rate for bad check passers is lamentably low.

A SLIPPERY SLOPE

Things have changed so much since my days as a check forger. Years ago, when a forger came to a city, there was a great deal of preparation involved if he wanted to forge checks. First, he would have to rent an apartment to establish a physical address. He'd try to find a place he could rent by the month so he wouldn't have to bother with a lease. Still, he'd have to pay the first month's rent along with a security deposit.

Then he'd go down to the County Bureau of Vital Statistics and search through the death records for the year of his birth. He'd find an infant who was born around when he was born and died shortly afterward. He'd copy the vital information off the infant's death certificate—the mother's name, the father's name, and so forth. Armed with this information, he could apply for a birth certificate. After he got the certificate, he'd go down to the Motor Vehicles Department and get a driver's license. Then he'd go to the bank and open an account. That was the risky part, because he had to identify himself to the teller to fill out a new account card and a signature card. Then he had to wait ten days for checks to be printed up. That gave the bank ten days to run a credit bureau report, ten days to check on where he said he was employed, and ten days to contact his previous bank to see how he maintained his account.

None of this is necessary today. You just buy your checks through *TV Guide*, one of the Sunday magazines you find in newspapers, or over the telephone. Anybody can order anybody's checks. We've made it so easy for people to steal from us. In fact, we're the only country in the world that does make it so easy. In every other country, you have to pick up your checks at the bank. In Australia, for instance, if you want to reorder checks, you have to physically go to your bank branch and place the order. When the checks arrive, you have to return to the bank and get them. Only recently have a few banks in Australia begun to entertain the idea of mailing reordered checks to customers.

This whole notion of ordering checks directly from vendors started in an entirely innocent fashion. About fifteen years ago, a woman in Colorado Springs, Colo., named Miriam Loo had a greeting card and gift company called Current, which she started in the basement of her home. She had the idea of selling novelty checks, personal checks with special designs on them. She began with dogs. There were so many dog-crazed people, she figured they'd get a kick out of putting their dog on their checks. Sure enough, orders flowed in for checks with Beagles and Cocker Spaniels. Then she expanded beyond dogs into sailboats, cars, birds, flowers, whatever you wanted. It was a nice little business.

The DeLuxe Corporation in Minneapolis, the king of checks, found out about this and said, hey, she's encroaching on our turf. DeLuxe went and bought her company and entered the personal check business. At first, DeLuxe sold only to banks. Then it began to sell directly to individuals by mail. Banks didn't like the idea, but DeLuxe didn't back off. The three other check companies said, well, we'd never do that. But one by one, they entered the business. Since the late 1980s, advertisements like this have appeared in newspapers and in direct mail: "Get two hundred checks for just $3.95. Or get one hundred fifty duplicate checks for only $4.95." There are more than 200 companies that sell checks through magazines and the Internet. And there are no controls over them. It's all perfectly legal.

People can get anyone's check. All they have to do is see it. Criminals nowadays will drive around until they find a ritzy neighborhood with million-dollar homes. They'll knock on a door. When someone answers, they'll say, "Boy, you've got a lot of leaves lying on your lawn. What'd you got, an acre here? I'll tell you what, my buddy and I will clean up your leaves, leave the place immaculate, and it'll cost you just seventy-five dollars." The guy thinks it's a great deal, the crooks clean up the leaves, and the owner pays them with a check for seventy-five dollars. That's all they came for: the check. Then they go to the Internet and order the checks of a guy from a million-dollar home, forge them, and start cashing them. Next time, the guy will rake his own leaves.

Or forgers drive to a wealthy neighborhood and park in a grocery store parking lot. They wait until you pull in in your Porsche or your Jaguar and they follow you into the store. You buy groceries. You have to write your check on a little pad that's sticking up on the counter. They're right next to you, loading items onto the counter. They look over your shoulder—most of them are women—and they can memorize your check in eight seconds. All they have to do is glance over your shoulder. You haven't gotten past writing the date, and they've memorized it. Everything on it. They go back and fill out an order coupon. Name and address you'd like on the check? They put your name and address on the check. Style of check? You've got flags on your check, so they order checks with flags. How many? Two hundred. Last question: if you'd like these checks sent to an address other than the printed address on the face of the check, so state here. They fill in a P.O. Box. Ten days later, they've got your checks.

And don't think these activities are limited to personal checks. A Fortune 500 company in Chicago got ripped off when somebody outside the organization ordered the company's business checks through a catalogue—and all he gave them to put on the check was the company's name and address. He didn't know where the company banked. He didn't have an account number. He didn't know who signed the checks. The person ordered two hundred of the company's checks and had them sent to him. Then he went to all the grocery stores he could get to and cashed them, because the company was a household word and employed thousands of people. Its checks were gold.

Not long ago, a company in Long Beach, Calif., got a disturbing invoice in the mail from its check printer. The company's checks were being shipped to 110th Street in Los Angeles. The problem was, the company didn't have an office there. Someone had reordered the company's checks and changed the ship-to location to 110th Street. The printer had gotten the reorder with an address change and had simply processed it. One way things like this happen is that criminals recruit company employees to steal check reorder forms. Or they buy them. A stolen check reorder form is worth one hundred dollars on the street.

WHAT TO DO

The solution is to order checks through your bank, not a mail-order catalogue. A crook can't waltz into Chase or Citibank and try to order your checks. And when you buy checks through a bank, they usually have more security features on them to prevent forgeries. Mail-order houses don't bother with these things, and that's why their prices are lower. [Although prices may soar if other states follow Illinois's example: Illinois, to my knowledge, is the first state to pass a law actually making it a felony to order someone else's checks. If you live in Illinois and a catalogue sells your checks to a crook you can sue the catalogue company.] Businesses also ought to order their checks through a bank, or else directly from one of the major business check-printing companies, which dispatch a salesman and follow strict ordering procedures to keep your checks from falling into the wrong hands.

HEARD OF THAT SPERM BANK?

A big reason for the proliferation of forged checks is that the tellers and clerks who cash them don't pay close attention to the IDs they get handed. Even if they do, it's so easy today for criminals to obtain bogus IDs that look genuine. Recently, a man showed up in Salt Lake City and went around to local banks claiming to be a Russian official doing preparatory work for the Russian Olympic team in advance of the 2002 Winter Games. He had a fake passport and other well-crafted fraudulent documents, and as an added precaution he brought along a young female accomplice who posed as his interpreter. In just three days, banks cashed $90,000 worth of worthless checks for him.

For the less creative forger, there are numerous check cashing stores that require no ID whatsoever, which is the reason they charge steep commissions. But the criminal doesn't care; the fee's not coming out of his account.

Too often, tellers and salespeople ignore an important precept, which is to be impressed with the check, not the person. Once, to demonstrate the point before a hidden television camera, I put on an expensive suit and drove up to a bank in a Rolls-Royce, where I managed to successfully cash a fifty-dollar check written on a cocktail napkin because the bank teller was more impressed by my appearance than by what I had handed her. Remember, the way someone looks, what he drives, or how friendly he is has no bearing on whether a check is good. It's all part of the scam.

I went into a store recently, and if this hadn't happened I wouldn't have believed it. I bought a piece of luggage and wrote a check for it. Within a moment, the saleswoman handed me the luggage on the counter and gave me my check back. I looked puzzled, and she said, "Oh, we have a new program. It's called e-check, from TeleCheck." I asked her how it worked, and she said, "Well, you wrote me a check, and I put it through this machine that looks like a Scotch tape dispenser. It read your account number off the bottom of it. Then I keyed in the amount of the purchase and it sent all of that data electronically to TeleCheck's file. Three days from now, the money is automatically deducted from your bank account and it shows up on your statement as an electronic deduction. In the meantime, your check is your receipt."

I was flabbergasted. I couldn't resist asking her, "What if I'm not Frank Abagnale? Since you didn't ask me for any identification, what if I happened to have forged this check? Where's your evidence?" This is a forger's dream come true. I write you a check, you give me the merchandise, and you give me the check back. When the police show up and ask for the forged check, you have to say, "Oh, we gave it to the forger." It's absolutely amazing. I'd like to know where this was thirty-five years ago when I needed it.

The truth is, people who cash checks today are often so blasé about it, that a forger hardly has to even try. You wouldn't believe some of the ludicrous checks I've run across that stores saw fit to cash. One check cashed in a grocery store in Houston, Texas, for fifty dollars, was literally signed, "I Screwed You." The bank wrote back, "unauthorized signature." I guess so. Another check was signed, "U. R. Stuck." A clerk took that one, too. Another check listed an ordinary person's name in the upper left-hand corner along with an address. The address read, "Your City, U.S.A." The bank was listed as National State Bank, also located in Your City, U.S.A. Still another check for ten dollars was cashed at a liquor store in Denver that was drawn off "The Sperm Bank of America." Must be a new financial institution. The television show, "Dateline," for a report on check fraud, managed to get a bank to cash a one-thousand-dollar check that had "void" written all over it and the message, "Please Don't Pay Me. I Am A Counterfeit Check!"

HOT CHECKS

The most common type of bad check is the proverbial "hot" check. A hot check is a check drawn from a legitimate checking account that lacks the funds to cover the amount, or has been written off of an account previously closed.

There are a number of ways to detect a hot check, but many people who cash checks fail to know the easiest one of all. Ninety percent of hot checks are numbered in check sequence between 101 and 200. A check numbered 118 would represent an account about three weeks old. A check number of 1315 suggests an account that's about three years old. Hence, many retailers over the years have become very leery of cashing so-called new account checks with numbers less than 200.

To circumvent this, bad check passers, when they set up accounts, try to obtain the highest possible check number they can get. This is usually done by asking the new accounts department to start their checks with a sequence number like 800. In many cases, they are denied. Most banks use a standard starter number of 101 for new checking accounts. Unfortunately, in recent years many new accounts departments have become very lax and, to oblige customers, will let them start their account with any number they request. Or they don't pay attention to unusual reorder activity, even though criminals reorder checks every twenty or thirty days so they can get a higher sequence number. If all else fails, a criminal can buy checks through the mail, requesting any sequence number he wants.

For this reason, you can't depend on the check number alone, but it's a good tip-off for when you should use discretion. If you get a low-numbered check, that would be the time to ask for additional identification, to call the bank if it's a large purchase, or to use a check verification company to guarantee the check. Remember: 90 percent of worthless checks are numbered between 101 and 200.

WHAT CAN BE DONE?

Over twenty years ago, a technique was developed that is referred to in banking as "date coding." A date code is a tiny three-digit or four-digit number that appears on the front of a check to indicate when the account was opened. For example, the number 879 would mean that this checking account was opened in August of 1979. This coding is done automatically by the check printer. No matter how many checks a customer orders or reorders, this number will always appear on the face of the check. The date code helps you determine the stability and credibility of the person writing the check. Even checks ordered through the mail from a catalogue will have a date code on them if it's required by the state where the person lives.

I recommend that all institutions date code checks. And I recommend that retailers teach employees how to read date codes on checks. The date code is sometimes found above the signature line or above the "pay to the order" provision, but most commonly next to the customer's name. The older the date code, the more established the person who has written the checks.

THOSE HANDY DEPOSIT SLIPS

I was speaking one day with a new acquaintance, and I asked him for a business card so I could stay in touch. After fumbling around in his pockets, he could only come up with a deposit slip from his personal checking account. He handed it to me with a smile. I smiled back and told him, "I'm the last person you want to give this to."

Deposit slips seem harmless enough. That's why most people write grocery lists on them, hand them out as business cards, or simply discard them when they run out of checks. But a deposit slip is actually an exceedingly valuable slip of paper. To a forger, a deposit slip is worth ten times more than a blank check.

The slips are used in a common scam called "less cash deposit" or "split deposit." After obtaining a blank deposit slip, the criminal will write a forged check to the person named on the deposit slip. He'll then proceed to the bank listed on the front of the deposit slip, and deposit a check in the amount of, say, six hundred dollars. In the line "less cash received," he'll write three hundred dollars back. The teller, especially a busy one, will think, Why should I bother to ask for ID? The person is obviously a customer of our bank and has enough funds in the account to cover the check. Plus, he's depositing more than he's withdrawing. She hands over the cash and the check writer drives away three hundred dollars richer. The bank is stuck with a worthless check. Less cash deposit scams occur more than two thousand times a day at drive-up windows of banks, savings and loan institutions, and credit unions.

WHAT TO DO

I advise tellers to pay very close attention to less cash deposits. Anytime you return more than twenty-five dollars to anyone you don't know, ask for identification. Deposit slips also have date codes on them. Look at them, because they can give you an idea of the stability and credibility of the account. And I tell everyone, don't give out blank deposit slips at the bar instead of business cards, or leave them in the grocery store cart.

STOP PAYMENT START-UPS

Many companies and municipalities have been burned by stale-dated stop payment orders. In these cases, dishonest recipients receive a check, then tell the issuer that it never arrived. So the company will place a stop payment order on the check and issue a new one. The second check is immediately cashed. The original check is saved for a rainy day, which usually comes about six months later.

Shrewd con artists know that stop payments at most banks are good for only 180 days. After that, they expire. At that point, they have to be renewed for another 180 days. The trouble is, few companies bother to renew them. The con artist will patiently bide his time for 181 days before negotiating the second check, which will pay almost every time.

WHAT TO DO

A little extra investment on the part of the company can easily prevent this scam. Put an extended stop payment period on the check, like 999 days. The bank's limit for a stop payment period needs to be a three-digit number, and 999 fits as easily as 180. Even the most patient con artist doesn't have that much patience. At most banks, stop payments cost between a dollar and two dollars a month. Many companies have dozens or even hundreds of stop payment orders in effect at any one time. Although the cost can add up, the exposure for loss is far greater.

FORGERY: HOURS OF FUN

Now, let's take a look at forgery. Forgery has increased considerably since 1975. The major reason for this is technology.

Twenty-five years ago, it used to take me twelve weeks to create a check. A truly sophisticated forger needed a four-color printing press that cost a quarter of a million dollars. Today, I can create a check with a laptop computer, a laser printer, and a scanner in my hotel room in twelve minutes. The *New York Times* once calculated that a forger can buy everything he needs for about five thousand dollars. Of course, it doesn't cost him anything. He pays by check.

A number of years ago, a business writer submitted an article to *Forbes* magazine, and the editors printed it, paid him, and also sent him a check in the amount of $333.33 to cover his expenses. The writer lived in a one-bedroom apartment in Boston, and he owned an old Apple computer, a printer, and a scanner. As an experiment, and with the blessings of his editors, he decided to try to demonstrate how easily he could transform that meager check into some real money. So he laid the check on the scanner and brought it up on the screen. Once it was on the screen, he could do anything he wanted to it.

He zoomed in on the amount box, locked on it, and removed the dollar amount of the check with his mouse. Then he went to the written legal amount of the check and deleted it. Then he asked the computer to identify the fonts. Back then, a home computer could match 122 fonts. Today, computers can match thousands of fonts. In just a few seconds, he was able to pretty closely match the font at the printer at the accounts payable department at *Forbes* magazine. Using that font, he typed in a new amount number. He put the machine on pause and went out to a stationary store. He asked for green basketweave check paper, which anyone can buy at Office Depot, and bought enough to serve his needs. He also picked up a mechanical number stamp and some red ink.

He went home with his supplies, took the white paper out of the printer, inserted the green basketweave paper, and printed out the new check. He forged the two signatures it required using two different pens. He needed the number stamp so he could reconstruct the ink of the check number in red. Using an Exacto knife, he cut the check out of the 8½ x 11 sheet so he could bring it down to the appropriate size. Once he was finished, he ended up with a check for $30,333.33, which he felt much better reflected the value of his services.

He deposited the check by opening up an account at Bank Boston. They told him there was a five-day hold period, and he said that was no problem. He didn't return for twelve days, at which time he withdrew all but a hundred dollars. Sixty-two days later, an auditor at *Forbes* caught the forged check, but by then it was a little late. The writer then crafted a story for *Forbes* about check fraud, in which he revealed the details of his own little charade. *Forbes* put a picture of the fraudulent check on its cover.

This little caper is called scanning, and it's one of the most popular forms of forgery and certainly the simplest. Scanning started to emerge as a problem in the early 1990s, and it has really caught on significantly in recent years.

In Springfield, Mass., a man changed a $3.00 refund check from L.L. Bean into one for $30,000. Then he changed a $2.39 bakery refund check for stale cinnamon buns to one for $15,552.39. In North Carolina, a well-dressed young man convinced an automobile dealer to accept a cashier's check for $50,000 from Wachovia Bank, in exchange for a new Mercedes 300SC. It happened to be six in the evening, when the bank was closed, but the dealer was not about to turn away a nice piece of business. Little did he know that the cashier's check had originally been made out for $5.00 and altered to $50,000, and that before the bank opened the next day the car would be two states away, with fake license plates and a new paint job.

DO YOUR BANKING WITH THE IRS

And sometimes, you don't even need all that technology. For example, people always seem to require extra cash around tax time, and criminals are no exception. So they get it from you. Say you've had your tax returns prepared and, like most of us, you owe the IRS some additional money. For argument's sake, let's say it's $1,500. You sign your return, insert a check made out to the IRS for $1,500, and drop it in the mail. As far as you're concerned, that ends the pain for another twelve months.

Not quite. The pain actually just doubled. Your package was "lifted" while in transit to the IRS. Envelopes to the IRS are common targets because of where they're going. The check was removed and the rest of the return trashed. With a few pen strokes, the thief easily altered the check so that it was made out to a Mrs. Smith, and deposited it into a fake account. All he did was change "IRS" to "MRS" and add "Smith" to the payee line. Not only did you lose the $1,500, but you still owe the IRS another $1,500, plus late charges. Talk about double taxation.

WHAT TO DO

The easy solution is to fill out the entire payee line. If you had written "Internal Revenue Service" instead of "IRS," this scam would not have worked.

SURE, YOU CAN TRY THIS AT HOME

Today, forgers drive around in industrial parks where there are big office buildings, and look into those large mailboxes standing in the parking lot. They'll tell you that five years ago, they used to have to fish into those mailboxes, sending a line down and yanking the mail out, but they don't have to anymore. Today, they drive up at a little after five in the afternoon, and there's so much mail stuffed inside that it's literally flowing out of the box. They just reach out of the car window and scoop it up. Any reasonable quantity of mail will always contain at least one envelope with a window in it that says, "Pay to." Inside is a check payable to a construction company or a public relations firm—it doesn't really matter who it's addressed to. It's not going to them anymore.

The odds are it's a laser check, and that's just what forgers want. Just about every company in America, no matter how big or small, has moved from a matrix printer to a laser printer to disperse payroll and accounts payable checks. It's faster, it's cleaner, and it's more efficient. With a laser printer, these companies can buy blank check paper, lay it in the cassette, and actually print the entire check—the company logo, the bank's logo, the routing numbers, the account number, even the signature.

Now a laser printer is a non-impact printer—in other words, there's no ink put into the paper. A matrix printer shoots ink into the paper. A jet printer puts ink into the paper. A typewriter puts ink into the paper via the ribbon. With a laser printer, toner is applied to the paper by heat, so the toner is sitting on top of the paper. Which is why we call it non-impact printing.

Years ago, when criminals stole, say, a thirty-thousand-dollar check made out to a construction company, they would bring it to a forger and explain that they wanted the forger to get rid of the payee name, so they could type in a new name and cash the check. Fine, the forger said, it'll be done in two weeks. The criminal was aghast. Two weeks? The forger said, hey, you're asking me to move ink off of paper. He had to extract the ink using bleaches, solvents, acetones, hydrochlorides, polarized chemicals, non-polarized chemicals. He had to take each letter, and do it slowly, or else the check would become abrasive and you'd notice it.

With today's laser checks, criminals have devised a new methodology. They take a piece of Scotch tape—the gray, cloudy kind that doesn't rip the paper when you peel it off—and put it over the dollar amount and over the payee name. They use a fingernail to rub it down hard over the check, and then lift the tape off. The dollar amount and the name and the address will come off on the tape. The toner attaches to the Scotch tape and gets pulled from the fiber of the paper. If there's any laser toner residue left over, a little high-polymer plastic eraser will take care of that. Sometimes forgers use dental picks, razor blades, or dry ice to remove the toner, but Scotch tape works quite nicely.

People are shocked when I tell them this, and then they go back and try it and sure enough that's what happens. So any idiot can take a strip of tape and remove the nine dollars off a check and type in nine thousand or ninety thousand.

And that's what the forger collecting the mail does. He uses tape to remove the payee's name and address, and of course, the amount. He types in his name and the amount he wants, and deposits it at the bank. Sixty days later, the construction company that was supposed to get the check calls the payer and says that it hasn't gotten its money. The payer calls the bank, but it's too late. The money is long gone.

It's that simple, because we make it that simple.

REVENGE OF THE SCIENCE GEEK

Forgers must have all had chemistry sets as kids, because another thing they love to do is to chemically alter checks. It used to be that the only chemical banks had to worry about was bleach. If banks used bleach-sensitive paper, they'd be protected. Today no forger uses bleach. Instead, all sorts of simple chemicals, like acetone, are used to modify checks. What's the product of choice from which to get acetone? Nail polish remover. It's 99 percent acetone.

If someone mails me a check today for nine dollars, but they're a Fortune 500 company and I know that they have a bit more than that in the bank, I do a little chemistry experiment. I take that check, put Scotch tape over the signature of the controller, put tape on the back of the check where the signature would be on the front, lay that check in a cake pan, take some nail polish—no other ingredient—and pour that bottle of nail polish over the check. In a matter of seconds, everything that was put there by a typewriter, laser printer, jet printer, matrix printer, ballpoint pen, or flair pen is off the check. Because acetone removes anything that's not a base ink. So the company's logo, the bank name, the check number, and the borders of the check will stay. But anything that's typed on or printed on by a laser printer disappears within fifteen minutes. It's called washing the check.

I take the check and dry it with a blow-dryer. I remove the Scotch tape which prevented the acetone from getting into the controller's signature. What's left is a nice dry blank check signed by the controller of a Fortune 500 company. I call the bank that the check is drawn on, and ask, "Would this account clear a check for twenty-thousand dollars?" "Oh, sure, the funds are available," I'm told. I stick the check in the typewriter, fill it out for twenty-thousand dollars, go down to the bank, they check the signature, and they give me the money.

A couple of years ago, four thieves cruised around the more prosperous neighborhoods in South Bend, Ind., as well as communities just over the border in Michigan, looking for mailboxes that had their flags up. The guy riding in the passenger seat opened the boxes and sifted through the outgoing mail. When he found someone who had paid their telephone bill or electric bill, he removed those checks from their envelopes and took them. The thieves washed them in nail polish remover, blow-dried them, filled in new names and much higher amounts, and cashed them at local banks. This mailbox caper goes on every day all over the country, usually near the last day of the month when the odds are best of finding checks. Since people generally leave outgoing mail in their mailbox before heading to work, criminals will steal checks in the morning, wash them, and cash them by the afternoon. A lot of the check washers are drug addicts. The same chemicals that they use to cook their drugs, they use to wash checks.

HOW BUYING TIME BUYS YOU MONEY

Often a forger needs to buy time to get away with passing fraudulent checks, and so he resorts to some other little modifications. First of all,

every good forger alters the numbers along the bottom of the check. Inside a set of brackets is a nine-digit number. That's the bank's routing number, and it's like a zip code. When you cash the check, that number allows the check to be sent back to the bank where your account is. The first two digits of that number signify the Federal Reserve Bank in your jurisdiction. For example, New York would be 02. There are twelve federal reserve banks scattered around the country; like a dozen eggs, there are a dozen banks. The numbers are assigned from east to west: for instance, 01 is Boston, 03 is Philadelphia, 08 is St. Louis, and 11 is Dallas.

Let's say you have a company check from a bank in New York and the company is in New York. You can color-copy fifty of them. That's quite simple. But if you start cashing them today at supermarkets in the New York area, by tomorrow the bank knows about it and the company will complain that these are forged checks. They call the police, and they send out a bulletin that you're out there passing bad checks. How many places could you get to in a day? Ten? If you got on the New Jersey Turnpike with all its traffic, you wouldn't get to the next exit.

But what if I drop the "0" and replace it with a "1"? When I cash the check, the clerk at the courtesy booth at the supermarket will look at the name of the bank and recognize that it's a New York bank, so it's a local check and he has no problem cashing it. But when the store deposits the check, by changing that number, just as if I had altered a zip code, I force that check to go all the way across the country to Hawaii to clear. When it gets to Hawaii, someone notices that the routing number is incorrect and puts a white strip called a Lundy strip across the bottom of the check over the old routing number and sends it back. But by the time that happens, two weeks will have passed. So I have fourteen days instead of one day to wander all over New York cashing bad checks. Forgers live on the theory that stall creates float and float equals profit.

WHAT TO DO

I always train people to know their Federal Reserve code numbers. If a teller in New York sees a New York check, that should have 02. If she sees 12, that tells her she's looking at a forged check.

Any government check always has as its routing number, "000000518." Forgers who forge government checks remove the first three zeroes and encode the check with the code of a bank in another state. That way the computer treats the check as an ordinary business check, and routes it to a destination other than the U.S. Treasury.

IN ADDITION, BE SUSPICIOUS IF . . .

Most forged checks don't have perforated edges. Real checks do. The only exception to this rule are United States Government Treasury checks. Forgers could create checks with perforated edges, but few bother as it's expensive. When forgers buy check paper, they usually buy standard 8½ X 11 sheets. They print out three checks on a sheet of paper and then cut them apart. When you're handed one of their checks, there is no perforated edge anywhere on the check. It's smooth on all four sides. That's usually a dead giveaway that it's a forgery.

Most forgers don't use magnetic ink to do the routing numbers. It's not because they aren't able to. Anyone can go into an office supplies or computer store, and buy a magnetic ink cartridge for their printer. Forgers don't do it because of the float. Meaning, if I put magnetic ink on the check and cashed it at a grocery store, the bank computers would read it overnight and reject it. But if I use regular blank ink, the computer in the clearing house can't read it. The next day, the check will have a Lundy strip put over the routing number. They'll reencode it with magnetic ink, but they'll still use the routing number that I put on the check. It'll still go to Hawaii, but now I've bought two more days. If you're passing six-hundred-dollar checks and you're doing ten a day, that's twelve thousand dollars more profit.

DON'T KEEP IT SIMPLE, STUPID

One of the main reasons forgers are so successful today is because we give away so much information. Businesses commonly establish an M.D.A., or maximum dollar allowed amount, for their checks. That puts a cap on the amount a check can be written for. A company, for instance, might set up its checking account with instructions that checks are not to exceed $1,500. The bank will lock that into their software, and if a check comes in for $1,500.01, it will reject it. It's a great feature, except many companies print those instructions right on every check: "Not valid over $1,500." That tells every forger, if you're going to forge this check, you better stay under $1,500. Why are you telling the forger how to defraud you?

Or a forger will pick up a check that says right on the face, "Two signatures required on checks over ten thousand dollars." He'll simply make sure he puts a second forged signature on the check.

Here's another way that companies unwittingly assist criminals in robbing them. If you look at the annual report of any Fortune 500 company, on page two or three is the signature of the chairman of the board, the chief financial officer, the treasurer, the controller, all in camera-ready art. That's where most forgers get their signatures for fraudulent checks, straight out of annual reports. A forger digitizes that signature, puts it on a check or letter of credit, and he's in business. Your business.

When you prepare an annual report, put in a picture of the officer, put in the name of the officer, and put in the title of the officer. But don't put in the signature. If you feel some obligation to show a signature, have an artist do a rendition of it rather than the true signature. If you do include the real signature, that signature is going to show up on a check that you won't be happy paying.

Except on large checks, what's remarkable is a forger doesn't even need a signature anymore. On most checks, banks don't bother looking at signatures, because everything is automated. Banks process 69 billion checks a year, and nobody really sees most of those checks. Banks practice "selective check inspection," whereby they set a limit below which they will clear checks without examining their signatures. It's rare nowadays for a major bank to look at any check for less than twenty-five thousand dollars. These checks whisk through a high-speed bank check sorter at a rate of two thousand items per minute, or forty checks a second. When the checks go down the sorter rails, they're traveling at a speed in excess of four hundred miles an hour! The machines could do it quicker, but the checks would catch on fire.

Thus, if the check is under a designated amount, no human eye looks at the signature. If I scribble an "X" or write "Elvis Presley" on a one-thousand-dollar check, or don't sign it at all, the check is still going to clear the bank as long as the funds are in the account. "Dateline," during its report on check fraud, had no difficulty cashing small checks signed by "Porky Pig," "Bugs Bunny," "Attila the Hun," and "Bill Clinton."

On those checks, you can't fault bank employees for missing suspicious signatures. But you can on higher amounts. At many institutions, there are rules for when someone from the site review area must verify signatures. At most community banks today, it's $5,000. At most mid-sized banks, it's $10,000. At the nation's top fifty banks, it's $15,000 to $25,000 before any human being in site review looks at that check. But here we run into another problem: there's not much emphasis on training anymore. Years ago, for instance, every city used to have a chapter of the American Institute of Banking, which was the educational arm of the American Bankers Association. When banks started to merge and began to create multiple branches, however, bank managers said, "I don't want to send my teller out to some training program that I'm not controlling, so I'll train my own tellers." A lot of banks teach the teller how to handle all the money in the window, but don't tell them anything about how you recognize a counterfeit bill or how you recognize a fraudulent check. And smaller banks simply don't have the resources to train their personnel. New hires get trained by whoever is standing at the next window. What that person doesn't know, new tellers will never know.

DON'T GET YOUR WIRES CROSSED

When someone wants to forge a company's check, one of the most promising ways that he gathers the pertinent information is by calling his victim and asking for it. When the company switchboard answers, he asks for the accounts receivable department. He tells them that he's getting ready to wire the company some funds, and asks for the wiring instructions. He could call up any company in the world, and as soon as he says that he's going to wire them some money, the company will tell him where it banks, on what street, in what city, what the account number is, and what the transit number is. What more could you ask for? What the forger is essentially asking is, how do I write drafts on your bank account? And you're the one telling him. Ten years ago, you had to corner someone in the parking lot and bribe him to write down that information on a piece of paper. Now you can get it for free with a simple telephone call.

WHAT TO DO

Obviously, any company getting wires every day has to give out the information over the phone, in order to allow people to electronically transfer money to its accounts. But there's a way to prevent this kind of fraud. All you have to do is open up what's known as a non-negotiable incoming wire account to receive your wire transfers. So when people call up and ask for that information, that's the account you give them. Funds that come into that account by wire can't be withdrawn, can't be taken out verbally, and can't be taken out electronically. The only thing you can do is put money into the account. Those funds are held there until the end of the bank day, at which point they're moved to the account that you write checks on.

THE BUCK STOPS WITH YOU—SO YOU'D
BETTER GET THE CHECK RIGHT

In the old days, the bank was entirely liable if it paid a forged check. At that point, companies would say, well, I don't care about my checks. If somebody forges a check, I'll catch it in my audit, take it down to the bank, and they'll give me my money back. And if they don't, I'll find another bank to do business with.

Because of changes in the law, it doesn't work that way anymore. If the bank can prove that you were negligent in any way, then they don't owe you the money. Say you work in accounts payable and asked a clerk to cut you a check for $63,000 to pay an invoice. The clerk cut the check and then brought it to you. It was five o'clock, time to go home. You were going to mail it with some papers, but you say, oh, I'll just do it tomorrow. So you put it all in your out box and go home. The janitor comes in, takes the check, cashes it, and it clears the bank. You ask the bank for your money back. Forget about it. You were negligent in leaving the check lying there, and your negligence led to that forgery.

Due to the shift in liability, businesses need to make their checks more secure. There are an array of security features to do just that. I do a lot of check designing, and I advocate the use of a technique called layering, in which a number of features are added to the same check. Why? Because different protection features respond differently to fraud methods. By combining several features, attempting to circumvent one security feature can enhance the protection provided by another.

WHAT TO DO

First of all, you need to use a check that's difficult to forge or alter. Too many companies just use that familiar green or blue basketweave check paper, because it's the cheapest. The companies run it off on the laser printer and they have no controls at all on the paper.

To guard against forgers who use chemicals to alter checks, you need to order chemically sensitive paper. You have to ask the printer, If someone touches it with bleach or ink eradicators, what's going to happen?

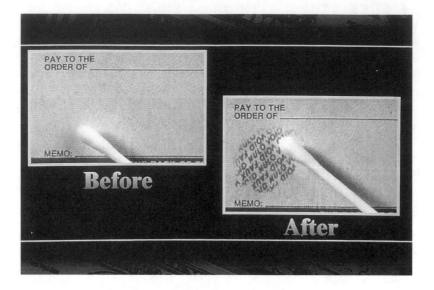

Good paper stock is sensitive to at least nineteen chemicals—chemicals like bleach, acetone, solvents, and hydrochlorides. Whenever these are used to alter a check, the word "void" appears in the background of the paper in three languages, English, Spanish, and French. The word should just appear right from behind the paper as soon as you touch it with any of those substances. At the very minimum, the check should change color. It should go from a blue check to a green spot or a brown spot on the check.

So if someone is issued a check and tries to chemically alter the amount, he's out of luck. He can't go back to you and say, "Look I tried to forge your check and this void showed up all over."

I told you about how forgers use Scotch tape to remove information off laser-printed checks. To solve this problem, when you buy laser paper for your checks you need to ask the supplier if it has "toner anchorage." Sometimes this is called "LaserLock" or "Toner Lock." This is a chemical that is put in the paper during the paper-making process to ensure that documents printed on a laser printer are secure. When the toner is applied, the chemical that is already in the paper is activated by the heat process and when the chemical and the toner mix, the toner is locked to the paper. It's impossible to scrape it off and tape won't remove it.

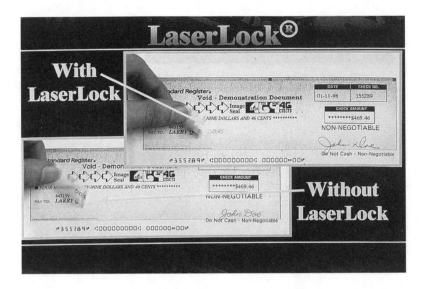

When you print checks, you should remember to use a font that is 12-point or higher. If you use small type, there's a lot less toner to take off. It's easier to remove with a piece of tape. If there's some residue, a forger just uses a bigger font to cover it up. A large font is less likely to be tampered with. It would take a forger all day with Scotch tape to remove the toner, and the process would leave a bigger area to cover up if anything does remain.

There are so-called "secure-number fonts" that make tampering with check dollar amounts impossible. Secure-number fonts are software that is loaded into your printer so that the dollar amounts print in a style that can't be altered. For instance, in the dollar amount box, the program reverses the toner, sending it to the back of the paper, so that numbers print white against a black background, and the toner background is permanent. The program will also print each numeral of a number in a different style, so that numerals can't be moved to change the amount. A secure-number payee font that does the same thing for the payee name is available as well.

A lot of times we number checks with a red ink or a black ink, and ink is removable. So I number checks with dye. It bleeds through the paper to the back of the check, and it stays on the check for the life of the check.

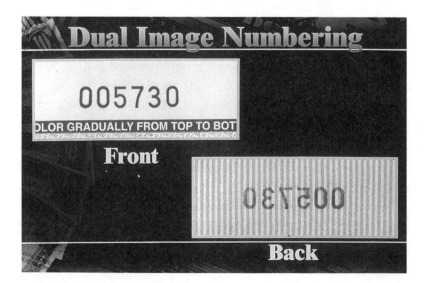

This is known as dual-image numbering (in Canada, it's called halo numbering), because you can see the number on both sides of the check, and it makes alteration nearly impossible.

Very often, I encounter companies that are more interested in company image than inventory control. All they have is blank-check stock with their company logo printed on the paper, handsomely done in four color up on the left-hand corner. Everything else is blank.

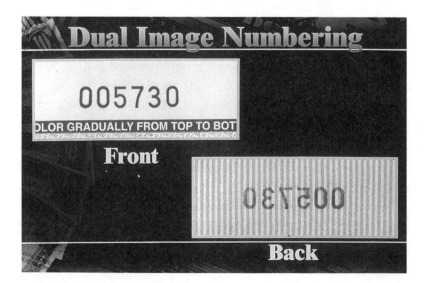

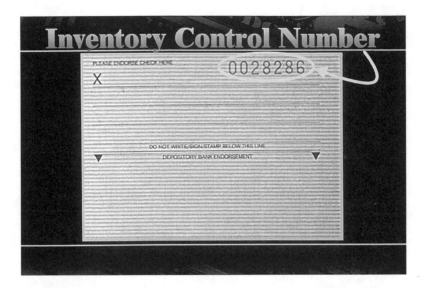

I always say to the company representatives, "What if I put one of these blank pieces of paper in my pocket? How would you know I had it?"

"Uh, we wouldn't."

"Well, think about that," I say. "I've just walked out of your company with your check. I've got a laser printer at home. All I've got to do is run it through the printer."

If all your company is going to do is have its logo on blank-check stock, you should ensure that inventory check numbers are on the back of each page. That number will allow you to control your unprinted check inventory.

One of the most basic and effective security features you can build into your checks is called a "void pantograph," which is printed in the background of a check. The way it works is the word "void" is put into the background in a dot pattern that isn't visible to the human eye. However, when a check with a void pantograph is copied or scanned, the word "void" appears along with it.

Look closely at some checks and you'll see what are called laid lines, which are evenly spaced lines on the back of the paper. I always put them on checks I design, because if someone takes a razor and slices the check and alters it, I want to know about it. Enhanced laid lines were intro-

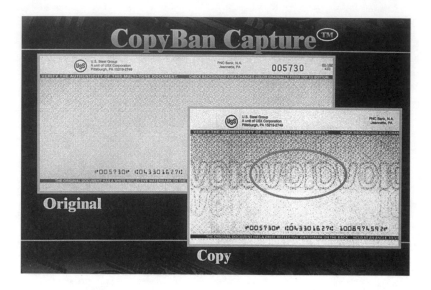

duced in 1997 that are similar in intent, but they use unevenly spaced lines and afford an even higher level of protection.

Another relatively new security feature is thermochromic inks, which disappear or, in some cases, change color when they react to heat and moisture. They will actually fade and then reappear again. Thermochromic ink can be found on the back of a check in a pink strip beneath the endorsement. Or it can be found on the front of the check in a corpo-

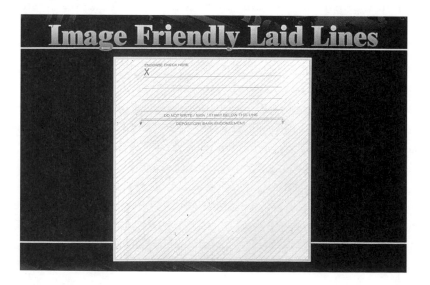

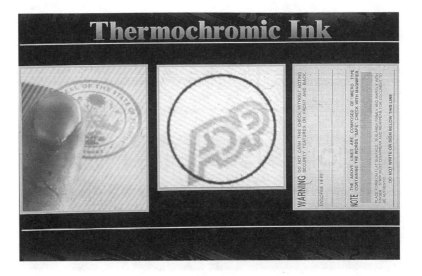

rate logo or seal. Run your finger over it and the heat from your finger will cause it to vanish. Let go, it comes right back. Day after day, year after year, just touch it and it disappears and then comes right back.

Other worthwhile antifraud techniques include artificial watermarks, messages that are visible only when the check is held at a 45-degree angle and aren't picked up by copiers and scanners; warning bands, which are statements printed on checks that point out design elements to look for

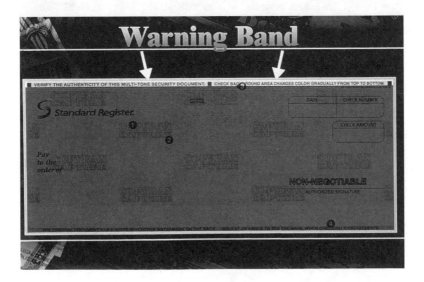

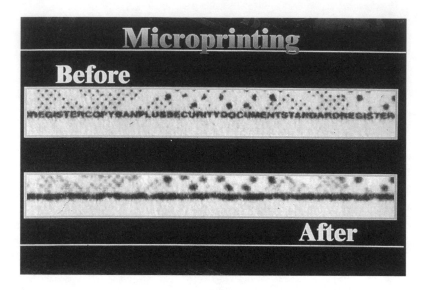

(no warning band is any good unless you add the words, "Do not cash," "Do not accept," or "Do not negotiate" before or after the warning); and microprinting, a technique where words or phrases added onto the check in letters so small they are legible only under a magnifying glass. It used to be that microprinting could only be done in a straight line, but circu-

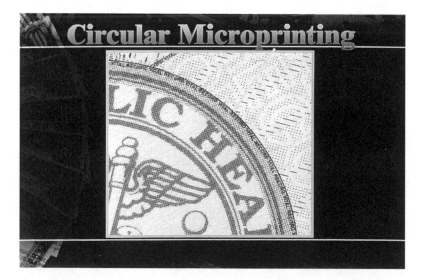

lar microprinting is now possible so you can put messages in as logos, or pictures.

Companies always ask me, "Well, we buy two hundred thousand checks a year, or a million checks a year, or two million, how much more will these things cost me if I incorporate them?" The answer is very little. With that kind of volume, adding these features won't add much cost. One other thing that I tell businesses is you need to secure all of your checks, not just some of them. All the time, I encounter companies that use secure features in payroll checks and accounts payable checks, but not in refund checks.

"Why not?" I ask them.

"Oh, they're always for small amounts," they say.

Their policy should be the exact opposite. Payroll checks go to employees who you know. Accounts payable checks go to vendors who you know. But refund checks go to complete strangers. They're the checks most in need of protection. Unfortunately, what criminals do today doesn't enter a comptroller's mind until his company suffers a loss.

BUT DO THEY WORK?

Believe me, these features really work. In 1993, Imperial Bank in California hired me to redesign its company check. The bank was having big problems with check fraud—to the tune of $3 million a year. I came in, and working with the printer, gave them some security features and helped them tighten their internal controls. The bank began to offer the new check to its customers at the same price as its regular check. It looks just like a regular check, and comes in a lot of colors and styles. The check-fraud losses fell to about $120,000 by 1996, a 96 percent decrease after three years of using the new check. This check is called SafeCheck, and is manufactured by a company that goes by the same name.

People often come up to me and say, You design these secure checks for corporations, why don't you design a check for me, the consumer? So I'm working to produce a secure consumer check. It will have twelve security features, including paper that reacts to twenty-four different chemicals, high resolution borders that are difficult to duplicate, white "chemical-wash detection boxes" that change colors with chemical tampering, and embedded fibers that glow under ultraviolet lights. But I've also told the manufacturers that whenever it takes an order, it has to verify the order with the person's bank. If someone changes his address, that has to be verified. It makes no sense to create a secure check if any criminal can order it.

When I design a check, I follow a little routine. I send a sample to three places: a graphics house in Australia, an Australian forensic document examiner, and a U.S. institute of technology. I ask each of them to create their best replica, so I can test how secure it is. At the institute, they select a smart student and give him access to the most sophisticated computer equipment, literally millions of dollars of gear. The last check I sent there, the student took a month's worth of manhours to produce a good replica. That told me I had a great check. As I've said, nothing is foolproof, but if it takes a clever student a month with millions of dollars of equipment to produce a counterfeit, I know few criminals have a prayer.

The other thing I learn is which features work best. Lately, I've been working with prismatic printing, which puts a multicolored, rainbow-like background on the check. It's very difficult to photocopy.

YOUR FIRST LINE OF DEFENSE IS YOU

If we're ever going to stop fraud, everyone has got to become a bit more vigilant. My guess would be that half of all Americans don't bother to reconcile their bank statements. They don't even open them. And what they don't realize is that they're liable for errors, because they generally have thirty days to notify their bank of a discrepancy, and sometimes less than that. Let's say I did get hold of your check and I filled it out for $2,000, and you never bothered to look at your bank statement. A month or two later, your husband says, "Hey, we're overdrawn at the bank." You say, "That's impossible. I've got $2,000 in the account." The bank says, "Oh no you don't, you're overdrawn." Now you go back and open that envelope and discover a check for $2,000 that you didn't write. You didn't sign it. Guess what? It's too late. The bank is not going to restore your money. But most people don't realize this until it happens to them.

A Wisconsin man named Borowski had two checking accounts with Firststar Bank. One was his personal account and one was for his father's estate. Borowski said that his fiancée stole $50,000 from his account, and $100,000 from the estate account. She did it with forged checks and unauthorized telephone transfers. She even left forged handwritten notes in the bank's night depository box requesting cashier's checks. When the monthly bank statements and $20,000 in cashier's checks were sent to Borowski, his fiancée intercepted them. When Borowski discovered the theft, he sued the bank to get his money back. Presumably, he also called off his impending marriage.

The case went to court. The bank pointed out that Borowski's signature card agreements required notification to the bank of unauthorized checks within fourteen days of the statement date. Borowski said he hadn't received the statements, because his fiancée got hold of them and lied about them.

The court ruled in favor of the bank. It said that as long as the bank had mailed the statements to the customer's proper address, it had upheld its part of the bargain. The court did rule in favor of Borowski on the $20,000 in cashier's checks, however, because the bank didn't include the handwritten notes with the bank statement.

GET GOOD BACKUP: POSITIVE PAY

There is a product out in the marketplace, and already about 60 percent of the nation's major banks offer it. It's called positive pay. I feel that positive pay is the greatest concept available to deal with the problem of forgery or fraud. In most cases, the bank provides it for a minimal fee. If it doesn't, look on it as an insurance premium to guard against losses from fraud.

The product is really quite simple. Say I'm a company and I write fifty checks a day. I could write five a day or five thousand a day, it doesn't matter. At the end of each day, I download a list to the bank over my modem of all the checks I wrote that day and sent out in the mail. The list, called an issue file, simply runs through each check number and the amount of the check. The bank doesn't want to know who I wrote the check to.

The file goes down to the bank and is stored in a program called positive pay. The checks go out in the mail and, lo and behold, a forged check shows up. I wrote a check to a guy for $250 and he color-copied fifty of them. I don't care. I'm on positive pay. I wrote a guy a check for $200 and he altered it to $2,000. I don't care. I'm on positive pay. The point is, when the forger goes to cash that check, it will go to the first bank of deposit, and then it will come to your bank. But because that check doesn't match a check on your list, it will be rejected. No match, no pay. If you didn't write it, the bank isn't going to pay it. The computer will say, I have one refund check for $250, but I don't have fifty, so I'll pay one and return forty-nine. I have one check for $200, but I've searched the file and I don't have one for $2,000, so it returns the check unpaid.

Now there are some small businesses that love the idea of positive pay, but they don't have a computer. I ask them, Do you have a fax machine? Yeah, they have that. Well, your bank can put you on reverse positive pay. At eight-thirty in the morning, your bank will fax you a list of all the checks written by you that came into the bank last night to be paid today. You'll have until two-thirty that afternoon to look over that list. If everything looks fine, you don't have to do anything, just throw the list away. But if you find a discrepancy, you call the bank and tell them to fax you that check. If you look at it and it's not your check, you tell the bank not to pay it.

This product literally does away with the threat of forged checks, altered checks, stolen checks, and counterfeit checks. And positive pay is also on the bank's teller line. So if I had taken your checks and they were drawn on, say, the Chase Bank, I would obviously go to a Chase branch to try to cash it. But when I go up to a teller at a Chase Bank and present a check, the teller would pull it up on the screen and say, "Sir, this check was never issued as of noon today. The company never wrote this check, so what is this?" So you're stopped cold right at the teller.

One of the most common questions I get about positive pay is, what if I send Frank Abagnale a check for five thousand dollars but a postal employee steals the check and Frank Abagnale never gets it? The employee types above my name, Bill Clark, and goes and cashes the check. The check number is the same and the amount of the check is unchanged. How will positive pay catch that?

It won't, but it's not meant to. That's because that is an altered payee, and under banking law, altered payee checks are the liability of the first bank of deposit, not your liability or your bank's liability.

Like any technology, positive pay is not foolproof. I recommend companies use both positive pay and a very secure check to close the loop, lock the lock, and throw away the key.

WAITING FOR THE PAPERLESS TOILET

A lot of companies and consumers figure, why worry too much about checks? With computers and debit cards, they won't be with us that much longer. Well, anyone who thinks that checks are going away is dead wrong. People are always asking me, "When are we going to see the paperless society?" I tell them, "When you see the paperless toilet. No time soon."

I'll be long dead, even if I live to a ripe old age, before checks will ever disappear. The amount of checks we write is growing at a rate of more than a billion checks a year. So they're not even declining in use. They're growing. I remember fifteen years ago, when we were writing 40 billion checks a year, people said it would never reach 50 billion, and now we're at almost 70 billion.

People happen to like checks. They're familiar. Many consumers will say, "I like this check. It has some float to it. I like that much better than when the bank immediately goes into my checking account and takes the money out. I also like the idea that I can get the check back and see who I wrote it to and have a record of it." And we have a very large generation that is not comfortable with smart cards and electronics. They're leery of new ways of payments, and they don't fully grasp them.

Electronic banking is still much more of an unknown frontier. And there's no forgetting the billions of dollars that banks have invested in electronic readers, sorters, and other check processing equipment.

We're not going to just scrap it and plow money into home banking. There are banks out there pushing electronics, but there are a lot of other banks that would just as soon stay with checks.

So if we're going to continue to use checks, you had better learn how to protect yourself. After all, awareness is 99 percent of solving the problem. The moment you accept the fact that fraud and forgery are so easy to accomplish, that's the moment you've taken the first step toward combating it.

3

[COUNTERFEIT **CAPERS**]

I once was interviewed about fraudulent documents by Sam Donaldson of ABC television. During the interview, I dug into my briefcase for a moment and pulled out a piece of paper. I handed it to him and said, "By the way, have you seen this letter?" He studied the sheet of paper and his eyes got very wide. "Wait a minute, where did you get this?" he said.

It was a letter of reference on ABC stationery, extolling the many virtues of Frank Abagnale. It was signed by Sam Donaldson.

"You sent me a letter two days ago confirming our interview," I said. "I scanned the ABC letterhead into my computer. I matched the paper— it was just standard linen paper—with paper I bought at the local stationery store. Then I wrote the new text and printed it out."

"But what about my signature?" he asked.

"I scanned that off your letter, too," I said.

That was just a fun thing I did to illustrate a point. But I'm far from the only one doing it. We're literally awash in phony documents, and I'm not talking simply about those fake IDs that teenagers buy in Times Square to allow them to purchase beer and gain entrance to clubs. Counterfeit documents of every imaginable kind have proliferated: birth certificates, death certificates, Social Security cards, driver's licenses, store receipts, medical prescriptions, product labels, traveler's checks, event tickets, amusement park passes, coupons, car titles, green cards, diplomas, college transcripts, passports, voter identification cards, and, the most counterfeited piece of paper of all, money itself. Almost anyone can professionally forge or counterfeit a wide variety of documents, day after day, for an investment of just a few thousand dollars.

Because so much fake paper is floating around, I caution managers that when they hire someone for a sensitive position, it's more than credentials that they need. They have to make phone calls. They have to write letters. Don't trust a piece of paper, because anything can be replicated. Just ask Sam Donaldson.

It's gotten so bad, even the FBI is changing its credentials. Since the days of Hoover, they've had the same ones—reused. When an FBI agent retires, he turns in his credentials and a new agent receives them. Now the agency is redoing them with holograms to make them harder to counterfeit.

A CHAIN IS ONLY AS STRONG
AS ITS WEAKEST LINK

The real travesty here is the chain-link effect of counterfeit documents. What happens is criminals use counterfeit papers as "breeder" documents. A breeder document is a phony document used to obtain a genuine one. Generally speaking, criminals will counterfeit a document that has little, if any, security features and then use that to get far more secure legitimate documents.

In most cases, a birth certificate contains next to no security features, so it has become an ideal breeder document. Criminals will create a fake birth certificate to obtain a genuine driver's license, then use those two documents to get a legitimate passport. Once you've got that first authentic document, you're pretty much on your way. After all, the right documents allow people to get unauthorized benefits, to land jobs they're not entitled to, to gain illegal entry into a country, to construct new identities, and to fraudulently obtain credit cards and loans.

There's always been a lot of Mom and Pop document fraud, and there still is, but there are actual document syndicates today that are as well-organized as major corporations. There's actually a standard counterfeit package that immigrants buy that consists of a resident alien card, Social Security card, and driver's license. Gangs in big cities like Chicago, New York, and Los Angeles sell these ensembles on the street. The criminals will brazenly approach foreigners in broad daylight and ask, "What do you need?" Estimates are that counterfeit and illegally-obtained documents cost the country something on the order of $25 billion a year. In late 1998, Immigration and Naturalization Service (INS) agents raided two storage facilities in Los Angeles and rounded up more than two million counterfeit identity documents. The agency estimated that the street value of that paper was in excess of $80 million. Hardly chump change.

GOODBYE PEN AND INK MEN

Technology has made life so much easier for the counterfeiter. Years ago, a document counterfeiter was known as a "pen and ink man." He worked meticulously by hand and needed steady nerves. That's all changed. To get an idea of the impact of technology on crime, consider the color copier. In late 1977, Xerox invented the machine called the Xerox 6500 Color Copier. And it was quite a machine. At that time, it was considered the most advanced copier in the world. People were reproducing full-color documents in a matter of seconds. All a forger had to do was lay a real check on the machine, close the cover, push a button, and out would come a duplicate check that looked just like the real thing. Forgers loved the Xerox 6500 so much so that they cashed more than $365 million worth of phony checks color-copied by the machine.

Twenty years later, it's an antique. These days, forgers interested in a wide array of documents use a product called the color laser digital copier, again found everywhere. The quality of the color copies produced by this machine is truly remarkable. Nearly anything on paper can be acceptably reproduced: gift certificates, traveler's checks, birth certificates, college transcripts, car titles, and even money. It can reproduce such magnificent colors that you couldn't tell the real thing from the fake even in a side-by-side comparison. Color copiers are so proficient at re-producing dollar bills that, in most cases, the bogus bills will go through a vending machine. They're so realistic that you find them in ATMs.

If you want to stop document fraud, you have to start building layers of security features into the documents. Because I'm in this business, I even have an array of features on my company letterhead. If Sam Donaldson tried to scan one of my letters the way I scanned his, he'd be in for a rude shock: "void" would show up all over the document.

YOU DON'T NEED A STORK

To counterfeiters, the birth certificate is one of the choicest documents of all, because so much can be accomplished with it. Since it's accepted by just about every government agency as proof of one's identity and cit-izenship, it's the key to getting a host of benefits and other documents. Thousands of state and local registrars' offices issue birth certificates in the United States. Many of them produce more than one type. Also, states have revised their certificates many times over the years, and both the old and the new variations are all in circulation. Add this all up, and there could be more than ten thousand variations of the U.S. birth certificate in existence. And that's great news to a counterfeiter. The more rendi-tions of a document, the harder it is for anyone to say that the one that you have is false.

Some birth certificates have very good security features. Some have none at all. I guess it's obvious that the best birth certificate to use fraud-ulently is a genuine one. Normally, it doesn't take a lot of effort to get one. In many states, birth certificates and death records are part of the public record and are readily available to anyone for the asking. I've seen estimates that more than 80 percent of requests for birth certificates are processed through the mail for people who gave nothing more than a name and a return address. Some states have a few requirements, but nothing so onerous that a smart criminal can't circumvent them. For in-stance, in certain states, only the next of kin or an attorney can request the birth certificate. But you don't have to go to law school to become a lawyer. All you need to do is pay a visit to a print shop and get some business cards and letterhead that will transform you into a lawyer, enough of one, at least, to get access to public records.

As with checks, forgers are adept at altering birth certificates. The biographical information is printed onto the surface of the paper. This means it's easy for the forger to remove it either mechanically or chemically, substitute new information, and be left with a genuine document imprinted with phony information, which can be very hard to detect. And with document scanners, computers, copiers, and the other technologies I've mentioned, it's quite simple to run off counterfeit birth certificates that will pass muster.

I've designed high-tech birth certificates for a number of states to guard against counterfeiting and alteration. The security features void the document if someone tries to copy it or chemically change it with bleach, acetone, or other substances. But I tell state officials, "This isn't going to stop an impostor from getting someone else's actual birth certificate. You need to make it harder for that to happen." And their response is, "Well, we know that, but that's another issue."

I no longer get involved in securing a state's birth certificate or driver's license, if they're not going to close the other loopholes. A few years ago, I worked on the Florida certificate. Florida makes it very hard to get a legitimate birth certificate. But the document itself was easily counterfeited. And with all the illegal immigrants down there, it was a highly desirable piece of paper. In Miami, a Florida birth certificate had a street value of five thousand dollars. So I designed a very secure document, and the counterfeiting problem has abated.

PICK A LICENSE, ANY LICENSE

Driver's licenses were initially intended simply to confirm that the holder had the right to drive in the state. But our customs have transformed them into commonly requested identity documents as well. And that has made them of keen interest to criminals.

The validity of a license is hard to determine, because there are so many in circulation and they differ so much. There are hundreds of variations, depending on when and where they were issued. In many states, you can get a legitimate driver's license simply by showing a driver's license from another state. Virginia, for instance, does that. So if you get away with passing off a counterfeit Kansas driver's license in Virginia, bingo, you can obtain a real Virginia one.

In California, they spent a fortune on their new driver's license. They put holograms on them, used sophisticated sealants in the printing, just poured a ton of money into the design. And a few months after the new license was introduced, the police arrested a forger with fifty licenses in fifty different names. Why? Because it was still easy for someone to go to the Driver's License Bureau and get a license with false identification. I told the state, "All you've done is stop some kid from changing the birth date on his license in order to buy a beer."

Either close all the loopholes, or you've closed none.

FEELING SECURE?

Another case in point is the U.S. passport. We all know how handy a fake passport is to a crook on the lam. So it makes a lot of sense to really secure it. The passport has long had some good features, and I added a new one a few years ago. For the U.S. passport, I helped develop with Standard Register a technique called Mirage Image, which adds encrypted information onto the passport photo. When you put a special piece of milled glass over the photo, your name and birthday are visible. The passport has become a hard document to successfully counterfeit, which is why a fraudulent American passport commands ten thousand dollars on the streets.

Unfortunately, the other loopholes haven't been closed. Nearly anyone can acquire a fake Social Security card and birth certificate that are good enough to get a genuine passport. Until these other documents are made more secure, the passport remains at risk. Right now, the U.S. Social Security card is about as vulnerable as it gets. Border Patrol Agents routinely intercept thousands of fake Social Security cards every year at traffic checkpoints. In 1999, they collected something like a hundred and twenty thousand of them, more than one every five minutes. This is frightening, because the Social Security card has become our ad hoc identity card, enabling the holder to collect government benefits and to certify that he's eligible for employment. When you flash a Social Security card, people know you're for real.

At the moment, there are more than twenty different versions of the Social Security card, and they vary a great deal in their security features. Earlier cards, meaning those issued prior to October of 1983, have no security features whatsoever. Those issued since then contain various things like intaglio engraving and microprinting. But criminals know that it's possible to get a genuine Social Security card if you have one of two other documents: a birth certificate or a resident alien card.

In recent years, the INS has been steadily tightening its own documents. Just a few years ago, the INS had twenty different types of Permanent Resident and Employment Authorization cards that were valid, too many for comfort. Now there are just five. No longer are the cards good for a lifetime, the way Social Security cards are, but expiration dates have been added, which enables the agency to update photos and implant new security features when a card is replaced. One new feature is a personalized engraving of the person's photo, signature and biographical data right on the optical stripe. These are important steps in the right direction, for they make it just about impossible for counterfeit cards to be mass produced.

BALL PARK PRANKS

Large public events of any type—sporting, political, religious—invariably draw a great many uninvited participants: crooks. Con artists go where the money is. Wherever there are crowds, there are opportunities for scams. You'd be amazed at how common it is for criminals to make counterfeit tickets and passes. It routinely happens at the World Series, the Super Bowl, and big golf tournaments. Two disasters at soccer matches where scores of fans were injured, some seriously, were attributed to stadium overcrowding. Why were the stadiums so crammed? Because thousands of people had gotten in after buying counterfeit tickets from scalpers.

I've worked on a lot of golf passes and the Disney World pass. Generally, I put an invisible dot on them. Then the guard at the entrance gate has a reader that reveals it. Disney also has cruise ships. Most of the employees are foreigners who need a special pass that allows them to get on and off the ship, and so I designed a secure version of that, too, which is printed by the Standard Register Company. With these documents, it makes no sense to incorporate the level of security features that you would put into a check, because you have to consider the value of what you're securing. If a pass is worth $30, it only pays to put maybe one security feature on it. But a check can cost you millions of dollars.

I served as a consultant to the 2000 Summer Olympics in Sydney, which, from my perspective, I envisioned as a possible gala fraud festival. Before I even got on a plane to go there, I realized that there were bound to be millions of dollars in losses from various cons at the games. At the Atlanta games, traveler's check fraud alone totaled more than $4 million, and there had been enough improvements in technology during the four ensuing years to make life easier for criminals.

I knew Australia was receptive to fraud. I had heard that there were something like three million more federal tax ID numbers issued in the country than there were actual Australians, which is not a promising sign. Plenty of counterfeit money was bound to be put into circulation—not the Australian currency, but American bills. Forgers don't do the local currency, because people are familiar with it. American bills were ideal, because newly-designed five-dollar and ten-dollar bills had just been released the month of the Olympics. Even Americans weren't familiar with them. When I visited the major Australian banks, they already had plenty of samples of fake bills that had crossed their teller windows.

At any event where there are limited tickets for which there is great demand, bogus tickets are always a nettlesome problem. I advised the organizers of the Olympics to use Australian printers to print the tickets for the games, because my experience has been that Australia has some of the best printers of secure documents in the world. In fact, I have all of my corporate checks and personal checks, even my business cards, printed in Australia. The printers there are not only good at making documents secure, but they're true craftsmen.

For whatever reason, the organizers of the games didn't follow my advice, and the contracts were given to a small company in Arkansas and another one in England. I thought that was an unwise decision. Even if those printers did a stellar job, there was all the handling of the tickets from America and England to Australia that presented opportunities for fraud.

WHAT TO DO

Since you can't expect ticket holders to differentiate between genuine and counterfeit tickets, electronic verification systems are necessary at the entry points to big events. As an added precaution, ticket holders should always carry their receipts with them in case someone turns up in their seat with a fraudulent ticket. And I tell people to be wary of anyone who offers to sell tickets for less than their true value; it's usually a sign that they're fake.

Because I'm always interested in how prepared people are for con artists, I went around with a reporter to some of the shops in Australia. We dropped in on a clothing store, and the reporter asked the clerk, "If someone came in here and wanted to buy a sweater and all they had was a hundred-dollar American bill, would you take it?"

"Oh, no," the clerk said, "I'd tell him to go to the currency exchange and bring back Australian money."

Satisfied that the man was on the alert, the reporter was ready to leave, but I wanted to rephrase the question. I asked the clerk, "Suppose someone came in and said, 'Gee, I really like that sweater. I see it's the equivalent of seventy-five American dollars. Listen, I'm in a big rush and I don't have time to get change. Why don't you take this hundred-dollar bill, and we'll call it even.' What would you do?"

"I'd take it in a minute," he said.

He would have sold a sweater for nothing. And the con man would have gotten a sweater for a bill that probably cost him ten cents in paper. See, the con man knows that the clerk wouldn't take the money. And he knows how to exploit human nature and go to the next step. That's why you can never let your guard down.

And the tricks never cease. A couple of years ago, I was hired by Go Transit in Toronto, the metropolitan transit agency, because they were being hindered by ticket fraud on their buses and trains. The ticket they used was a thick piece of paper, with the same fare information printed on both sides. Kids were taking tickets home and putting them in the freezer overnight. When they took them out, the paper was split perfectly in two. Most paper will split when frozen. So they now had two tickets. Go Transit was losing something like a couple of million dollars a year from the scam. I redesigned the ticket using a special paper that won't split, making for a lot of grumpy kids who had to start paying the full fare again.

MY DENTIST FOR LIFE

There's nothing that you can look at today and be certain that it's real. And that opens a lot of doors. Interested in getting some drugs? That's not a problem. You put on a nice suit and go down to a dental office in a wealthy part of town at eight forty-five in the morning and tap on the glass. "Excuse me," you say, "I woke up this morning with this abscessed molar. I'm in serious pain."

The receptionist asks if you're a patient. "No," you say. "I just moved to town, but everyone told me he's a great dentist and if I can slip in this morning and see him, he's my dentist for life." The receptionist checks with the dentist, and comes back and tells you that he's booked up solid, but he'll stay late and squeeze you in at the end of the day. He's sympathetic to your anguish, she says, so he's given you a prescription for a painkiller. You take the prescription, make fifty copies of it, go to fifty pharmacies, and you've got fifty bottles of painkillers to sell on the street.

For a new college graduate to get a good job, or to get into a top-notch graduate school, he needs the best transcript possible. But if his actual transcript doesn't quite pass muster, that's easy enough to rectify. He scans his transcript into his computer and, in a revisionist touch, improves his 3.0 grade point average to a perfect 4.0. Many employers and graduate schools require applicants to send in their transcripts through the registrar's office, but that's fine. You simply call your university and ask them to mail you a university application. When you get the material, which comes with a nice letter from the registrar, you scan the university's logo, letterhead, registrar's envelope and signature, and mail it off. One thief had the nerve to put a counterfeit degree and transcript from the University of South Florida up for auction on eBay. He offered it for fifty dollars. Seventeen bids later, it went for $356.

Here's another clever idea made possible by new technology. Crooks today can go to a junkyard and find a late-model Lincoln Continental that had been totaled in an accident and buy it for one thousand dollars. The car is such a wreck that they can't even drive it, so they tow it to their home. They say, "Why don't we go down to the credit union and get a loan against the car? They'd give us twenty thousand dollars on it easily. We give them the car title for collateral, they give us the loan. The car title doesn't say the car is a wreck [only recently have some states started issuing different titles for damaged cars]. A week later, we'll default on the loan. We'll go to another credit union and get another twenty thousand dollars. Then we go to another, and another. In just a few trips, we're out of here with one hundred thousand dollars from a car that won't go around the corner." One of the crooks might wonder, "But how could we get another loan when we gave the first credit union the car title?" And one of the others will reply, "I didn't say give them *the* car title, but give them *a* car title, a copy that we make."

Five years ago, that was impossible to do, because in all fifty states car titles had to be intaglio engraved. In order to reproduce the engraving, it would take at least a half million dollars in equipment and considerable skill. Today, with a digital copier, I just place the car title on the machine, put a piece of paper in the cassette, and make a copy. I pick up the copy, put it back into the cassette, make another copy, and then another and another. Each time I make a copy I'm building up toner over toner over toner over toner. After the fifth copy, I have the exact raised lettering, the exact engraving, the exact seal of the original. And that's why con artists regularly pull off precisely the scam I described above.

MALL MADNESS

You go to the mall nowadays, and invariably, some guy will ask you, "You want to buy a gift certificate for the mall?" So you take one for two hundred dollars. He asks you what name to put on it. You tell him that you don't know who you're going to give it to, just leave it blank. You go home, type in a name, make fifty color copies at the local copy shop, and return to the mall. Companies that issue gift certificates vastly underestimate the quality of color copiers. Most gift certificates can be copied without a single telltale sign. In fact, in many cases the color copies actually look sharper and brighter than the originals.

These new mall gift certificates are wonderful, because they're honored at virtually any store in a mall, as well as any store in other malls handled by the same management company. This is a great consumer benefit, and a great criminal benefit. A criminal will go to a mall in Miami, buy a gift certificate, make a hundred copies, and spend that same gift certificate in New York, Los Angeles, Atlanta, and fifty other malls around the country. What a terrific way to travel during the holidays!

During the Christmas rush period, harried and inexperienced sales clerks haven't a prayer. So you take your $200 gift certificate to the Gap, buy some $50 jeans, and get the $150 change in cash. You go to the frame shop, buy a $28 frame, get the change in cash. One of the things criminals love about gift certificates is they're as good as cash. Most stores are happy to give cash when making change after a purchase. And since many companies reconcile their gift certificates only on a sixty-to-ninety-day cycle, criminals have plenty of time to complete their holiday shopping.

The security people at the malls call me all the time and say, "Hey, the mall's getting killed. Thieves are hitting us with all these color-copied gift certificates."

I tell them, "You have to put out a bulletin to all your store managers about the names on the gift certificates."

"Uh, we don't put names on them."

"Well, you need to send a bulletin out about the serial number of the gift certificates," I say.

"Uh, we don't put numbers on them."

"Well then, you need to tell me where you're calling from so I can come and buy some of those gift certificates."

Remember, if they have value, they'll copy them.

SHOP 'TIL YOU DROP

Con artists have a particular fondness for store receipts. They're a living in themselves. I was once visiting with the head of security for one of the big discount chains, and he was telling me how incredibly secure his stores were with all their cameras and gadgetry. "Really," I said. "Well, let's see." I walked with him outside the store entrance, rooted around in the trash receptacle there, and fished out a receipt. Customers are constantly throwing away their receipts as soon as they leave a store. I examined the receipt and noticed it included a toaster oven. So I went with the security head to the small appliance area and picked out the same model toaster oven. I told the security director, "Now all I have to do is go to customer service, tell them I just bought this and need to return it, and I've just conned the store."

Criminals aren't content to just go with what they find in the garbage, and so naturally they make their own fraudulent receipts. Several years ago, Macy's had a nagging problem with criminals. Armed with fraudulent receipts, the criminals went to the store, picked out the items they had listed on the fake receipts, and then returned them for cash. The clerks at Macy's had no way of distinguishing a real receipt from a counterfeit one. I was brought in and redid the receipt by adding "Macy's" on the back in thermochromic ink. Rub your finger over the word and the body heat causes it to disappear. Macy's trains all of its help to check receipts with their fingers, and the problem has been cured.

A few years ago, there was a guy who drove all over the country in a white Cadillac who had his own inventive scam. One of the big store chains would regularly put its fine jewelry on sale for 50 percent off. This guy would anticipate these sales and go in and buy a necklace or bracelet at full price. The chain had an arrangement where, if you had bought an item of jewelry just prior to the sale, you could come in with your receipt and it would give you the difference back in cash. First, he would take his receipt to a local copy shop and make two hundred copies. Then he'd return the necklace and hit the road. Whenever he encountered another store in that chain, he would bring in one of his fraudulent receipts and get a refund of half the price. He didn't need to show the necklace, just the receipt. He did this for years. He'd park his Cadillac illegally in the fire lane outside a store, dash in, collect his cash, and head to the next store. Eventually, the chain figured out how to stop him. It ceased offering the cash-back arrangement.

Some of the techniques used to fleece businesses are surprisingly simple, but they can be raised to the level of art by rings of criminals. If I had to anoint the King of the Receipt Scam, it would be Rondal Vickers. Vickers is a sixty-two-year-old Florida man, and an Air Force veteran with a generous white beard. He goes by the name Santa Claus. It's an unlikely nickname, since he was the ringleader of a crime group composed of as many as twenty thieves known as the Vickers Gang. For more than thirty years, it carried out an elaborate refund scam that was reliant on counterfeit receipts and UPC labels. (In their spare time, the gang indulged in gift certificate fraud and insurance fraud, once collecting insurance claims six times on the same Corvette.)

Santa Claus pretty much had theft in his blood. He got started as a checkout cashier at a Winn-Dixie and augmented his paycheck by never ringing up purchases of beer. Whenever someone had beer mixed in with his groceries, he would pretend to have forgotten to ring it up, hit "no sale" on the register, and then ask for the amount, which he pocketed. From that beginning, he built a formidable organization. One of the masterminds was a fifteen-year-old runaway named Jodi Vickers, who became Santa Claus' wife. The gang traveled all over the country, generally in "sprees" lasting six to eight weeks, and then they would return to their home base in Florida until they needed to steal some more money. They preyed on the national mass-market retail chains like Wal-Mart, Kmart, and Target. Santa Claus was particularly fond of Target, because it kept enhancing its security in order to foil him. To feed his ego, he relished the challenge of beating the toughest system, so he'd often send his soldiers to the other chains and devote his own devilish energies to Target.

The Vickers Gang had multiple scams in its arsenal, but its most common dodge was something it referred to as "marking down." Members of the gang would visit one store in a chain and identify a sale item. For instance, they'd pick out a tent that was on sale for $19.95. They would jot down the UPC number, and with a hand-held UPC gun anyone can get from a retailer supply house, would make a counterfeit UPC label. They'd return with the label cupped in their hand and stick it over the actual UPC label of a higher-priced tent, say one selling for $129.95, and then put the tent in their shopping cart. They'd mosey around and pick up a shirt, some pants, a bottle of shampoo, maybe some chips and dip, enough other goods to get that receipt high enough to exceed $129.95. Say they'd get it to $149.95. At almost all stores, the receipts didn't have what's known as line-item detail. When you returned something, the store computer would read only the header at the top of the receipt. That header gave the date and time of transaction, as well as the total amount of the purchase, in this case $149.95. But the computer won't search the list of items on the receipt and see if they matched a purchase record stored in the computer.

Once they got out of the store, the crew members would remove the phony UPC label. They'd scan the header of the receipt and then print out a counterfeit receipt containing that header, but with a new list of items, including a tent for $129.95. They would use distraction to steal cash register paper right out of a cash register, so they could print the fraudulent receipt on the actual paper of the chain. Finally, they'd go to a sister store in another town with the receipt and return the tent, earning $110 for their effort. When the customer service representative looked at the receipt, he'd see the tent there and the computer would satisfy itself that the header included a sufficient amount of money. The Vickers Gang would print up additional phony receipts to return as much as possible of the other items, though some of the things they kept because they needed them. In this way, they made as much as $4,000 a day during busy shopping periods. They liked tents because there was such a wide price range. They also liked golf clubs, and for a while they made a killing returning submersible water pumps to Home Depot.

BUT THERE ARE ALWAYS RULES AND REGULATIONS

The Vickers Gang operated like a well-oiled business. Santa Claus schooled his members in a list of professional rules and routines they were to faithfully obey. For instance, the Vickers Gang never did their marking down in the morning, except around Christmas when the stores are continually packed and clerks are easily distracted. Otherwise, they avoided mornings because that's when clerks and other store employees are most alert. The Vickers Gang would do its shopping in the afternoon, after the clerks have been there for four or five hours. By then, everyone is worn out. Cashiers just want to get you out of there, because they're ready to go out on a date or pick up their kids, and they just want the last two or three hours at the store to end.

They were told never to return something in Minneapolis with a receipt they got in Chicago. Clerks get confused with out-of-state receipts, because the chains often have different style receipts in different states. They won't recognize them and will then call the manager. You never want the manager to get involved. Another rule was not to return something with a receipt dated thirty minutes ago to a store an hour away. Also, they were forbidden to return the same type of item twice to the same store. If you bring back pots and pans one day, don't return pots and pans next week. You can bring in a jacket or a microwave, but not the same thing. There's always the risk that the store will have figured out the pots and pan return after you left.

Determined to stop the Vickers Gang, Target was fastidious about incorporating fresh security features into their receipts. But when company officials go to sleep at night, criminals stay up late working on new ways to beat the system. The genius about Santa Claus and the Vickers Gang was their ability to adapt. Within days of a retail chain making alterations in its systems, they would make the appropriate changes in their operations. After all, when they began, there were no UPC codes, just ordinary price stickers. So they counterfeited the price stickers. Stores had manual cash registers. So the Vickers drove around with an NCR cash register in their trunk, and would make their counterfeit receipts on the register. When clerks looked at a receipt when he was returning something, Santa Claus would sometimes joke, "If you don't like that receipt, I can just get another one from my trunk." When stores moved to computers, they followed suit. At one point, Target switched to a restricted cash register ribbon that printed in two colors of ink, so that the top half of a number might be black and the bottom half red. The Vickers Gang tried unsuccessfully to buy one of the ribbons, and finally managed to steal one.

The Vickers Gang had a long and prosperous run, and some narrow escapes. Sensing she was being watched, Jodi Vickers once had to peel off a bunch of labels she stuck on some pots and pans and chew them up. Both she and her husband got caught in a Kmart but were let off with probation. But the work of Target investigators and law enforcement agents finally succeeded in catching Santa Claus and his gang in Florida in the mid-1990s, and he was sent to prison. He never paid any restitution. While he was in jail, Target became one of the few chains to switch to line-item detail on its receipts, which is what I strongly recommend. When you bring something back to Target now, the computer in the store will not only read the header but also search for that particular item and see that it matches the purchase record in the computer's data base.

Jodi Vickers agreed to cooperate with prosecutors and received probation. The last I heard, she was remarried, working for the Florida Motor Vehicle Department, of all places, and writing cookbooks for people with gout. Toward the end of 2000, Santa Claus was released from jail. His feet were in bad shape from gangrene, but Target and other retailers put their stores on alert that he was once again a free man. Even at this late date, no one is willing to bet that he is planning to go straight.

THE JOYS OF TRAVEL

Traveler's checks are another favorite document for criminals to counterfeit, because they can be readily converted into cash. Traveler's checks are pretty secure. The problem is not enough people who take them know how to recognize the security features, even though it's not hard, since there are only four brands of traveler's checks in the world to remember.

The first thing to know is that all traveler's checks begin with the routing number, 8000. This is the number assigned to traveler's check companies. Forgers who forge traveler's checks go to a great deal of trouble and expense to engrave them. In order to make their money back, they need a lot of time to pass them. To give themselves this time, they will remove the 8000 code and insert the check code of a bank located a far distance from where the checks are being cashed. This will give them just enough time to float those checks, so they can cash them. So remember, the only acceptable routing code on a traveler's check is 8000.

Every traveler's check also has security features in its paper. For instance, if you hold the Thomas Cook traveler's check up to eye level, you will discover the image of a Greek goddess to the right in a circular wa-

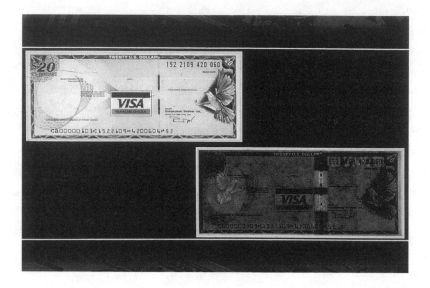

termark. It's visible front and back. If the lady's there, the check is legal. If you don't see her, it's worthless. Don't feel it, don't look at it, simply bring it up to your eye and see if she's there.

If I give you a Visa traveler's check, there will be a big white spot over on the left. If you bring it up to eye level, there will be a two-tone dove flying in it, visible front and back. And the line where you sign your

name, as well as the countersignature line, are not truly lines but the word "Visa" repeated over and over in microprinting visible under a magnifying glass.

The Citicorp check has a white spot on the right. If you bring it up to eye level, a Greek god's face appears inside the spot.

The American Express check has a centurian printed on the left, but when you look closely, there's a centurian on the right in a white spot. If you still have any doubt about the authenticity of an American Express traveler's check, turn it over so the back is facing you. Take your finger, wet the tip, and run it across the left denomination. If the image smears, then it's good. If it doesn't smear, then the check is worthless. American Express treats the left denomination with a chemical enzyme so that on contact with saliva or water, it instantly smears. Remember, only on the back left-hand denomination. You can go after the one on the right with Comet cleanser and a toothbrush and it won't change.

Finally, on the front of American Express traveler's checks, you'll notice that it says, "Pay this cheque to the order of United States dollars." Many times, Canadian-issued traveler's checks will pass as U.S. currency. On Canadian checks, it says, "Pay this cheque to the order of Canadian dollars." Make sure that when you're cashing it you're cashing it for the right country's currency.

DOES IT GET ANY BETTER THAN THIS?

If you're going to counterfeit something, I guess it doesn't get any better than money. As it turns out, the most counterfeited currency in the world is the American bill. That's because it's easiest to reproduce. Most foreign currencies are made up of at least six to eight colors of sophisticated background and etching. In comparison, the American bill is made up of just two colors. With today's technology, counterfeit American currency comes quite close to the real thing. And there's a lot of it out there. In 1999, $52.7 million in fake currency was recovered in the United States.

In 1995, 0.5 percent of all the counterfeit money in circulation was done on the personal computer—in other words, none of it. Back then, the Houston police arrested some counterfeiters and brought them into their interrogation room. Where'd you get the money? they asked. The counterfeiters admitted that they worked for a printing company. They had a key to the back door. On the weekends, they would go in, cut the alarm, and print stacks of money on a high-speed printing press.

Now when the police arrest counterfeiters, they hear an entirely different story. It turns out that more than half of all counterfeit bills are produced on a personal computer in the privacy of a home, and by someone younger than nineteen. Kids are sitting in their rooms, fooling

around, and one of them will say to his friend, "Look at this. I place this twenty-dollar bill on the scanner and watch what comes up on my screen." "Wow," the friend says. "Check the detail."

So the kid goes down to an office supplies store and buys some rice paper, the closest paper to currency paper you can buy, loads the paper into his color ink-jet printer, and prints out bills that look great. He could pass them anywhere. So he goes to the school cafeteria, buys his friends lunch, and the cashier doesn't bat an eye. He takes a trip to the mall, and no one says a word. So he starts printing them all the time, and his parents no longer need to give him an allowance. He can give his parents an allowance.

Now, if your kid is more of a purist, he can try this scam. Go into a bank and ask to buy five hundred one-dollar bills. If the teller questions him about why he needs all of those singles, he can say, "Well, it's not your business, but if you really want to know, our school has a school project and they take money at the commissary, and we need change." He goes home and washes the bills in a washing machine with a bleach eradicator that washes all the ink off so they come out as blank bills. He scans a twenty-dollar bill, puts the bleached bills in the printer, and ink-jets twenties. Now he's got real currency with inflated amounts on them. It's a trick that started in Colombia and has been imported here.

Another common type of counterfeit bill is the paste-up bill. This is where a dollar bill is converted into, say, a twenty-dollar bill or a five into a fifty or a ten into a hundred. Most commonly, however, the paste-up artist converts ones into twenties, because they're easiest to pass. The paste-up artist never changes the back of the bill, only the front. And all he changes are the denominations in the corners. The giveaway is that George Washington is still staring out from the center instead of Andrew Jackson, and there's a one written across the seal. So it's worth paying attention to who's in the center when someone gives you a twenty-dollar bill.

One more thing kids love to do is copy five-dollar bills. They take the bills to a local copy shop. They place them on the machine and copy them right onto white bond paper. They only copy the front. They don't bother with the back. Then they cut out the copies and go to the video arcade, the laundromat, or the car wash, or anywhere that has a change machine. All change machines work on the same principle. Inside the machine is an optical scanner, and it only scans one side. If a facsimile is within 5 percent tolerance, it goes through every time, and these copies make the cut.

FIGHTING FIRE WITH FIRE

The way we fight technology is with technology. Real money has always had its protective features that have made counterfeiting something of a challenge. Genuine money is printed, then engraved, then intaglio engraved, which gives it depth. The intaglio engraving is what makes it tough to duplicate. On real money, the portrait of the famous American in the middle looks three-dimensional. The eye sockets look sunken, the hairline recedes. This is three-dimensional engraving. On a counterfeit bill, these items appear flat, like a picture in a newspaper or a magazine. The real bills are printed on special paper made under government control; it's fibrous and strong, and red and blue fibers are visible. Over the Treasury seal are tiny hash marks which make up the word or number of the bill's denomination. On real money, you should be able to read the words on the seal clearly. Even on the best counterfeit bill, the hash marks become bars, making it difficult to discern the words of the seal.

But technology has overwhelmed these safeguards, and so the gov-

ernment has battled back with a new round of technology. In 1996, for the first time in seventy-two years, the government made changes in the currency. Over the last few years, these new bills have been introduced with additional security features. Then the government said, don't worry, we won't change them again for another twenty-five years. Actually, they'll be changing them in 2003 to multicolored bills with additional safeguards, because technology has already found ways to defeat them.

The new bill is actually not a bad bill, but the problem is that the people who take it have no idea what to look for in order to gauge whether it's real or fake. Management hasn't taken the time to teach them. What management prefers to do is go out and buy them a cheap one-dollar pen. It tells them, just take this pen and mark the bill and if it stains then you know the bill's good. That pen is ridiculous. All it has is a chemical that checks the Ph level of paper. That's all it does. Money has a very high Ph level, because the paper is bleached white in order to engrave it. But so do about thirty-five hundred other stocks of paper that are sold at office supplies stores. And even if you didn't have that paper, take a sponge, dip it in a pail of Clorox, wring it out, and pat it on the paper you're using. When it dries, the paper will have the same Ph level.

We've become so utterly convinced of the authority of this pen. A clerk will run the pen over a bill and say to the customer, "Well, even though you've got a misspelling on this bill, as long as it's got that mark on there, no problem, I'll take it."

WHAT TO DO

I tell people who handle a lot of money, take five minutes and learn the proper way to identify a genuine bill. Let's consider the new hundred-dollar bill. To the right of the portrait of Ben Franklin is a registered mold watermark. When the bill is viewed above eye level, an image of Franklin appears on the far-right side of the bill, front and back. It shows up right away. If you have to hunt for it, you don't have it. A counterfeiter cannot reproduce this watermark, for it requires a $200 million paper mill. There are only six in the world, and only one capable of doing it in the United States.

The New $100 Bill Note: Issue Date 4/96

Current Security Features: To prevent counterfeiting, the government has included a number of security features in U. S. currency.

Security Thread
This polymer thread is embedded vertically in the paper and indicates each bill's denomination. The words on the thread can be seen only when held up to a bright light but cannot be duplicated by photocopiers or computer scanners. In the 1990 Series Notes, the security thread appeared only on the left side of a bank note. Now, to improve authentication, the thread is in a unique position in each denomination in which it is used. As an additional enhancement to currency authentication, the new security thread will glow red when held under an ultraviolet light.

Portrait
Since most people focus on the portrait to verify a note's authenticity, the enlargement of the portrait of Benjamin Franklin makes it easier to recognize, while the added detail in the design makes it harder to duplicate. The portrait is now off center, providing room for the watermark and security thread. Also, this modification reduces the wear and tear on the portrait caused by folding bank notes in half.

Microprinting
Because they're so small, microprinted words are extremely hard to replicate without blurring. Originally located around the left of 1990 Series Notes, microprinting has been modified for the new design. Examples of microprinting, which can be read under magnification, now can be found in two places on the front. "USA 100" is microprinted within the number in the lower left-hand corner, while "The United States of America" appears on Benjamin Franklin's lapel.

Federal Reserve Indicators
Instead of designating the Federal Reserve district from which a note was issued, the new universal seal now represents the entire Federal Reserve System. A letter and number near the serial number identify the issuing Federal Reserve Bank.

Concentric Fine-Line Printing
This series of fine lines is very difficult to reproduce with color copiers, computer scanners and other traditional printing technologies.
It is used on both sides, for the background behind both Benjamin Franklin's portrait on the front and Independence Hall on the reverse.

Color-Shifting Ink
Color-shifting ink changes color when viewed from different angles. This ink is used to print the number in the lower right-hand corner on the front of the currency. The ink looks green when viewed straight on, but changes to black when the paper is held at an angle.

Watermark
A watermark has been added on the right front side of the note depicting the same historical figure as the portrait. This watermark portrait is only visible when held up to a light source and does not reproduce on color copiers or computer scanners.

Serial Numbers
The serial number is a combination of eleven numbers and letters on the front of the note in the upper left and lower right. An additional letter has been added so that no two bank notes of the same denomination have the same 11-character serial number.

The New $20 Bill Note: Issue Date Fall/98

Current Security Features: To prevent counterfeiting, the government has included a number of security features in U. S. currency.

Security Thread
This polymer thread is embedded vertically in the paper and indicates each bill's denomination. The words on the thread can be seen only when held up to a bright light but cannot be duplicated by photocopiers or computer scanners. Now, a vertically embedded thread to the far left of the portrait indicates the $20 denomination. The words "USA TWENTY" and a flag can be seen from both sides against the light. The number "20" appears in the star field of the flag. The thread glows green under an ultraviolet light.

Portrait
Since most people focus on the portrait to verify a note's authenticity, the enlargement of the portrait of Andrew Jackson makes it easier to recognize, while the added detail in the design makes it harder to duplicate. The portrait is now off center, providing room for the watermark. Also, this modification reduces the wear and tear on the portrait caused by folding bank notes in half.

Federal Reserve Indicators
Instead of designating the Federal Reserve district from which a note was issued, the new universal seal now represents the entire Federal Reserve System. A letter and number near the serial number identify the issuing Federal Reserve Bank.

Fine-Line Printing Patterns
This series of fine lines is very difficult to reproduce with color copiers, computer scanners and other traditional printing technologies. It is used on both sides, for the background behind both Andrew Jackson's portrait on the front and The White House on the reverse.

Color-Shifting Ink
Color-shifting ink changes color when viewed from different angles. This ink is used to print the number in the lower right-hand corner on the front of the currency. The ink looks green when viewed straight on, but changes to black when the paper is held at an angle.

Watermark
A watermark has been added on the right front side of the note identical to the historical figure in the portrait. This watermark portrait is visible from both sides when held up to a light source and does not reproduce on color copiers or computer scanners.

Serial Numbers
The serial number is a combination of eleven numbers and letters on the front of the note in the upper left and lower right. An additional letter has been added so that no two bank notes of the same denomination have the same 11-character serial number.

Microprinting
Because they're so small, microprinted words are extremely hard to replicate without blurring. Originally located around the portrait of 1990 Series Notes, microprinting has been modified for the new design. Examples of microprinting, which can be read under magnification, now can be found in two places on the front. "The United States of America" is on the lower edge ornamentation of the oval framing the portrait. On the front of the note, "USA 20" is repeated within the number in the lower left corner.

Counterfeiters use a grease pen and merely pen a little sketch of Ben Franklin. When you hold it up, the light bounces off the grease pen mark and you thought you saw a watermark. In reality, you saw a grease pen mark. If you rubbed it, it would smear. If you turned it over, you wouldn't see anything. So you have to make sure the watermark is visible, front and back.

At the bottom right-hand corner of the bill is the numeral 100, indicating the denomination of the bill. That number is printed in a shiny, sparkly metallic green in what is known as OVI, or optical variable ink. When you tilt the bill slightly forward, the green color of the numeral will turn a dull jet black. Color copiers can't pick up the changeable appearance of this ink. What's more, this ink is made by just one company in the world, located in Switzerland, and the ink's use is tightly restricted. Trying to replicate it is extremely difficult.

If the color doesn't change, you don't have a real bill. Counterfeiters in the United States use a Revlon metallic nail polish and paint the number in so it's shiny. In Bogotá, they add flakes to the ink to make it sparkly. It's a nice try, but it doesn't change color from green to jet black.

The greatest tool we can give a bank teller is a little magnifying loupe. On the bottom left-hand corner of the bill is another 100. If you look at it through a magnifying glass, you will see that what appeared to be shad-

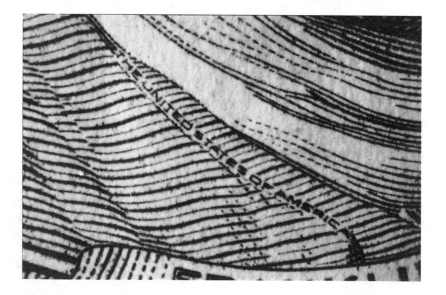

ing is actually the words "USA 100" repeated one hundred times in microprinting. Copiers can't see it. Scanners can't see it. So when we examine money out of Bogotá, it looks great, but if you study the numeral under a magnifying glass, you can't read anything. The microprinting is just a blur. Then if you move the magnifying glass to the left side of Franklin's collar, you'll see the words "United States of America," again in microprinting. On a counterfeit bill, there's just another blur.

Making bogus money is one of the oldest crimes known to man. Back in the time of the Civil War, when individual banks issued their own currency, about a third of all money was thought to be counterfeit. I'd hate to see those levels reached again, because counterfeit money can destroy a country's economy. Sadly, it's looking more and more likely. Every day, I learn of someone buying a McDonald's meal or getting change for a fifty at a yard sale with counterfeit money. The other day I read about a priest smuggling in counterfeit bills from South Korea. I guess his vow of poverty slipped his mind. Stories like these are disheartening, because when people are getting something for nothing, the cycle of greed continues. Still, until technology advances once more, the simple steps I explained are entirely reliable in separating the real from the fake. All we have to do is use them.

4

[THE THIEF
AT THE NEXT DESK]

An auditor arrived for a routine review of the books at a foreign automotive company that had its offices in New Jersey. The office was one of those tall, angular buildings that seemed to be made entirely of glass. All morning, the man sifted through the voluminous records, matching invoices and payments, and everything seemed to be in good order. But there was one pattern that struck him as a little odd. There were quite a number of bills to replace windows—$600 for this window, $1,200 for that one, $800 for another. Was that normal? Was everyone who worked there a klutz? Well, he shrugged, the building was almost all glass. Glass cracks easily enough.

At lunchtime, he took a break and headed down to the company cafeteria. He selected a seat next to the windows so he could look out on the day. As he was munching on his sandwich, he happened to notice something that made him sit up straight: a date was stamped on the bottom left-hand corner of the glass that signified when the window had been put in. This one had been intact for years. He began to wonder. The auditor got up and proceeded to wander through the building, floor after floor, looking at nothing but windows and the little dates stamped on them. He couldn't find a single one that had been replaced anytime recently.

The auditor confronted the head of maintenance with his findings, and, sure enough, the man was in cahoots with a glass maker in an ongoing embezzlement scheme. The glass maker sent invoices for "ghost" windows that the maintenance head approved. The company paid the bills, and the two of them split the proceeds. This had gone on undetected for a long time.

The maintenance head ended up being quietly fired. The only reason he wasn't prosecuted was because the president of the company was paying him with company money to cut his lawn and do work on his house, and he didn't want that getting out. Months later, when the auditor returned for his next audit, he happened to notice that the man was working at the building across the street. It was all glass.

A DUBIOUS DISTINCTION

There are a million ways that employees embezzle money from their employer, and to catch them it usually takes a stroke of luck like a keen-eyed auditor who happens to take his lunch by the window. And so it is small wonder that, at every imaginable type of business, from the corner deli, to the muffler shop, to the seafood restaurant, to the industrial parts maker, to the leaders of the Fortune 500, employee theft is escalating. Embezzlement has ranked as America's No. 1 financial crime for more than thirty years, and I have no doubt that it will continue to hold that sorry distinction for many years to come. About a third of all the fraud that goes on in this country is embezzlement. Banks, for instance, lose five times more money to embezzlement than to armed robbery. Workplace larceny can be so devastating to the company that is victimized that almost a third of all bankruptcies are attributed to embezzlement.

The dimensions of the problem vastly exceed what the surveys indicate. Only about 10 percent of embezzlement cases ever get reported to

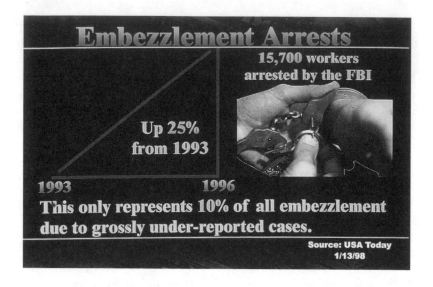

the authorities. Many companies, leery of negative publicity, are loath to admit that they have been snookered by their own worker, and simply fire the employee and keep the incident under wraps. They just swallow the loss.

Embezzlement schemes can involve little thefts that run into the hundreds of dollars or large ones that run into the millions. No matter how small they are, they're annoying to the victim. A toy store chain told me about a nimble little scam that had bedeviled one of its store managers. A cashier would peel off a UPC sticker from an inexpensive toy, something like a beanbag for $9.95. He'd stick it on the inside of his wrist. Then an accomplice would come to his register loaded up with forty- and fifty-dollar video games and other more expensive items. The cashier would pick up each of the purchases and swipe his wrist across the scanner while appearing to be swiping the product. So everything went through at $9.95. A sale that should have been hundreds of dollars was a fraction of that.

The main reason people steal is because of opportunity, followed by need and greed. One thing I always say is, if you make it easy for people to steal from you, they will. It's a simple principle, but my years in the fraud business have proved to me that it holds true time and time again.

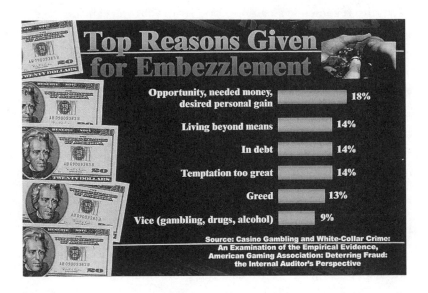

THE IRS IS YOUR FRIEND

Embezzlement fascinates me, because we know how to prevent it. For over one hundred years, the accounting tools have been in place. This is why we have auditors. This is why we conduct audits. This is why we have internal auditors. This is why we have due diligence. This is why we have best practices. This is why we have controls. This is why we have segregation of duties.

The problem today is, the bigger companies have become, the less controls they have. The more they merge with other companies, the fewer controls that stay in place. Accounting staffs that used to be six people are now one person. You can't segregate duties with one person. If I have a bookkeeper who writes checks, signs checks, and reconciles checks for me, then it's just a matter of time before I have a bookkeeper who steals from me. So today, we've taken all of those controls that we've learned in accounting for one hundred years and thrown them out the window.

Even if you catch an embezzler, don't expect to get your money back. If you have an employee who stole $60,000 from you and you went to court and the employee pleaded guilty, he'll get probation and there's no restitution. You're out $60,000, while he's driving a brand-new car and living in a great house on the lake. There is one recourse. It's rarely used, but it's my favorite. If someone steals $60,000 from you, you can file a 1099 on that employee with the government. The 1099 is a wonderful tool. It gets you a write-off on your taxes of $60,000, and you may get as much as one-third of the money back from the IRS for reporting someone who failed to pay taxes on earned income, even if it was earned by theft. The IRS will go after the person, and it has the power to take his home, take his car, and garnish his wages, things that you don't have the power to do even in a successful civil action. It's always been my experience that the threat of a 1099 is far greater than the threat of a lawsuit or prosecution.

THE GUY NEXT DOOR

One thing to keep in mind is that the culprit is often the last person you would suspect. That's the curious thing about embezzlement. It's rarely the new worker who's a total mystery to you. It's not the guy with the shifty eyes and the sinister glare. Embezzlers are frequently some of the nicest people in the world. They're the ones who sit at the next desk, who have lunch with you, who are in the adjacent pew at church on Sunday.

Far more often than not, the embezzler is the guy who's been at the company forever and who you trust implicitly. That's one of the reasons why embezzlements often persist for years without being detected. There was a recent case of a fifty-one-year-old woman that worked as a payroll and employee benefits administrator for a sizable Arizona plumbing company. She was very sociable, very well-liked, and very involved in the community. Everyone found it hard to believe when they discovered that over an eight-year period, she had embezzled nearly $2 million. Just about every week, she signed and cashed fraudulent insurance checks. She began her scheme practically the day she was hired. By the time she was caught, she was cashing checks at a rate of $40,000 a week.

Then there was the bookkeeper for a Manhattan magazine publisher. She was fifty-four, an esteemed senior employee, earning $150,000 a year. She decided to give herself a raise. She inserted her name as an additional payee in the books she kept. That gave her another $15,000 a year. Year after year, she added her name to more and more checks. After ten years had passed, she was receiving more than fifty checks, in amounts ranging between $15,000 and $75,000. Just like that, she was earning $1 million a year. By the time an audit finally caught her, she had embezzled something like $8.2 million.

Her lawyer claimed she had a psychological problem that compelled her to steal from the rich and give to the poor. It was pointed out that she sent much of the stolen funds to charities in the Philippines, where she was from. Perhaps. But she also happened to own expensive cars, homes in New Jersey, California, and Florida, real estate in the Philippines, and an entertainment and production company. So she was pretty charitable with herself.

ALL WORK AND NO PLAY

One of the weird things is, the harder someone works, the better the chance he could be an embezzler. Someone who never takes a vacation, stays late, comes in on weekends—that's the person you have to wonder about. It may not be devotion to the company. It may be devotion to an embezzlement scheme. Often these schemes need daily, or at least weekly, maintenance to keep them from being detected. Any number of scams have come unraveled when the crook got sick and couldn't get into work for several days. He can't very well call up someone else at the office and say, "I'm under the weather, could you do me a favor and take care of covering my embezzlement scheme?"

Most embezzlement cases begin small. Everyone in his or her life has a desperate situation, whether it's a child who's sick, or an investment that went bad, or a gambling debt, and they need money. So they say to themselves, "I can take this ten thousand, and they'll never know it. I'll put it back as soon as I can." But they never put it back, and ten becomes twenty, twenty becomes fifty, and fifty becomes a hundred thousand. Just like that, a small loss has snowballed into a large one. Greed and hunger change human character.

A common technique of embezzlers is known as "lapping" or check-kiting. It works like this: An employee with responsibility for recording payments will pocket a payment for an outstanding bill. He then covers the shortfall by applying part of a larger and later payment by a second customer to the incriminating invoice, thus "lapping" the two accounts. A payment from a third customer will then be used to cover the second

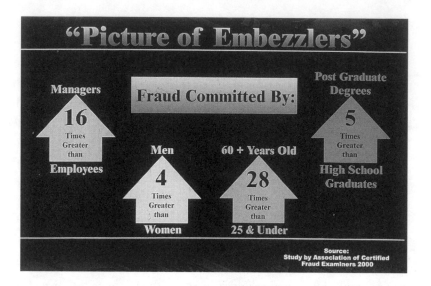

account, and on and on. A skillfully done lapping scheme can keep the money flowing undetected for years, as long as the employee stays on top of it and doesn't take time off. I heard about one guy who succeeded in lapping receipts for twenty-nine years, quite possibly a lapping record. He was basically a career lapper. He rarely took a day off, and his scam was only discovered when he no longer came in at all. He had reached retirement age.

A recent study by the Association of Certified Fraud Examiners offers an interesting picture of embezzlers. It found that fraud committed by managers was sixteen times greater than fraud by rank-and-file employees. Fraud losses caused by men were four times those caused by women. People sixty and older committed twenty-eight times the fraud committed by people twenty-five and under. The losses from workers with post-graduate degrees were five times as great as those caused by high school graduates.

When you think about it, this picture starts to make sense. In order to steal a lot of money from a company, you've got to be in a position of some power and trust. Otherwise, you don't have access to the company's assets. So that's likely to be someone who's well-educated and in a senior position. It's not often going to be some young person on a low rung.

ERODING ETHICS, GROWING ENTITLEMENT

It's obvious to me that one of the key reasons that employee theft has gotten so pervasive is that ethical standards have fallen to appalling lows.

Back in the 1960s, if a company found out that an employee had embezzled some money, say ten thousand or twenty thousand dollars, he would be called into the head office and confronted with the crime. Under questioning, he would eventually break down, apologize profusely, and explain that he stole the money because his kid needed a heart operation. He would promise to pay back every cent.

By 1980, a bold new ethic had taken hold. This time, when an employee was caught stealing company funds, he would again be ushered into the head office. But his response would be completely different. He would launch into a diatribe about how he was entitled to take the money. He actually deserved it, he would insist, because the company paid him poorly, offered a vile healthcare plan, and didn't in any way properly value him. He would practically expect his boss to thank him for taking the money.

By 1990, we reached yet another level of entitlement. When an employee was called in to account for his theft, he wouldn't even bother with explanations or excuses. He would simply shrug his shoulders and say, "So what?"

It's a pretty sad state of affairs, but it's a reality. Another undeniable factor for taking at the office is economic envy. Top executives make so much more than ordinary workers, and there is so much publicity about all the millionaires created from stock options, that some workers rationalize that they deserve their cut. They don't feel that there's anything shameful about robbing the company. A cavalier attitude has taken hold.

SIZE DOESN'T MATTER

By now, I've seen just about every type of scam imaginable, and to my mind, embezzlement is the most difficult to detect. It's a crime of stealth and subterfuge.

Here's a case that typifies so many. There was this small company, doing about $1.7 million in revenues, with just seven employees. The company hired a temporary woman to come in and do some bookkeeping. They liked her well enough that they asked her if she'd like to work full-time. She did and was hired.

Every month, the bank that the company dealt with sent along the company's statement to the president. He faithfully opened it, looked through the checks, and reconciled the account. Then he would tell the bookkeeper, "Here's the statement. I've already gone through it, go ahead and post it." In time, he came to trust the woman enough that he asked her to take care of this chore, which he never much cared for anyway. Fairly quickly, the woman realized that she was balancing the books, and the president didn't even know how much money he had. Each month, she began to write herself a check for one thousand dollars. Sometimes, she wrote one for five thousand dollars, and she made some out for fifteen thousand dollars. She did this for a year and a half. She stole a total of $178,000 from the company.

Finally, she wrote a very large check, and the bank called the company to check on it. For several days in a row, the bookkeeper told the bank that the president wasn't available. Suspicious, the bank officer called the president at home one night. He told him about the check and explained that he wanted to verify it. At this point, the president went through the books and discovered the losses. He prosecuted the secretary, but the bank said they weren't responsible for replacing the stolen funds. The president protested that he would sue the bank, because these were forged checks and the bank should have caught the signatures. The bank explained that it didn't examine checks for as little as $1,000. It would never have seen the signatures of most of the checks. And no one challenged the bank statements sent to the company.

I was asked to testify in the case, and I supported the bank. No bank looks at one-thousand-dollar checks. What's more, the company president was negligent in not going over the statements himself, as he used to do. It was his mistake that allowed the loss to happen.

It's very important to reconcile bank accounts promptly, and always within thirty days of when the statement was mailed. So many companies don't bother to do it. I know there's nothing interesting or fun about reconciling a bank statement. You'd rather read the Congressional Record. But it's important to your financial health. If you fail to reconcile accounts, you've extended an open invitation to employees to embezzle, because they know their actions won't be discovered for a long time, usually after they've resettled in Bermuda.

Unfortunately, that was a small company. A loss like that would probably be enough to bring it to the brink of bankruptcy. If you're Delta Airlines and somebody rips you off for $250,000, you contact your insurance company and tell it that the bank refuses to cover your loss. The insurance company says, okay, here's $150,000, your loss minus your $100,000 deductible. Then Delta takes the loss off of its taxes and ends up being shortchanged $50,000, which it can certainly absorb as part of its operating costs.

But if you own six dry cleaning stores, and an employee embezzles $50,000 and takes off with her boyfriend, the bank's not going to give it to you and you're through. The smaller you are, the more you need to worry about these things and be aware that embezzlement is prevalent, and it's a real threat.

MAILROOM MAYHEM

The mailroom is where stealing frequently starts. For the criminally-inclined, a mailroom is as opportune a place as a bank vault. Much of the company's money passes through there in the form of incoming and outgoing checks. Criminals frequently seek mailroom jobs for this reason.

A Fortune 500 company in Cleveland hired a twenty-four-year-old woman as an accounts processor in its mailroom. One of her jobs was to go get postage for the meters in the building. So she would walk in and ask to requisition a check. She would say it's for the post office, two thousand five hundred dollars. Someone would sign out the check, called a Quick Check, and give it to her. It consisted of an original and two copies on a voucher. She would stick the check into an IBM typewriter and make it out to United States Post Office, two thousand five hundred dollars, and take the check in to an assistant controller, who would sign it and give it back to her. Then she would return to her office, pull the check apart, file the two onion-skin copies, and put the original back into the typewriter. Since she had a self-correcting typewriter, she would lift off the words "United States Post Office" and type her name on the check, her real name. She would deposit these checks, or cash them, at her bank. She did this for about four years. At the end of that time, she had taken $278,000 of the company's money.

During those four years, no one questioned anything about these instances. Every month when the checks came back from the bank, she would go down the hall to the person who had received the incoming returned checks. She would tell her that she needed to see the checks, she was looking for one that her department wrote. She would take them into her office, remove the originals, and destroy them on a shredder. All the reconciliation for the company was done by the onion skins, not by the original checks, which matched.

Personally, I will not use a bank that won't give me my canceled checks back. The big thing today is to give images of your checks. But only images of the front. Thus, I don't see who endorsed the checks. How do I know someone didn't forge a signature and cash it? How can I notify my bank in thirty days that a check was forged, if I never was allowed to see if it was forged? So I get the actual checks returned to me.

No one wondered why the young accounts processor had a new car almost every year, went to Jamaica three or four times a year on vacation, and always had new jewelry. When she was finally caught and admitted it, there were questions like, didn't the company notice that it's postage cost went up 300 percent? Wasn't anyone the least bit suspicious that every month this woman had to look at the checks? As a matter of fact, when it was all said and done, only two checks were available for the court trial, because all the others had been destroyed in a shredder.

Embezzlers tend to be compulsive, and the money they steal they spend freely. Thus, one of the obvious giveaways that someone is stealing from you is that the employee starts living a suspiciously lavish lifestyle. When the mailroom worker drives up in a new Ferrari, you have to wonder. But it never fails to amaze me how often employers accept lame excuses for unorthodox spending. There was the case of the budget director for a California school district. He earned $76,000 a year. That's not a bad living. But how could that be enough for the fur coats his wife started wearing? The fancy house they lived in? How did that pay for a Mercedes and a Rolls-Royce? Nobody who works for my school district drives a

Rolls-Royce. When anyone wondered, he simply replied with a sly smile that outside investments paid for these frills. The real answer was he had managed to embezzle about $2 million by writing checks to himself out of an old health-insurance account that the other school administrators thought had been closed years before. He diverted money to that account from the district's building programs, food services, and insurance rebates.

THE BURDEN IS ON YOU

I believe that companies have a moral obligation to their employees to have controls in place. It's entirely unfair to put an employee in a position where it's very easy for him or her to steal. People are people, and by not having controls, you're basically putting up a sign that reads: "Steal from me. I'll never know." A study that was done a few years ago concluded that 10 percent of employees would steal all the time, another 10 percent would never steal, and the remaining 80 percent would steal given the right motive. That's a scary survey. It's telling a company it has to worry about 90 percent of its workforce.

So I think that if you don't have temptations in place to begin with, you avoid a lot of problems. It can be simple things. One restaurant chain furnishes its workers with uniforms without pockets. It sounds silly, but it takes away temptation. My experience with embezzlement has led me to come up with a series of steps that I feel represent the best internal controls to deter theft, and I'd like to run through them.

The most important thing is to review your hiring procedures for permanent and temporary positions, so you keep people with dubious backgrounds out of your company. We have to get back to common business practices and good sense. In most of the embezzlement cases I get involved in, the employee who stole from the company also stole from the previous company he worked for. If the company had run a sound background check on that employee, then the loss would probably not have occurred. I believe trust is a good thing. I believe controls are better. I believe a preliminary employment application is best.

And you have to make phone calls, not just look at pieces of paper. I know that if I walked into a New York hospital tomorrow and applied for an internship, as long as I presented credentials, I doubt anyone would make a call. But as I told you in the last chapter, anyone can create credentials. When you check references, you need to pay particular attention to dates and time gaps in a resumé. What was going on then? Had the person been fired and unable to get another job? Was he in jail?

When you're filling a position in a particularly sensitive area, think about hiring an outside firm to tackle a complete background check. Run a credit bureau report on that employee. Does he have a gambling problem, which would show up on a credit report? Is he deep in debt? Is he about to file for bankruptcy? These are the elementary things you should know about him before you allow him to handle your money. Call up the former employer. He may not be willing to tell you, "Oh yeah, that guy stole us blind and we had to fire him." But you can ask, "Would you hire this employee again?" If he says, "No, we wouldn't," then that tells you there was an incident there.

I'm not saying you need to go to these extremes with everyone. If a guy is going to paint my building, as long as he can paint, I'm not too worried. But it's got to be done with anyone who puts his fingers on your money and who regularly goes into secure areas. All the time, when I go into a secure room at a company where they keep their checks, I ask them who has access. And all the time, they say, "Oh, only three people, and we've checked them out twenty different ways and they have ID cards that have to be swiped." I say, "What about the janitorial service?" "Oh yeah," they reply, "they come in and clean." Well, you've got to check out the janitor, too. When using temporary employees in financial areas, have them bonded. And rotate personnel in financially sensitive assignments on a regular basis.

VET YOUR VENDORS

You absolutely must protect the accounts payable and procurement functions by restricting access to the master file records of your vendors. Changing or adding new vendors should require supervisory approval and supporting documentation, because otherwise any employee can set up a company name and have the company start billing and getting paid off of accounts payable work. I was involved in a case in Atlanta, at a billion-dollar company, where a woman who had been there for three or four years set up a vendor file with her own initials. She called the company by those initials, WJK Inc., and then simply started billing the company for services and, of course, they were in the vendor file. And the company paid the bills. After about three years, more than $4 million was stolen.

Someone who's independent of the buying and payment functions ought to review all new supplier entries. That review should always include a telephone call to the new supplier, and get that number from directory information to make sure it's the real one. When you make the call, verify the name, address, and Federal tax ID number.

If you want to guard against payments to ghost employees that don't exist, as well as improper changes in pay rates, you also have to restrict access to the personnel master file records. A supervisor ought to have to approve adding any new employees or changing anyone's pay rate. Otherwise, you're going to find yourself paying a dishonest worker five checks a week—or fifty. A fellow in the business office of the German Army regularly paid checks to a battalion that didn't exist. He was the battalion, and he was just lucky he never got summoned into battle.

Another practice that should be carefully monitored is outsourcing. Businesses outsource so many things today, including accounts payable. How do you know the people you outsource to aren't cheating you? One company outsourced its security detail; the guard firm assured the firm that it had checked out everyone. Well, they missed one guy. He had an arrest record for stalking. Fortunately, he didn't stalk anyone in the company, but he did steal a bunch of laptop computers. So you've got to be careful, and I don't believe in ever outsourcing accounts payable. You're not saving a lot of money and you're relinquishing control. You can outsource payroll, but not accounts payable.

YOU NEED MORE THAN BREADCRUMBS

A really basic thing to do is to create audit trails, but businesses have gotten away from this practice. Most companies create no records whatsoever. If you ask them, "Who authorized this change?" their answer is, "Gee, I don't know." Thieves aren't going to suddenly have a moral awakening one day and turn themselves in. You need evidence of wrongdoing. That's why audit trails were invented.

All access to master file records should be protected by a password and restricted by job function. Computer systems should then automatically create an audit trail of all changes made to those master records, including who made the change. A report of the changes should be printed and reviewed by someone independent of the employee who made the changes. This report is sometimes called an "access matrix." Checking the access authority of each employee should be part of this review. Determine a standard "access profile" for each employee, and restrict the master file records to these employees. And immediately investigate any unusual or suspicious activity. Most computer systems are designed with audit trail capabilities, but companies rarely use them.

In one recent case, an accounts payable supervisor at a major manufacturer felt his mortgage was a little too large for his comfort. So he did a touch of editing in the master file that contained the company's suppliers. Since he had no oversight, he could pretty much do as he pleased. He changed one of the vendor names to the name of his mortgage company, and edited in a reference to his loan number. Instead of his company sending a check to the supplier, it sent a sizable principal payment to the employee's mortgage holder. What tripped him up was that mortgage companies generally won't accept a large principal payment without specific written instructions. Since the guy wasn't able to intercept the payment to include a written note, the mortgage company returned the check to the manufacturer and the fraud was uncovered. It would have been caught with an audit trail.

CHECKS AND BALANCES

It's essential that you separate the accounts receivable and banking functions. Receipts and deposits must balance each day, and different people should perform these functions. Different groups should also process payments, disburse checks, and do bank reconciliations. If you don't split up these duties, then a dishonest employee can issue a check to himself, or to a co-conspirator, remove the check from the bank statement, and alter the accounting records to hide the embezzlement.

No one person, no matter how much you trust him, should ever be in complete control of a transaction. I remember when bank loans, up to a certain limit, were issued on the say-so of one officer. Often, that officer could make loans of as much as one hundred thousand dollars. Say you're a bank officer and I'm your college buddy. I come in and beg you that I'm desperate and need this loan. You say, "Okay, but I want something for myself." So I give you a ten-thousand-dollar kickback and probably default on the loan. There's a reason a committee now approves loans in banks. The same thing must happen in all businesses with all transactions.

I've spoken about how vulnerable companies are through their mailroom. It goes without saying that mailroom personnel must have absolutely clean backgrounds. And you need to put in internal safeguards to discourage theft of incoming or outgoing checks. So many companies that have been the victim of an altered payee check scam have traced the source of the original checks to their own mailroom.

One important step is to replace your company name and address on disbursement envelopes with a simple post office box number. This box should be solely for returned checks. And you've got to segregate the processing of returned checks. Any checks that get returned should not be returned to the area that originally processed them. A person independent of the payment function should handle these and investigate why they were returned.

CHECK CHECKING

Company checks should be made secure by using some of the techniques I mentioned in the chapter on checks. All checks and cash equivalents, whether they're preprinted or entirely blank, should be stored in a locked facility and only those employees who truly need access should have it. A physical inventory should be conducted at least once a quarter to account for every check. Zero amount checks and checks that have been canceled or voided should immediately be written or stamped "void" or "canceled" so they're unusable. All canceled or voided checks that have a signature on them should have the signature removed. And someone other than the accounts payable processor who handled the original transaction should be responsible for accounting for all voided or canceled checks. Too often, checks that are to be canceled or voided are left lying in someone's in-box, even though they're still "live" checks. Employees aren't dumb. They know that a replacement check was issued for the canceled or voided check, and so the canceled check won't be missed if they take it.

An accounts payable department of a city office out West had the bad habit of throwing away any checks that had been crumpled by the printer. The checks weren't voided. A member of the cleaning crew had his own habit, which was to rescue those checks from the trash, forge signatures, and cash them for increasingly large sums of money. The thefts weren't discovered until the account was overdrawn and more than $1 million was gone. The city, it was discovered, hadn't reconciled its accounts in more than a year.

All obsolete check stock should be shredded as soon as possible. Often, when bank accounts are closed or when highly secure check stock replaces old checks, boxes of the old checks are left unattended outside the locked cabinet where the new checks are stored. Some companies even store old checks on a pallet in a warehouse. Their rationale is that there's no need to worry about checks drawn on an account that has been closed. Checks are checks. Even though an account has been closed, someone could steal the old checks and pass them on to an unsuspecting third party. And guess what? The company would be considered negligent and be held responsible for the loss.

I tell every company I visit, make sure you empty the laser printer tray of checks and return them to the locked storage area after every check run. All too frequently, unused checks from the last check run are left in the printer tray. Anyone could find them and use them. And change keys or entry codes periodically to prevent unauthorized access to all of your secure areas.

There was an apparel maker in the Northwest that lost a lot of money from forged company checks that an employee had stolen. The company was puzzled. It thought it had really tight controls. An audit firm was brought in and traced the problem to a handful of blank checks left lying on the printer.

SEND US A POSTCARD!

And don't forget this one: make people take vacations, especially the ones who handle your money and financial records. Every employee has to be out of the office and without control over transactions for at least one week a year. Large embezzlement schemes, as I have already pointed out, often must be maintained daily, and key figures in the scheme will resist being away. And remember, most sophisticated embezzlement schemes are conducted by the long-tenured, trusted bookkeeper, controller, or chief financial officer. If any of them never takes a vacation, find out why.

As I've said before, nothing is foolproof. But I'm convinced that any company that follows these steps is removing a lot of temptation. Someone who wants to embezzle is probably going to apply for a job elsewhere, where the taking is easier.

5

[THE ROCK IN THE BOX
AND THE MUSTARD SQUIRTER]

A few years ago, a young man living in New York contacted the local phone company and asked to speak to customer service. When he was connected, he explained to the representative that he gave advice over the telephone on the stock market, and he wanted to start charging for his insight.

"Oh, so you need something like a 900 number," the representative said.

"Yes, exactly," the man said. "What I want to do is charge thirty-five dollars for the first minute, and then a dollar a minute after that."

The customer service representative told the man that they had a number of area codes that could be set up to do exactly that: 900, 847, and a few others. "Give me an 847," he said. He chose that code deliberately. Many people, from calling astrology or other self-help numbers, know that you have to pay when you call a 900 number. But, with the flurry of new local area codes that have been introduced in and around New York, not many people know about 847 and some of the other codes.

In short order, the man was all set. And not to give any kind of stock advice. He sat down at the phone with the Yellow Pages. He began at the front of the directory and moved alphabetically through it. He'd pick a category: air conditioners. He'd phone a supplier and be routed to sales. Often enough, he'd get someone's voice mail. He'd leave a message to the effect of: "I'm from Aurola Sales. I need about ten pretty good-sized cooling units, as soon as possible." He left his new 847 number.

A salesman would hear the message and get right on the phone. The guy would pick up, "Sorry, you have the wrong number." Bam. He just made $35. The salesman would figure he misdialed. He'd call right back. "Sorry, wrong number." There was another $35.

The man would do this day after day. He'd mark his page in the Yellow Pages at night and in the morning would resume from where he had left off. Sometimes, he was given pager numbers, and he'd go ahead and page people to call him at his 847 number. Because these were businesses he was calling, they all incurred large enough phone bills that they would never detect an extra $35 or $70. For the young man, it added up quite nicely. It wasn't long before he had cleared more than $1 million. And he was never caught.

LOW RENT DOESN'T MEAN LOW RETURN

It's a deceptive world out there today, and I have to give criminals credit. They're clever. On top of hot checks, counterfeit documents, and embez-zlement at the office, there's a whole patchwork of little scams that pro-lific con artists play on a gullible public, some of them puckishly insidious. Many of them have a shape so surprising that their place in the annals of con artists is insured. They involve irresistible forces that en-tice even highly intelligent and wary consumers. The artful confidence man can extract money from just about anyone, because he's an astute student of human nature and knows the power of deception.

I think of these as low-rent scams, because they don't involve much in the way of investment and are easy to perform, but, as you can see from that devilish telephone caper, they can generate surprising returns. In

Short-Change Artist

Short-change artists always deal with cash transactions. Victims of short-change artists often do not know exactly what happened or how it happened. The short-change artist is hard to spot because he or she looks like everyone else.

The Artist May:
- be any age, even an elderly person or a small child,
- look ordinary and respectable,
- act pleasant and unsuspicous, and
- easily gain confidence and trust.

The Artist Will Usually Do The Following:
- purchase a small item (often less than $1.00),
- pay for the item with a large bill (a $20, $50 or $100),
- request that change be broken down even further,
- try to create confusion about the amount of change involved in the transaction.

The following is a sample Short-Change situation:

"Good afternoon, miss. Let me take these razor blades."
"98¢, sir."

"98¢? Here's a $20 bill, miss."
"Thank you sir, that's 98¢ out of $20."

"Here's your change. 2¢ makes a dollar, that's 2, 3, 4; 1 is 5; 5 is 10 and 10 is 20. Have a nice day, sir."
"Tell you what, miss. I really didn't want all this change. Do you think I might just trouble you for a $10 for $5 and 5 ones?"

"Certainly sir. Here is a $10."

"And here is the $5 and 5 ones. You might want to count that. Make sure I gave you the right change."
"Thank you, sir."

"I'm glad you said that. You only gave me $9.00. I'm afraid you owe me one more dollar."
"Look miss, this is ridiculous, what did you do with my $20?"

"It's right here on my register, sir, where it is supposed to be."
"I'll tell you what, miss, let me just get my $20 back. You say you have $9.00 there?"

"Here's $1 makes $10 and here's $10 more, makes $20. Have a nice day!"

How much was she short-changed? $10. If she had been given a $50 she would have been short $20. If she had been given $100 she would have been short $40.

To Stop the Short-Change Artist

Never try to do more than one transaction at a time. Always close out the first transaction before moving on to additional ones. Always have the customer's money before you make change.

fact, the Federal Trade Commission (FTC) reports that, in contrast with crimes like bank robberies, where a lot of money can be obtained in one act, there has been a significant increase in frauds that realize relatively small amounts of cash each time they're pulled, but defraud many more people.

For example, a dry cleaning scam was making the rounds not long ago. Managers of well-heeled restaurants were getting a letter in which a man claimed he had recently eaten at the restaurant and a clumsy waiter had spilled food on his suit. He insisted that the restaurant pay the nineteen-dollar dry cleaning bill. The amount was modest enough that many managers simply paid it. They didn't seem to think it was odd that the return address where the check was to be mailed was a P.O. Box. The letters went out to enough restaurants that the nineteen-dollar payments added up to real money.

IF IT AIN'T BROKE . . .

Some of these scams have been practiced practically from time immemorial, while others are new inventions. But many of the oldest and most clearly defined ones have a lot of vitality left in them and are more popular today than ever. One way criminals look at it is, the more tried and tested the scam, the better. If a scam has worked for decades, it's almost like it comes with a warranty. There are literally thousands of different scams out there, of varying complexity, but let's take a look at some of the more prevalent ones, and see how you can guard against being hoodwinked by them.

One of the oldest scams around is still going strong, and that's the short-change scam. It's a classic. Deftly performed, it can be deadly. Back in the old days, I used it myself on more than a few occasions. Just about any con artist who's had any success is pretty proficient as a short-change artist, and practitioners show up in abundance at all major public events. Hundreds of short-change artists worked the recent Summer Olympics in Australia and took away plenty of gold.

Here's a simple version of how this persistent scam operates. I go into a deli and pick up a can of soda and a bag of chips. At the register, I pay for it and collect my change. I'm about to leave when I turn back to the clerk and say, "Oh, by the way, can you break a twenty for me?"

"Sure, no problem," he says.

The clerk hands me a ten, a five, and five ones.

I examine the bills in my hand, and say, "Actually, I didn't want all this change, could I trouble you for a ten for this five and five ones?"

"Certainly."

While he's fishing in the drawer, I keep up a patter of idle conversation. When you're pulling a scam, inane conversation is your best accomplice, because it distracts someone from concentrating on what he's supposed to be doing.

The clerk gives me a ten and I hand over my bills and say, "You might want to count that, just to make sure that I gave you the right change."

The clerk proceeds to count the money and discovers that I gave him a five and four ones. He tells me, "I'm sorry, sir, there's only nine dollars here."

I say, "Let me tell you what, so we don't get confused let me just get my twenty back. You have nine dollars, here's one more to make ten and here's ten to make twenty."

"Fair enough," the clerk says. "Thanks much."

What's wrong with this little scenario? I just short-changed that clerk out of ten dollars. Add it up. I gave him twenty. He gave me twenty in change. We're even. I gave him nine dollars. That means I've got twenty-one and he has twenty-nine. Then I take my twenty back and hand him eleven. I'm left with thirty and the clerk has twenty, giving me a net gain of ten. It's a quick little profit that can be duplicated over and over again at store after store. If I had started out by giving the clerk fifty, he would have been short twenty dollars. If he had been given a hundred, he would have been out forty.

WHAT TO DO

To protect yourself from being short-changed, the important thing is to never do more than one transaction at the same time. Always complete one transaction before you begin the next one. Short-change artists try to confuse you with two transactions at once, change for a twenty and change for a ten. If you're confused, you can rest assured that the short-change artist has it perfectly clear in his head what's going on. And never make change until you have the full amount in your hand.

When someone starts talking to you while you're handling money, ignore them and focus on the exchange at hand. A good short-change artist is like a magician; a moment's lapse in concentration and you'll be had. Johnny Carson once invited me onto the "Tonight Show" and dared me to fool him while he was fully expecting to be scammed. I had no problem shortchanging Johnny out of twenty dollars twice in five minutes. The audience loved it.

One final note. The short-change artist can be on either side of the counter. It can be the cashier short-changing the customer, or it can be the customer short-changing the cashier.

PHONE FOOLERY

I don't know how con artists made ends meet before the invention of the telephone, because for a long time, the telephone has been a con artist's handiest weapon. You can make a lot more with a phone than you can with a gun, and it doesn't require a mask. Phone scams exist in all shapes and forms.

The ringing pay phone is one of the most common. You're in Grand Central terminal, and you need to make a pay phone call. When you get to a bank of phones, one of them starts ringing. You pick it up, and say, "Hello?" There's no one there, so you hang up, then pick up the receiver again to make the call.

Guess what? If you didn't hang up for thirty seconds (as opposed to just five or ten seconds on a home phone), there's still someone on the other end, and not who you'd like it to be. When you dial your number and your credit card, someone has a tape recorder on the other end and is recording those beeps. A criminal can very easily translate them into your credit card number.

When I hear a ringing pay phone, I pick it up, hang it up, then go use another phone.

There are a whole host of variations on the call-back scam like that first one I told you about that exhausted the Yellow Pages. One that regularly shows up in people's e-mails and on their answering machines involves a message to immediately call a certain number beginning with the area code 809. The reason why will vary, but it will be something designed to get your attention: a relative is very ill, a friend has been arrested, you've won a vacation in Tahiti. With all the new area codes these days, most people don't get hung up on the unrecognizable code but go right ahead and place the call. You'll either get a lengthy recorded message or someone will do their best to keep you on the line as long as possible. Meanwhile, a huge charge is being run up on your phone bill, a bill that can run into the hundreds and even thousands of dollars. I've heard of people getting bills in excess of twenty-five thousand dollars.

Here's what's actually going on. The 809 area code is located in the British Virgin Islands. It's a "pay-per-call" number, similar to 900 numbers in the United States. But since it's not located in the United States, the number isn't covered by American regulations of 900 numbers that stipulate that you must be notified and warned of all charges. There is also no requirement that the company offer a time period during which you can hang up without being charged. And, unlike with 900 numbers, you can't put a block on your phone to avoid these calls.

The whole thing is such an obvious rip-off, and you've done nothing wrong. But trying to fight those charges can be nearly impossible. After all, you did make the call. Your local or long distance carrier will not be much help. They'll probably tell you they are simply providing the billing for the foreign company. That leaves you with a foreign company that will argue that it has done nothing wrong, either. So the solution is, beware of calling a number that you don't recognize, particularly one with an unfamiliar area code. By calling the operator, you can quickly determine precisely where that area code is.

Then there are the scams that combine the phone and the credit card. A guy calls you up on the phone: "Mrs. Jones, I'm delighted to inform you that you've just won a brand-new, nineteen-inch color Sony TV."

"Oh yeah, what's the catch?"

"No catch at all. Nothing to sign, nothing to buy. We simply ask you to pay freight and we'll ship it to you today."

"Oh yeah, how much is that?"

"It's just nineteen dollars. And you can put it on your credit card."

"Okay, great. Let me get my card and give you the number."

Mrs. Jones's TV is not on the way. But her credit is on the way out the door. Never give information over the phone to someone you don't know. If an offer sounds too good to be true, then it probably is.

The same thing goes for advertisements. A man was arrested in Florida and found to be bilking consumers in thirty-four states. His con was simple and straightforward. He ran ads in magazines that promised to send people a Visa card or a MasterCard with a $10,000 limit. There would be no credit check, and no questions asked. All that was required was a fee of $32.95. People sent their money and heard nothing. Sure there were no questions, but there was also no card. The con artist did see fit to send some of the respondents a generic list of banks that issued credit cards. In many of the cases, the victims simply swallowed the loss and never even reported the crime to the police. That was good for the perpetrator. By the time he was caught, he had bilked more than five thousand people.

A man in Kentucky pulled a similar scam. He set up a website that offered to provide credit cards for people with bad credit histories for $99. The site was called Credit One Financial. Payments were to be made to Capital One Financial, which sounded similar to but was unrelated to Capital One Bank. The man collected $200,000 in six weeks before he was caught.

FORGET THE FREE LUNCH

Unsolicited business opportunities that promise fat rewards for the most prosaic efforts are always something to steer clear of, and there are many variations that use the same basic technique. The solicitations are unfailingly tantalizing: earn one hundred fifty dollars a day or earn one thousand dollars a day by starting your own business. You don't need any employees, you don't have to have any meetings, you don't even have to do any selling. Someone else will do all the work. Oh, sure.

These offers are always very long on promises and very short on details. And that's the tip-off that they will lead to nothing but misery for you. One of the most common scams of this variety is the envelope-stuffing scam. "Earn two dollars every time you fold a brochure and seal it in an envelope," is the come-on. You'd be surprised how many people are tempted by it. Of course, there is a small fee of thirty-five dollars or fifty dollars that you'll have to pay to get started in the envelope-stuffing business. Not to worry. You'll recoup your investment in no time at all.

I'd recommend the work myself, if it were only for real. Often, you get nothing back at all for your money, except a tax write-off. Or you're actually told how to set up a bulk-mailing operation and begin stuffing envelopes. But the organizer refuses to pay you. He claims that your work just wasn't up to their high-quality standards. Sometimes, the con artist does nothing more than send you instructions on how to send the envelope-stuffing ad in bulk mailings of your own. In other words, he's turning you into an accomplice. If you ever do earn any money, it will be from others who fall for the same trap.

There are similar craft assembly scams, but no matter how exquisitely you assemble the crafts, the promoter always finds something lacking in them. And there's also a scam where you're invited to staple books. The trouble is, there are heavy duty machines to do that, not individuals. Keep in mind, there are very few effortless roads to riches.

Charity ruses are extremely popular as well, because people let their guard down when they hear a sob story. Recently the FTC took action against a company called Handicapped Industries that was selling products at steep prices—light bulbs, for instance, at ten times normal prices—and making the sales because its telemarketers told people that all of the workers were handicapped. They weren't. In settling the FTC case, the company agreed to stop misrepresenting its staff.

In a 1995 study, the FTC found that 10 percent of the money donated to charity that year was misused or given to fraudulent organizations. So don't believe what you hear. When in doubt, always ask for written information about the charity. Any legitimate one will be glad to send you material. Also, be careful of similar-sounding names, because lots of phony charities use names that sound or look like legitimate ones but one letter in the name may be different. The local Better Business Bureau or the state regulatory agency can tell you if a charity is for real.

STREET SMARTS

Many scams are executed by invisible thieves, scams that require no acting skills. But there is a whole repertoire of street scams that get pulled on the unsuspecting. One of the all-time classics is the Mustard Squirter.

A man comes up to you and says, "Do you know you have mustard all over your back?"

Startled, you glance over your shoulder, and say, "No, I had no idea."

"I've got some tissues," the man says. "Let me wipe it off."

He proceeds to blot out the stain with tissues.

"Great," you say. "Thanks so much, I've got a business meeting in an hour."

"You're welcome," he says. "I think it's all gone now."

"Thanks again."

You were just a victim of a mustard squirter. Before you were aware of him, the con artist squirted some mustard on your back. It doesn't have to be mustard. It could be ketchup, chocolate, or lotion. In any case, it was a distraction. While he wiped it off, he picked your pocket, or an accomplice working with him did the theft. It happens a lot in crowded areas. Be suspicious of any good samaritan. If someone offers to wipe off some mustard, hold on to your wallet while he does it.

Then there's the well-worn Jamaican Switch. The con artist, generally a foreigner, approaches you on the street and confides that he just arrived and has all his money in this package he's carrying, most of which he plans to give away to the church. He opens it and shows you a thick wad of bills. He says he has no bank account or anything, and is worried about the money being stolen from him. He wonders if there is some way you could deposit it for him in your account until he makes arrangements. He'll even pay you a fee when he picks it up. If you agree, he makes one more condition. He'd like you to give him some good faith money to prove you can be trusted. Once you do, he hands over the package and quickly leaves. The package, however, no longer contains money, but rolled-up paper.

A very popular stunt at tourist destinations is the camera scam. You're strolling with your spouse, with your camera dangling around your neck. A friendly guy, looking like he's having a good time himself, approaches you and asks, "Would you like me to get a picture of you?"

"Hey, great."

He takes the camera from you and suggests, "Why don't you go over there, so I can get that view behind you."

The moment you turn around, he takes off with your camera.

If you want someone to take your picture, you pick the person, because although most people are honest and friendly, many people act friendly and honest but aren't. They strictly want to take advantage of you. Always be suspicious of anyone who volunteers to take your picture. If someone asks you, the odds are good that there's a reason and you'll go home without your picture or your camera.

HOLD THE ROCKS

So many different goods are being sold on the street these days by vendors: cameras, phones, VCRs, televisions. And the vendors are very persuasive, the prices always bargain-basement.

"Twenty bucks, it's a New York bargain," the vendor boasts. "Hey, anyone want a calculator for twenty bucks? C'mon, twenty bucks, a New York bargain."

You stop and take a closer look. It's a name-brand calculator that you've seen in all the office products stores for twenty dollars more than that.

"Twenty dollars, that's all?" you ask.

"That's right. It sells in the stores for thirty-nine ninety-nine."

"It's got everything with it?"

"Yeah, it's all here. Warranty. Instructions are in the box."

You know that the guy on the street has no overhead. You figure he probably can make a profit for himself selling the calculator for twenty dollars. So you buy it. The guy hands you a cellophane-sealed box.

Well, the guy actually will make a lot more profit than you imagined. When you open up the sealed box, you'll find a nicely-wrapped rock. This is the famous rock-in-the-box scam, and it works well with a wide variety of products and rocks of all dimensions. I've seen people who thought they had bought a TV, but had actually bought a carton with some pretty good-sized boulders in it. The rock in the box has been going on for years, and you can find it wherever vendors sell merchandise on the street.

There's an easy way to avoid it: If you buy anything on the street, open up the box before you pay for it.

And never sign things on the street. You know those collapsible card tables you see set up on the street or outside a store, advertising a sweepstakes or a lottery of some sort? The ones with the smiling girl who says, "All you have to do is fill out this form, fill out all the information, and sign at the bottom. You'll win a car or a vacation."

Stop. Don't get sucked in. Carefully read any document before you sign it, and always read the fine print first. That's where the trouble usually lies. Then consider: Are they asking you to give too much information, your Social Security number, even your address or phone number? You could actually be signing up to switch your phone service or purchase something you really don't want.

THERE'S NOTHING LIKE A MAN IN UNIFORM

There are a whole host of scams that get carried out with little impersonations. A guy in a postal uniform shows up at the door and says, "I have a COD package for a Mr. Clark."

The woman who answers says, "Mr. Clark? That's my husband. He died two days ago."

"Oh, I'm terribly sorry," the delivery guy says. "Well, it's a COD package for a hundred dollars."

"Well, what is it?"

"I really don't know. All I know is I have to collect a hundred dollars."

"Well, since my husband ordered it, I'll get the money."

Mrs. Clark won't find anything in that box. She's just been the victim of the COD scam. It's a common one, and criminals target widows in particular. They read the obituaries in the newspaper to locate their marks. Never trust the uniform that someone is wearing. Anyone can get one.

You come to the bank after-hours deposit box to drop in a deposit. There's a handwritten sign beneath the box: "Box is out of order. Please leave deposits with security guard." Standing next to it is a man in a bank security uniform with a four-wheel dolly. He tells you, "I'm sorry, the box is out of order. Just drop your deposits here. I'm with the bank."

There's no way I'm going to fall for that. I've done it. Thirty-five years ago as a teenager, I pulled the scam myself. I dressed up in a guard's uniform, put a sign up on a night box at an airport, and said it was out of order. People came by and put their money right in my bag. I made thirty-five thousand dollars in about an hour. Sometimes it's a night box that criminals use, and sometimes they even use mailboxes.

It's a fairly easy rip-off, because the only props that are required are an "out-of-order" sign, a receptacle of some sort, and a standard issue security guard uniform. And even though it's a pretty low-tech scam compared with so many of the financial swindles that go on today, it's an "evergreen." A few years ago, a financial institution in Livingston, New Jersey, told me that someone had dredged up the caper out of the archives and walked away with thousands of dollars on Christmas Eve.

The tip here is quite simple. A box cannot be out of order.

Home repair schemes of one sort or another are a small industry in their own right. You're outside watering the lawn with your wife. A guy in a workman's coveralls comes up to you carrying a clipboard. He introduces himself, "I'm Tom Lindsay, from Quality Driveways. I've just noticed that your driveway is about due for resurfacing."

"I guess that's right."

"Well, let me tell you what I can do. I just did a house two streets over, and I bought too much asphalt. I'm stuck with this extra load and I want to do something with it, I don't want to waste it. I'd be glad to do your driveway just for the cost of the materials. No trucking, no labor, just the cost of the asphalt on my truck right now. What do you think?"

"It sounds good," you say, and you turn to your wife and ask, "What do you think?"

"Let's do it," she replies.

The workman has you sign a contract and asks for a 20 percent deposit.

It may sound like a good deal, but it probably isn't. Before you agree to anything, check out his company and assure yourself that it's reputable.

GREAT OAKS FROM LITTLE ACORNS

Phony prizes, phony awards, phony grants—con artists try them all, and people nibble and bite. There never is any money and the end result is generally a gratified con man with a big grin.

A science researcher at a southern university in need of research funding was among a diverse number of people who received an opportune overture from a man who identified himself as Dr. James E. Lipton, chairman of the Lipton Trust. He explained that he was the heir of Sir Thomas Lipton, who developed the Lipton Tea Company and died in 1931. The Lipton Trust, he elaborated, gave grants for worthy endeavors and was considering the scientist for funding amounting to $200 million. However, if he wished to hold a spot as a potential recipient while final decisions were being made, he needed to put $350,000 in an escrow account. Others got similar come-ons, including a lumber executive looking to do a real estate investment in Asia. Some of those contacted were resourceful enough to call Unilever, the conglomerate that owns Lipton Tea. They discovered there was no Lipton Trust and no Lipton heir. Sir Thomas Lipton died without heirs and left much of his fortune to the city of Glascow, Scotland, where he was born, to aid the poor and build hospitals. The professor managed to avoid losing his money, but others weren't as lucky. Always be suspicious if you're asked to put up money to get money. It's almost always a ruse.

Small and simple scams can escalate and, if they work, become massive in scale. For years, one of the most ubiquitous scams going has been the Nigerian Letter Fraud, a swindle that has become so large in scope that it has been said to rank as Nigeria's third-largest industry. It's actually a new construction of one of the oldest scams on record, the Spanish Prisoner. In that old con, a man shows the dupe a picture of his sister, a beautiful young woman who he says is being held captive, along with their fortune, in Spain. If the person would be willing to front money to get her out, he would reward him with a portion of the fortune, as well as the sister. There is, of course, no sister and no fortune.

The Nigerian Letter scam takes myriad forms, but the basic idea is that you or your business get an unsolicited "top secret" letter from someone identifying himself as a functionary of a Nigerian company or government ministry. Usually it's something like the Nigerian National

Petroleum Company or the Ministry of Mines. The writer asks for your help in getting "trapped" money out of Nigeria. He would like to use your bank account to park something in excess of $20 million. Typically he'll name an imprecise sum like $30.3 million for credibility.

For your help, you'll be paid anywhere from 15 to 40 percent of the sum. You're told the arrangement is "risk free." All you need to do is furnish your bank account information so the funds can be transferred. Sometimes the letter will inject an added sweetener, as if millions of dollars for doing nothing were not enough. One version offers "as a token of our appreciation" as much as 500,000 barrels of automotive oil at less than market price.

Needless to say, there are no funds and no oil. It was the account number that the Nigerians wanted. They proceed to use it to illegally withdraw your money or your company's money.

Other variations target members of religious organizations. The letter writer will claim to be of the same faith and will say that he is being persecuted in Africa for his religious beliefs. He explains that he has made considerable profits, some of which he wants to entrust to you to do good work. Just send the necessary bank account numbers. Yet another version goes to veterinarians and is supposedly from a fellow Nigerian veterinarian, though it's often the same guy who works at the Nigerian National Petroleum Company and at the Ministry of Mines.

Too often, greed overwhelms reason when these letters arrive. Millions of dollars have been lost to the Nigerian enticements over the years, despite the fact that law enforcement authorities have heavily publicized them and warned against giving out your bank account number. I can't stress that enough. Never, ever, give out banking information in such a carefree way. And I would also be careful about what you do about getting your money back. Some of those fleeced have taken trips to Nigeria in pursuit of their money, and some of them have been killed.

So have the Nigerians stopped?

Hardly. Some of them have gotten so bold that they've even contacted previous victims. Posing as Nigerian government officials investigating the schemes, they request an upfront fee to fund their attempts to recover the victims' money, thereby adding to the sum that needs to be recovered.

And they've introduced a new, easier-to-swallow twist. They send out letters that again mention the desire to move money out of Nigeria, but they don't ask for your bank account number or any sort of personal information. They simply offer to send you $4 million, or some such impressive sum, to hold in exchange for a commission. All you have to do is check "yes" or "no" in the boxes below.

Well, even if it's a fraud that sounds harmless enough. You say to yourself, "What do I have to lose? I just check 'yes' and if the check clears, I've got $4 million. If it doesn't, I've lost nothing, because I haven't given away anything."

When the scam artists get your response, they send you a beautiful, official-looking check drawn on the Bank of Nigeria. You deposit it. It gets routed back to the Bank of Nigeria, and in fact into the hands of the con artists. Of course it doesn't clear; it's a fraudulent check. But now the Nigerians have just what they need: your bank account number and your signature.

These schemes require a lot of mailings to seduce enough people to make them pay. You'd imagine that the Nigerians run up some pretty serious postage bills. Don't be concerned. They use counterfeit stamps.

UNMARKED AND UNREMARKED

Scams that prey on the elderly irritate me the most, particularly the ones that could easily be averted if someone in the know had only intervened. Here's one that goes on all the time. A little old lady pays a visit to her bank and makes a deposit. She doesn't notice two well-dressed men loitering outside, but they notice her. They follow her home. Once she's inside, they knock on the door. When she opens the door, they identify themselves as agents from the FBI.

"We believe an employee where you bank is stealing money," they tell her. "We'd like you to help us out."

"Oh, that's horrible," the woman says. "But what can I do?"

"We'd like you to go to the bank tomorrow and take out all of your money and bring it home. We'll pick it up and get it marked. Then we'll give it back to you to redeposit. If you help us, you'd be doing your government and your bank a tremendous service, and there'll be a reward for you."

It sounds like someone would have to be awfully credulous to bite on this one, but this scam has been going on forever and people still fall for it, and usually the people who can least afford to be ripped off.

I get angry at the banks over these schemes, because they don't take them seriously enough. When I hear about another one going down, I'll ask a bank officer, "This is an elderly lady. Why would you let her take out twenty thousand dollars or forty thousand dollars in cash?"

Their invariable reply is, "Well, it's her money. You can't ask too many questions."

I don't buy that. The real issue is that since the bank's not liable for the loss, it doesn't care enough to do something about it. As far as I'm concerned, that's not good enough. I tell banks, if an old person makes a sizable cash withdrawal, have an officer sit down with the customer and ask a few questions. If an officer simply asks, "Did anyone talk to you about marking bills?" that alone can be enough to foil a theft.

As you can see, all these scams are artful dodges meant to part you from your money. There's nothing occult about them. Once you know how they're done, they seem so rudimentary, little more than child's play. But they wouldn't still be around if they didn't work. With just a bit of knowledge and a healthy dose of suspicion, you can avoid their temptations.

[CARD **GAMES**]

Outside Miami International Airport, a new rental car franchise opened up a few years ago, begun by several enterprising young men. It was billed as one of those Rent-A-Wreck places that rented less-than-perfect cars at lower rates than the major chains like Hertz and Avis. The deal here was an awfully tantalizing one: a wreck for ten dollars a day, and no mileage charge. People arriving on flights took a look and thought it was a terrific price. The cars moved briskly.

In subsequent weeks, a spate of fraudulent credit card transactions were confounding law enforcement agents and credit card companies. They were on all sorts of cards and dispersed around the country in almost haphazard fashion. The authorities looked in vain for some sort of pattern, some fragile thread that might connect them. One finally emerged. It turned out that every card that had been used in the fraudulent purchases had also been used legitimately by the cardholder at the new Rent-A-Wreck at the Miami airport.

A little more investigation broke the case open. It seems that the young men weren't really interested in making a living renting cars at extraordinarily low prices. That was simply their cover. Their true business was recording the credit card numbers of everyone who came through and selling them to a ring of credit card thieves. The thieves then used them to make the illegal transactions.

In the world of fraud, it helps to remember that things are never what they seem. In fact, they are often the opposite of what they seem. I'm reminded of that little demonstration in the David Mamet con artist movie, "House of Games." Two men, one a soldier, are waiting at a Western Union office for money that's supposed to be wired to them. They don't know each other. The other man tells the soldier he sure hopes his money comes, and the soldier says the same thing. You know, the man says, if my money comes in first, I'll give you some of it, because I know you'll pay it back and I know you'd do the same for me. The soldier is warmed by this generosity. But of course no money is being wired to the man. He's the scam artist. When the soldier's money comes, he offers to give some to the other man and he'll never see it again. At the Miami Airport, people thought they were renting a car and they were actually donating their credit cards to thieves. It could be happening anytime you use your credit card, if you don't know who you're dealing with.

CUT THE CARDS

We all understand "sticker shock," that numb feeling you get when you go shopping for a new car. Well, now there's "statement shock." That's when your credit card has not left your wallet for weeks but you receive your monthly bill and it looks like you spent the entire month shopping on Rodeo Drive. Most likely, you're a victim of counterfeiters helping themselves to your credit. As I pointed out earlier in the chapter on checks, check fraud far outstrips credit card fraud. But plastic fraud is an accelerating problem, too, and new card tricks keep getting devised to enable crooks to enrich themselves.

Federal law generally limits a cardholder's liability for use of a stolen credit card to just fifty dollars. If you report the stolen card promptly, the issuer will typically waive that fifty dollars as well, as a goodwill gesture. So it's not the consumer who is hurt by card theft, but the issuers. All fraud losses, though, get reflected in higher prices, so, one way or another, the money ultimately comes out of everyone's pocket.

In the 1990s, it became commonplace for forgers to start altering existing credit cards. The simplest thing criminals do is to tell garbage collectors that for every intact card they find in the garbage and turn over to them, they'll pay them thirty-five dollars. Even though credit card companies repeatedly admonish cardholders to cut up their old cards before discarding them, I'm amazed that most people don't. They assume that because the card's expired, it's worthless, so just toss it in the trash.

Once they've got the cards, the thieves can't go out and use them, because verification machines will reject them as expired. So they need to make a few appropriate modifications. They take a handkerchief and lay it over a card. Then they put a hot iron over the handkerchief. The heat and weight of the iron melts the embossing. In other words, it flattens the raised letters and digits that constitute the name, account number, and expiration date. Putting the card in boiling water will accomplish the same thing. With a card embosser, which is easily and inexpensively obtained from an office supply store, they put on a new, illegally-obtained name, number, and expiration date.

Finally, they turn the card over, and with a paper clip, put a scratch in the magnetic stripe. Thus when they go to use the card, the damaged magnetic stripe won't work when a clerk swipes it through the verification terminal; instead, he'll be forced to read the newly-embossed number over the phone to obtain the authorization code. Clerks need to be told to proceed with caution when a card's magnetic stripe will not operate with their card swipe unit. It may be honestly bad or it may be intentionally bad.

To catch people embossing new numbers on cards that have been ironed flat, card companies have been printing the card number again on the back of the card in small type, often just above or on the magnetic stripe. The number is flat, so an iron won't melt it off. Sounds good. But crooks have figured that one out, too. They print up little stickers that say, in one instance, "Warning. This card registered" and then showing an American Express logo and a toll-free number to call for assistance. Then they put the sticker right over the account number on the back. It fools clerks every time.

For its credit cards, Citibank came up with the enterprising idea of af-
fixing a person's picture to the card as an added security measure. As a
further precaution, anyone receiving a card has to come into a Citibank
branch and get their picture taken there. For the most part, this was a
good idea. There's just one problem. If you live out of state and thus can't
get to a Citibank branch, the bank allows you to mail in your photo. But it
has no way of knowing if that is actually your picture. There's always a
loophole.

Criminals even have a way of making invalid cards work overtime.
Forgers will replace the magnetic stripe with a test stripe of their own
that causes a verification machine to read a dummy approval code without transmitting the information. This instant approval registers on the
machine less than a tenth of a second after the card is swiped. One way to
identify a fake card is to slowly swipe the card. The approval code, instead
of quickly appearing in its entirety, will print out, number by number, in
the display window. That's impossible with a valid card. Newer verification machines can't be fooled by this maneuver, but there are still a lot of
older ones around.

WHAT TO DO

As a consumer, the thing to remember is, don't toss away an expired card
intact, and put the pieces in at least two different garbage receptacles. If
I'm traveling, I'll toss one half in the garbage at the airport I'm leaving
from and I'll carry the other half with me and throw it away in the airport
where I land.

ONE PERSON'S TRASH IS ANOTHER'S TREASURE

You must be continually proactive. If you buy a club for the steering wheel
of your car to protect it from being stolen, why wouldn't you do the same
thing for your credit? People get notices in the mail every day telling
them they've been preapproved for a Visa card. They already have a wallet stuffed with plastic, so they throw the whole thing away. The garbage
collectors pick them up, open them, take out the coupon and check, "Yes,
I want it." Has the address changed? They check "yes" and write in the

new address. And they get your Visa. Rip those envelopes up before you throw them out. Don't make it so easy for criminals to take advantage of you.

Everyone needs to be a little more circumspect with credit card numbers. Merchants dealing with account numbers lapse into a kind of autopilot and treat them as if they were no more significant than last night's baseball scores. I was riding in a cab once when the dispatcher's voice crackled over the radio: "Hey, I didn't get that last credit card." "No problem," the cabbie said. "I'll read it to you again." And he proceeded to do just that, while I'm sitting there within earshot. All I had to do was scribble down the information and then start charging things on the phone or the Internet.

Sometimes, credit card companies find it convenient to have you write your account number on the outside of your remittance envelope. Criminals will drive up to your mailbox, look for just those envelopes, and take down your account number. Once they have it, they'll access your account to get credit. Never write your account number on the outside of an envelope. You might as well take out a newspaper ad advertising your credit to the world.

BEWARE HELPFUL HANK

There are innumerable dodges credit card thieves use to get hold of valid credit card numbers. To try to stamp out fraud, credit card issuers stopped using carbons of card imprints a few years ago, because people would leave these carbons behind, or toss them intact into the garbage, and crooks would get the account numbers off them. Thieves called these carbons "black gold." But other techniques have been developed to pick up the slack. One familiar approach is to dupe a merchant into giving you a number. That might sound like a lot to ask for. It isn't. What a criminal will do is call up a small local business—a gas station, a pet store, a florist—anyplace that does steady credit card business. He hopes to get a gullible clerk, and he usually will.

"Hello, this is Joe from MasterCard," he'll say. "I'm returning your call."

"What call?"

"I just got word that there was a problem with your verification machine. Are you encountering any difficulties with it?"

"Uh, no, not that I'm aware of."

"Well, you know what happens is, when something goes amiss on a transaction, the machine will automatically send out a signal to our central processor indicating that there's a problem. That must have been what went on here. Did you just do a transaction?"

"Yeah, maybe five minutes ago."

"Good, that must be the one. Let's check that transaction. What was the card number?"

He'll read off the card number from the store's receipt.

"Now, what's the expiration date?"

He'll read that off.

Just to keep the ruse sounding good, the crook will ask for the amount of the purchase, although that doesn't interest him. He's already got all that he needs.

Crooks usually pull these little capers in the evening, when there are always a lot of transactions and when the manager has gone home. Managers are a lot less likely to fall for this routine than a clerk, but you'd be surprised how often a manager will bite, too.

WHAT TO DO

It can be that easy. And it can be just as easy to avoid that ever happening. All you have to do is teach your employees that if they ever get a call purporting to be from a credit card company, tell them you'll call them right back. Then make sure that's where they're from. Don't take someone's word on the phone for who they are. Often, it's a con artist, and you know how good his word is.

And when you've handed your card to a salesclerk to make a purchase, take the time to examine it when you get it back. The vast majority of the time, you get the same card back. But not always. Dishonest salesclerks will pocket your card and hand you a fake or expired card, the old "bait and switch" scam, because they know most people will put the card back in their purse or wallet without even glancing at it.

Have you ever gotten home and received a phone call from someone who tells you he found your wallet at the store you just came from and he'll put it in the mail to you that afternoon? You check, he's right, and you're immensely relieved that your wallet was found by such an upright citizen.

You shouldn't be. Too often, the guy who stole it out of your purse is the one who's calling, and with that telephone call he's buying himself time. Now, because he's called to tell you he's sending you the wallet, you don't contact your credit card companies and cancel the cards and he's got an extra day or two to use them. Never delay in reporting a credit card lost or stolen, or the next pickpocket will take a vacation on you.

SO *THAT'S* WHAT HIGHER MATH WAS FOR

The number of people who potentially have access to your credit card or credit card number can be mind-boggling. For instance, the job of a worker for Northwest Airlines was to load and unload mail on Northwest flights arriving and departing from Metro Airport in Detroit. He would transport the mail back and forth between the planes and the airport's postal facility. Not all of the mail made the flights. He would make a point of stealing a certain amount of letters and rummaging through them for credit cards or credit card numbers. He shared his bounty with some associates, who used the cards to purchase merchandise. When he was caught, police found more than six thousand letters in his home and car.

There are cheap dates and there are cheap bribes. Seven clerks who worked in the New York offices of the Social Security Administration were willing to accept between ten dollars and seventy-five dollars to reveal a person's birth date and mother's maiden name to a group of Nigerians, ones apparently taking time off from sending out letter scams. The Nigerians needed the information to activate new credit cards they had intercepted before they got to their rightful owners. A common security feature credit card issuers use is the requirement that a cardholder receiving a new card must call a toll-free number and give his mother's maiden name, date of birth, and other information. Over a relatively short period of time, the Nigerian ring rounded up a breathtaking twenty thousand cards and charged more than $10 million on them.

But it's not even necessary to steal credit card information. That's usually for the amateur crook. A true criminal knows exactly where to go to get it, and that's from what we call a credit card generator. There are maybe a dozen or so websites around the world that are maintained for criminals by other criminals, a nice little service in the intricate fraud network. If you know the code to get into the website, you can get any information that you want. The people who maintain the sites generally charge someone five thousand dollars to ten thousand dollars for regular use. It may sound like a lot, but it's a bargain considering what you get for your investment.

Once you get onto the home page of the site, you enter a code. That takes you to the next screen. You're asked what information you want. Do you want an American Express card number, Diner's Club, Discover Card? Maybe you just want a utility company account number? Whatever you click on brings you to the next page. Say you check Visa. Then you're invited to select an institution: Citibank, Bank of America, Household Bank. You click on one, and within twenty seconds you get the names, numbers, and expiration dates of valid cards. Number after number after number. Each of these generators contains thousands of card numbers. I've checked them out, and I've never logged on and not gotten a valid card.

There are also software programs that will essentially pluck valid credit card numbers out of the air. Legitimate card numbers generally end with what's called a "check digit." It's a number added for the purpose of validating the authenticity of the card number. This check digit is derived from the card's other numbers by what is known as a Luhn formula or Mod-10 algorithm. I'm not going to get into higher math, but suffice to say, a quick way to verify a card number is to run the algorithm and compare the check digit you get with the check digit encoded with the credit card number. As it happens, the Mod-10 algorithm is fairly widely known and assorted computer programs use it to churn out numbers likely to fool authorization checks.

Now, these don't always prove useful, as the issuing bank will normally confirm the number, expiration, and mailing address when you make an Internet purchase, thus thwarting any software-generated account number. But for inexpensive purchases, generally those under twenty dollars, and often higher amounts overseas, banks commonly run a "stand-in" check, a quick authorization that does nothing more than see that the account number is valid against the "check digit." Consequently, thieves armed with these computer-generated numbers will log onto online merchant sites and type in number after number until they find one that gets taken, and then they make a blizzard of small purchases.

In so many ways, the Internet has opened up a wide new avenue for crooks to get hold of your card number and use it for nefarious purposes. I'll discuss this and other computer crimes in further detail in a later chapter on the Internet.

MING'S BOOSTER RING

Account boosting is yet another popular trick of credit card thieves. This is a scheme where criminals acquire legitimate credit cards and accrue balances on them. The criminal then sends the issuer a payment by overnight delivery using a stolen or counterfeit check. The payment exceeds the balance, and thus "boosts" the account's credit line. Under Federal law, banks have to post card payments before the checks clear and so they have no choice but to credit your account. The next day, the criminal goes to a bank machine and withdraws the excess amount on that card. Later, of course, the check bounces.

A Vietnamese criminal named Minh C. To, also known as Big Ming, headed up a credit card ring that recruited legitimate cardholders to overpay their credit card accounts using counterfeit checks. Once the accounts were boosted by the checks, Big Ming and the recruits would start buying merchandise. Big Ming would fence the goods and split the profits with the recruits. To cap off the scheme, he had the recruits file for bankruptcy so they wouldn't be liable for the debt. Before Big Ming was stopped, the ring defrauded credit card issuers of more than $100 million.

So it pays for card companies to be very suspicious of any payments that exceed what a cardholder owes.

BANKING ON YOUR EMBARRASSMENT

And there are endless ingenious schemes criminals employ to tack on charges to your credit card. A group of thieves, apparently from Russia, created a phony adult porn website. They then stole 3 million credit card numbers from a computer database, and had the site bill each account ten dollars. Otherwise, they didn't use the cards. The amount was so small that many customers didn't even notice it. Others did, but were too embarrassed to report it as being unauthorized to the bank. Those ten dollar charges added up to $30 million in charges. Oddly enough, law enforcement authorities were convinced that the real purpose of this game was to launder money.

DEBIT CARDS—THE DOWNSIDE

A lot of consumers like the idea of using a debit card rather than a conventional credit card. With a debit card, money comes right out of your own bank account when you make a purchase. There's no bill thirty days later. By using a debit card, you're deprived of a month's worth of float, and since we're a country built on float, most people don't like them. I'm one of them. But there's another issue with them that bothers me. Since the money is immediately extracted from your account when you make a purchase, it becomes harder to contest a fraudulent charge. On a credit card, if something is on your statement that you didn't buy, you refuse to pay for it. With a debit card, the money's already gone and you've got to try to recover it. And the law doesn't protect you as well. If you don't report a lost card within two days, you can be liable for up to five hundred dollars. And if you don't report an unauthorized transaction within sixty days of when your latest statement was issued, there's no liability limit at all, just the size of your bank balance.

I don't own a debit card myself. Two of my three sons, though, use them. They tell me they don't like writing checks and that's why they have them. Young people, it seems, are bothered by the chore of writing checks, so it may be a generational thing.

SEARCH THAT WAITER

In the last few years, an entirely new approach to credit card fraud has opened up. A case that was reported in *Time* magazine told about a crook in Miami who had charged more than five hundred thousand dollars against a hundred different American Express cards. American Express had determined that none of the cards had been stolen. That meant they had to be counterfeit. But that was a lot of cards.

American Express ran elaborate computer analyses of the account numbers and their recent activity. What it found was startling. Each of the victimized cardholders had recently eaten dinner at one of two New York restaurants. What did that mean?

Federal agents in New York obtained the cooperation of the owner of one of the restaurants, a Brazilian steak house called The Plantation. He was an honest and reputable owner, and he was as puzzled as anyone about the seeming connection between his restaurant and the fraudulent cards. In short order, after searching the employee dressing room, the agents found the answer in an open locker: a skimmer.

A skimmer is one of the newest and much-prized toys on the front-lines of fraud. It's a compact, battery-powered black device, not much larger than a hand-held Palm or a cell phone. It has a slit in the front, and Velcro is affixed to the back. When a credit card is swiped through the slit, the skimmer reads and stores all of the data that is embedded on the card's magnetic stripe—the card number, the cardholder's name, and the invisible encrypted verification code. The chip in the skimmer can hold information for up to three hundred cards. The data can then be readily downloaded onto a computer and used to make counterfeit cards.

That's precisely what was going on in The Plantation. A waiter kept a skimmer concealed inside his jacket. When a customer gave him his card, he stealthily swiped it in his skimmer before taking it to the cashier. He did it in a flash. He then sold the numbers to a criminal ring.

This sort of chain has become increasingly common. It goes on in department stores, hotels, and gas stations, as well as restaurants. Card numbers are picked up by the sales help and then e-mailed to card-cloning mills, all for money. Often the mills are run by organized crime syndicates, and they could be anywhere in the world. In essence, these rings operate counterfeit card factories. With a thermal dye printer, they put the colored graphics onto what's known as "white plastic," a blank card with a magnetic stripe on the back. Next, an embosser adds the victim's name and account number. Then an encoder puts the verification code onto the magnetic stripe.

The final touch is to apply a hologram onto the face of the card. Since 1981, credit card companies have used holograms to guard against fraud, but one upshot of this has been the emergence of sizable counterfeit hologram operations in Taiwan, Hong Kong, and China. Smugglers regularly bring fraudulent holograms into the United States, and sell them for five dollars to fifteen dollars apiece. On a legitimate card, the hologram is embedded in the plastic when the card is manufactured. On a counterfeit card, a hologram decal is attached to the card. If you examine the card closely, you should be able to feel a decal protruding slightly above the surface of the card.

Skimming is an immense problem. With stolen credit cards, the criminal has a narrow time frame in which to make purchases, but with skimmed cards nobody knows these cards are out there until a victim gets his statement, which can be more than thirty days after the crime took place. That's a lot of time to rack up illegal charges.

The skimming threat has worsened because the skimmers have gotten smaller. A few years ago, the forerunners of today's tiny skimmers were devices the size of portable computers. They would be concealed under gas station counters, where attendants would run cards through them without the customers' knowledge. The miniature versions came out in early 1999.

Some of the credit card companies are trying to use computer analyses to fool skimmers. Say someone in Taiwan tries to buy something with a card that hours earlier was used in Wisconsin. The computer could be programmed to reject the transaction. But given the gigantic number of cards in circulation, it gets expensive to do this and isn't practical on a large scale.

THE FUTURE GETS SMART

The technology of the future is Smart Cards. These are credit card–sized plastic cards that contain an integrated circuit chip instead of a magnetic stripe. It's the chip that makes it "smart." In essence, it's a credit card outfitted with a "brain." The card is actually more powerful than the first desktop computer. That little chip can store a hundred times more information than a magnetic stripe, which is limited to just three lines of information: your name, the account number, and your PIN number.

A Smart Card chip can be configured to include everything a person needs and replace all of his other credit cards, phone cards, and health care cards. For example, you go to a store and buy a turtleneck sweater and hand the clerk a Smart Card. The clerk asks what account do you want it on: Visa, American Express, Macy's? They're all on that chip. So your Smart Card is a full-fledged electronic wallet. Someday, we'll even have a Smart Card driver's license. When the police stop you, they run the card through a reader and your entire driver's record will come up. Hawaii has already been experimenting with these.

Smart Cards were invented in France and have been around for about twenty years. Billions of them are already in use throughout the world—in Western Europe, South America, Asia, and Australia—but it's going to be a few more years before they become widespread in the United States. For that to happen, merchants have to be willing to invest in Smart Card readers and junk their credit card verification equipment. And Americans still like checks and credit cards, so there will have to be a cultural shift.

Are Smart Cards invulnerable? No, nothing is. They're tougher to defeat than conventional cards, but they can be defeated. Criminals with extraordinary knowledge of encryption have broken the encryption codes. Indeed, computer experts have bragged that there is no chip they can't penetrate. A graduate student at the University of California at Berkeley used a network of about two hundred and fifty workstations to crack one type of chip. It took him four hours. Other thieves have found that if they can force the chip on the card to make a calculation error, that error can be used to extrapolate the data that validates the card when it gets used. One way to force an error, they found, was by bombarding the card with radiation. Some accomplished this by sticking the card in a microwave oven. Criminals have even popped out the chips and replaced them with their own.

In 1999, a French engineer, after four months of work, managed to make counterfeit French Smart Cards that he used at an automatic machine to buy tickets for the Paris Metro subway system. He offered to sell his technique to the bank consortium that issued the Smart cards for $1.5 million. Instead, the bank chose to have him arrested.

And any card is only as good as the internal controls at the card issuer. If a clerk in charge of encrypting the cards wants to sell the codes for $10,000 to some thieves, it will happen without reliable controls.

No matter what sort of card you have, the most important safeguard is to always carefully check your statements, and that goes for the five dollar charges as well as the five hundred dollar ones. While issuers and con artists continue their taut battle of one-upmanship, it's the only reliable way to tell if you're being scammed.

I must admit, there are days when I have to wonder if a criminal needs to even try all that hard. Not long ago, I was shopping in Neiman Marcus with my wife, and I saw a shirt I really liked and decided to buy it. My wife had a Neiman Marcus card, so she told me, "Here, use my card." It had her maiden name on it and her signature, but if there was a problem I was going to tell the clerk, "My wife's right over there, it's her card."

The clerk rang up the shirt, and put down the sales slip for me to sign. She took the card and flipped it over to look at the signature, my wife's signature. It wasn't the same name, no less the same signature. She held up the slip I had signed, held up the card, compared the two, thanked me very much, and handed me my shirt.

7

[BEATING **THE MACHINE**]

 few years ago, the head of security at Bank of America called me at home at night. I could immediately tell from his tone of voice that he was a little flustered. "Say, we've got a really serious problem, and we need your advice," he said. "We're losing something like $40,000 a day out of our ATM machines. It's got to be a ring, but we can't figure out how they're doing it."

I asked him if the cash-dispensing machines being targeted were high-profile ones, those found in heavily-trafficked, very visible locations. He said they were. I told him he had shoulder surfers. Go out to some of the machines, I advised him, and look for a van parked within a block of any of them. The culprits were caught the next day.

"Shoulder surfers" is the name that's been bestowed on criminals who lurk behind you, trying to peek over your shoulder at what you punch into the automated teller machine (ATM) keyboard. However, it's become something of a misnomer because savvy criminals don't stay that close anymore. That's too obvious and too dangerous. They've become long-distance surfers who camp out fifty or more yards away, and pick off personal identification numbers (PIN) numbers with a high-powered camera or binoculars. This was a team who would set up in their van across the street from an ATM and then train a video camera on the machine.

In this caper, one of the conspirators would first go and take twenty dollars from the machine under surveillance. He'd examine the receipt, which would show the time of the transaction. Then the video camera in the van would be synchronized to that time. As customers used the machine, the camera would be locked on the keypad and would record their finger movements. The thieves weren't interested in seeing you, no matter how good-looking you were. They were interested in your fingers. By taping them, they could tell what your PIN was.

After they retrieved their cash, nine out of ten of the people using the machine did the typical thing: they took a quick look at their receipt and tossed it into the wastebasket. At machines where the bank hadn't provided a wastebasket, the crooks were courteous enough to furnish one of their own. At the end of the day, one of the thieves hustled over to the machine with a garbage bag, emptied the receipts into the bag and took them with him.

When they got back to their house, they dumped the receipts on a table and began to sort them by the time stamped on them. They then stuck the videotape into their VCR, played the tape of all those fingers, and matched the receipts to the fingers. In that way, they attached the account numbers printed on the receipts to their respective PIN numbers. The beauty of the receipts was that they allowed the thieves to see the balances in the accounts. Oh, this guy's got fourteen dollars left. They'd throw it away. This guy's got five hundred dollars. That's a keeper.

Once they had the account numbers and PINs they wanted, they went to an office supply store and bought some blank credit cards. With a hand embosser, also easily acquired, they encoded the cards with the account numbers, took them to ATM machines, and began withdrawing money.

This was one case at one bank, but it goes on all the time.

There's no denying that the swift growth in ATMs has revolutionized consumer banking. But ever since their introduction in 1973, ATMs have been viewed as attractive targets by criminals, luring everyone from brazen armed robbers to crafty scam artists. Despite all this, I think that ATMs are pretty safe, a lot safer than your checkbook. Generally, you can't withdraw more than two hundred dollars in a single day from any one account, which is an effective safeguard. In addition, an account holder is only liable for up to fifty dollars if an account and PIN are compromised, and banks typically waive that. ATMs, therefore, are not the problem that fraudulent checks and embezzlement are. Still, the ATM machine is how we get our money every day, and wherever there's money, criminals lurk.

There have actually been some astounding sums withdrawn with a single card in just a few days of frenzied activity. A woman in Gresham, Oregon, was at a high school football game on a Friday night. She had left her bank card in her purse in her van out in the parking lot. Two men and a woman who were working together broke in and stole it. Leaving it there was mistake No. 1. Mistake No. 2 was that she had scribbled down her PIN number on her Social Security card, which was also in her purse. The thieves, I'm sure, were quite thankful that she was so obliging. They wasted no time in satisfying their needs.

Within minutes, they were at a bank machine a few blocks from the football field. Before the next series of downs was completed, they had made their first withdrawal. They kept on going, traveling at a hundred miles through five counties, stopping pretty much every time they spied an ATM. Even though the standard limit on a withdrawal in a given day on one card is generally a few hundred dollars, there had been a computer program change at the credit union where the victim banked, and there was no limit at all on that particular weekend. In a 54 hour time frame, the thieves made 724 withdrawals from 48 bank machines. They collected $346,770. Talk about being lucky. Before they were caught, largely because of hidden cameras at five of the machines, they even managed to find the time to buy a new pickup truck. So you can see why it's vital for banks to keep a lid on how much cash can be withdrawn.

THINKING OF GLUE

In terms of ingenuity, one of my favorite ATM scams took place at the Miami Airport. Like a lot of cash machines, the ATMs there used to have little revolving doors on them. Once you punched in your transaction, the door opened and you stuck your hand into this little well and collected your cash. The well had a small light inside it that told the machine that a hand was reaching in there, so don't close on it. This criminal went and used one of those superglues to glue the door shut. When a customer tried the machine, the door didn't budge. Assuming the machine was malfunctioning, the customer would press "cancel" and nonchalantly move on to the next machine.

Just because the door didn't open, however, didn't mean money wasn't being dispensed. The cash would get spit out of the bowels of the machine, bounce against the rigid door, and just sit there in the well. Another customer would come; more money would pile up on top of that money, and more and more. After about ten people had used the machine, the guy would come up to it, put his card in, and hit the door with his fist. The door would pop open and reward him with a fat stack of twenties.

So you've got all this technology and all these safeguards built into the machine, and yet no one thought of the possibility of a criminal gluing the door shut. These days, new machines are no longer manufactured with doors. They simply have slots that shoot out the money. But there are still plenty of older generation ATMs with doors on them. If a door doesn't open, don't shrug it off. Notify security.

Sometimes you'll put your card into the ATM slot and, tug as you might, it gets jammed and you can't get it out. So you leave it there, intending to contact the bank when you get to a phone or the next morning if it's after banking hours. While it might be a broken machine, I wouldn't bet on it. The odds are it's a card-withholding scam.

Here's what happens. A thief puts an adhesive of some sort inside the card slot. He steps aside and waits until someone comes and tries to use it. When someone does, the card gets glued to the slot. Then the crook slips into line behind that person and watches him enter his PIN. Sometimes, just to be on the safe side, the thief will position a sign on the ATM machine that says, "If your card gets stuck, enter your PIN three separate times to retrieve it." If the thief can't pick up your PIN number after three tries, he needs to find another line of work.

After you leave, frustrated by the experience, the thief moves in and removes the card with a pair of pliers. He then proceeds to use your card at other ATMs.

In Massachusetts, two men worked a card-withholding scam in ten towns in the Boston area, preying on young women. When a woman's card got stuck, they would come up and sympathize, meanwhile memorizing her PIN as they tried to help her remove the card. Once she left, the thieves would extract the card using a fingernail file. If they weren't able to get the PIN, one of the men would later call the customer and pretend to be a bank official or ATM security officer and get the number that way. The men stole more than ten thousand dollars from twelve different women before they were caught.

WHAT TO DO

The tip to remember here is, before you insert your card into a slot, take the time to inspect the card slot for any residue. If you notice any, don't use it. And if you see a notice on a machine advising you to enter your PIN multiple times, don't even think of using that machine. Believe me, the bank didn't put that sign there.

Police in New York arrested a man who had been stealing PINs at ATM machines in Manhattan and then tricking his victims, usually senior citizens, into reinserting their card under the guise of "clearing the machine." Once the customer did so and left, the thief would linger, punch in the stolen PIN and make additional withdrawals. There's no need to "clear a machine." Once your transaction is done, there's never any reason to insert your card again, no matter who tells you to.

Common sense is always the best defense against any form of crime, but it astounds me how often people neglect to use any sense at all. Consider this con that succeeded in netting its perpetrator a nifty one hundred fifty thousand dollars. The man positioned himself outside the locked door of an ATM enclosure, and posed as a bank security officer. When customers approached the enclosure to use one of the ATMs, he would introduce himself and tell them he needed their assistance in catching a dishonest bank employee who had been driving management crazy. Could they please leave their bank cards under the locked door?

He'd personally assure them he would get their cards back to them by the next day.

For those who complied, the con man would then fish the cards out from under the door. The next day, an accomplice would call the cardholder and report that the employee had been apprehended. He wanted to thank him for his help. Then he would point out that since the dishonest employee had come into contact with the card, the bank would have to give the customer a new PIN. Could he please have the old PIN to verify that he was speaking to the actual cardholder?

Incredibly enough, more than three hundred ATM users fell for this ruse. As enthralling as it sounds, I can assure you that a bank is never going to use a customer to assist it in nabbing a crooked employee. It will use a security guard or enlist a police undercover detective. Real life is nothing like the movies.

AND WITH SOME HEAVY EQUIPMENT . . .

Some criminals will physically assault an ATM. A thief in Norfolk, Virginia, broke through the ceiling of an ATM enclosure and used a crowbar and a blowtorch to try to get into the machine and collect the cash inside it. The machine put up a good fight, but it really took a pounding. There were scorch marks on the ATM from the blowtorch. There were scars from the crowbar. The handle of the door was broken off. The combination lock was destroyed.

A crook armed with the proper tools can break into many ATM machines within fifteen minutes. ATMs are actually rated on how resistant they are to physical assault. A certain model may have a TL-15 or a TL-30 rating, the number indicating the time it would take for a skilled thief to break into it with the right tools, and given a suitable environment. But a thief rarely has that much time, because ATMs are outfitted with detectors sensitive to things like vibration and heat. These detectors are usually silent, so the criminal doesn't know the police are on the way.

There was a mechanical engineer, however, who was very successful at breaking into ATMs. At one time, he used a burning bar on ATM vaults. Later, he used an industrial magnetic drill. Then he manipulated the locks and combinations on the ATM chests. He was ultimately caught, but not before he did a lot of damage and collected a good deal of money.

I always tell banks, keep the ATM area well lit and free from obstruction. Don't create hiding places with bushes or ornamentation near the machine. Put video cameras in the ATM enclosure to record criminals on tape. There are various types of alarms and time locks and relocking devices. If time locks are used, you can bet that no criminal is going to wait around for the time to elapse.

Generally speaking, it's not that easy to find an environment where a crook can spend even as little as fifteen minutes with a blowtorch opening up a machine without attracting attention. That's why crooks who are after the cash inside a machine—a convenience store machine may have as much as ten thousand dollars in it and one at a bank could contain something like seventy-five thousand dollars—will more likely just cart the whole machine off with them. A few years back, two criminals walked into a convenience store and identified themselves to the seventeen-year-old clerk as representatives from the bank. They said the ATM needed to be repaired, and they put it on a dolly and made off with it.

For the most part, though, relatively few thieves bother risking pulled muscles when they can make so much more money by ripping off card numbers.

THERE'S NOTHING LIKE OWNING YOUR OWN

Criminals are pretty nervy, and I've learned to never be surprised by what someone will try to get away with. And, given the right circumstances, you can get away with almost anything—up to a point.

The nerviest form of ATM fraud is when the thieves actually set up their very own bank machine. Here's a case that I still shake my head over. One weekend a few years ago, two men dressed as bank employees arrived and set up a perfectly ordinary-looking ATM in a popular shopping mall in Manchester, Connecticut. Mall officials had swallowed their con that they were from a New Jersey outfit called Electronic Cash Machines. I'm not sure they did any background check on them whatsoever.

In any event, the machine didn't dispense money. It wasn't even connected to a phone line that would have enabled it to be linked to a bank network. It was simply plugged into an electrical outlet. What the bogus machine did do was record the card numbers and personal identification numbers of customers who inserted their cards in futile attempts to get some cash. That was all the thieves needed. They then manufactured counterfeit cards with the customers' numbers, went to working machines in New York, and gradually drained their accounts.

Even though the phony machine was real in appearance, it did take a certain leap of faith for customers to actually try to use it. Or perhaps I should say, it took downright gullibility. After all, the machine wasn't tucked into a wall the way real ATMs are. Instead, it just sat there on wheels, outside one of the mall's busier department stores, looking like it was still waiting to be installed. There was no bank name inscribed on it, just a few stickers affixed to it advertising various ATM networks.

And the machine never spit out any money, even though one of the thieves, posing as a repairman, spent an awful lot of time crouching next to it, doing his best to look like he was industriously working on its mysterious problems. Again and again, he would pronounce it fixed, and yet it never was. But he was a nice-looking young man, and he sounded persuasive. "I think it's fixed now, c'mon and try it," he would invite people. "I think it was a problem with the dedicated phone line."

Incredibly enough, more than a hundred and twenty customers went ahead and gave the machine a try, much to their subsequent regret. There was a man who sold Nordic Trak equipment who worked nearby. He'd notice customer after customer using it, never once getting any money. He'd see that same persistent repairman constantly at work on it, never seeming to make any headway. So what did he do? He went ahead and swiped his own card in the machine. A few days later, two hundred dollars was missing from his account.

The machine remained in the mall, standing on its wheels, for a full two weeks, collecting more and more card numbers and PINs. By the time the authorities finally caught on to what was transpiring, after customers complained about missing funds, the crooks had gotten away, and so did the machine. Apparently deciding enough was enough, the two men came in one day and loaded it onto a white truck. They informed the mall that it had to be taken in for repairs.

It was unclear how the thieves got their hands on the bank machine. It was speculated that they bought it on the used ATM market. Or they might have stolen it. Not that long before, there had been a wave of thefts in New England, during which a band of robbers wrested bank machines off of their foundations and took them away in trucks. In actuality, though, there are companies that make portable ATMs and will gladly sell them to anyone who wants one. You'd be amazed at the things that the general public can buy. There's only one state in the country, Oklahoma, that doesn't allow just anybody to buy a pay phone.

The Connecticut thieves managed to realize more than one hundred thousand dollars from their audacious crime. What tripped them up was they made the mistake of using their counterfeit cards for withdrawals in Manhattan bank machines. New York has a law requiring cameras on every teller machine. By inspecting photographs and withdrawal records, the police apprehended the two men about a month later. One of the thieves was a computer specialist. The other had a background in finance. When they were arrested, the authorities discovered that they had five ATMs, including the one used in the Connecticut caper.

There have been other extravagant variations of the open-your-own-ATM scheme. In a number of instances, a criminal has ventured into hotels, asked to see the manager, and introduced himself as a representative of a business that installs ATMs in commercial locations. He outlined a deal where he would put a portable machine in the hotel's lobby. Every time a guest used it, his company would collect a service fee of one dollar fifty cents. He'd give one dollar of that to the hotel. It's a deal that sounded great. The hotel would have a new convenience to offer its guests, and not only would it cost the hotel nothing, but also the hotel would make money off of it. So the manager said, go ahead, put it in.

The criminal rolled it in, and unlike with the mall caper, he loaded it with $1,500 so it functioned like a legitimate machine and actually dispensed cash. He didn't mind this little investment, considering the returns he anticipated. His machine wasn't connected to a bank phone line, either. It was simply registering card numbers and PIN numbers to allow counterfeit cards to be generated.

So don't be fooled into thinking a machine must be real if it dispenses money. Criminals aren't that cheap. They're perfectly willing to invest some cash if the returns are much greater, as they inevitably are in scams like these. I'm always mistrustful of portable ATMs, and use them only if I have no alternative. When I go to a stand-alone machine, though, I always take a look behind it to see if it's connected to a phone line. If it isn't, it's a fake.

JUST SKIMMING ALONG

The latest approach to ATM theft is skimming. Skimmers similar in function to the ones I spoke about for credit card fraud are specially manufactured for ATMs. Criminals fit them over the card slot on a standard ATM, and they have a magnet in the back that holds them in place. The skimmer is motorized, so that when you put your card in, the motor nudges the card along so it actually penetrates the real hole as well. That allows the machine to function normally. But while the card passes through the skimmer, your card information is stored on its chip. At the end of a day, the criminal retrieves his skimmer, as well as dozens of account numbers and PINs.

Anytime you notice something protruding from an ATM, be suspicious. The card slot should be flush. Someone I know once encountered a skimmer, yanked it off the machine, and went in and handed it to a bank officer. "You might be interested in this," he told him. "I found it on your machine."

WHAT TO DO

It's the simple things that can prevent you from becoming a victim of ATM fraud, and so let me review the key safeguards to keep in mind. Never give out your PIN to anyone, especially someone who maintains that he's a bank officer or a security guard. All a crook needs is your card and your PIN, and he can go to town. If others are waiting in line behind you to use the ATM, don't be lackadaisical, and block the keyboard when you enter your PIN. Some banks have redesigned the ATM keyboard or enclosures to make it particularly difficult for an observer to watch the cardholder punch in his PIN, but even then you need to be watchful.

Never write your PIN on your card or on a piece of paper that you keep in your wallet or purse. I know some people who put it on a little sticker and attach it right to their ATM card. That's credit suicide. If your ATM card is lost or stolen, immediately report it to your bank so that card can be disabled. Crooks move fast, and you need to move faster.

Don't consider using an ATM unless you've checked out the area carefully. If people seem to be loitering by the machine, don't assume they're there for innocent purposes. And check across the street for people with cameras or binoculars, those long-distance surfers I mentioned. If something about an environment makes you uneasy, err on the side of caution and come back later or use another machine.

If you feel threatened while processing a transaction, press the "cancel" button and leave the area. If you sense someone is following you, drive to the police station or nearest business with a lot of people around. Once you're done getting your money, don't just stand there at the machine and count your cash, advertising your withdrawal. Put it away, leave the area, and count it once you're in your car or back in the office.

The receipt that gets spit out of an ATM machine is a nice convenience for the customer. It's also a great convenience for the criminal. It has part of your account number on it and how much money is left in your account. In some cases, it even has your PIN. Until a few years ago, federal law mandated that ATM receipts had to carry your full account number on them. That made it too easy for crooks. I was among those who testified in behalf of a change in the law, known as Regulation E. It was finally changed, and now receipts only have to carry half of an account number.

Even so, don't throw away your receipts at the ATM machine in those receptacles banks (or crooks) put there. Criminals retrieve them and use even fragments of information to carry out shoulder surfing scams. Rip the receipts up before you throw them away, or take them with you. If you're going to leave them behind, you might as well leave your bank card, too. When I use an ATM, I always choose the option, "No receipt."

All ATM cards have a daily limit that prevents the cardholder or any other user of the card from withdrawing more than a certain amount of money in any one day. Cardholders, however, are seldom aware that certain banks allow a cardholder to go into the bank and withdraw larger amounts on the card using only the PIN and card. No further identification or signature is required at these banks. This allows a thief who has a person's card and PIN to withdraw the maximum allowable at the ATM and then, after checking the account holder's balance, to go into the bank and withdraw additional amounts at the teller. If my bank did that, I'd have them put the same limit on a teller withdrawal, unless further identification is furnished.

And here's some advice about PIN numbers: be a little bit more inventive in your choice of number. Surveys of our habits are interesting fodder, but—guess what—criminals read surveys, too. They know that 70 percent of people use their birthday or their street address as their PIN. If a thief gets hold of your purse or wallet, he's got your street address. If it's a four-digit address, that's probably your PIN. Any number of cards in your wallet will have your birthday. Another common choice is the first four digits or the last four digits of your Social Security number. Thieves love that, too. Use an easy-to-remember number that's not tied to you, a number that isn't going to be found on any piece of personal identification. I have three sons, and so I use their birthdays for my PIN numbers. I never forget my kids' birthdays, and yet no one can find those dates on anything in my wallet.

LEAVE MY EYES OUT OF IT

Because PIN numbers are the weak link in the system, there's been a lot of discussion about doing away with them. The hot new technology for ATMs is biometrics, which is the statistical measurement of biological phenomena. An array of devices have been invented that will identify people through physical characteristics, whether by hands, faces, voices, eyes, or even smells. One of the most promising is a machine that identifies you by your eye. When you insert your bank card, a pea-sized camera locates your face, homes in on the eye, and snaps a digital image of your iris. It can do this from as far away as three feet. The computerized "iris code" then gets compared with one that the customer furnished to the bank. If the two codes don't match, the ATM won't work. The entire process takes not even two seconds.

The key to mass deployment of these systems is that they work no matter what contingencies arise. For instance, face recognition systems

get foiled when a man grows a beard or a woman dyes her hair. If someone puts on a significant amount of weight and his face gets pudgier, that
alone will throw off the machine. But the iris systems work, even if a customer wears glasses or contact lenses. They work at night and in dim
lighting. Face recognition systems are thwarted by twins, not that theft by
one twin against another is one of the world's major crime problems, but
even twins have unique irises.

Fingerprints can change from injury or deliberate alteration. But not
irises. From the time someone is about eighteen months old until a few
minutes after they die, their iris is unchanging. For the purposes of an
ATM machine, that's plenty of time. And you can't fool the machine by
holding aloft a picture of the cardholder. The first thing the camera
checks is whether the eye is pulsating, and thus alive. If the camera fails
to detect blood flowing through the eye, then it concludes that it is looking at a picture or at someone who's dead.

It's fascinating technology, but I'm personally against these devices. I
just think the whole idea is ridiculous. We've given up enough privacy in
this modern age, so why should we be asked to give up anymore? The
bank has enough information on its customers. Now it's saying that it
wants them to give up their irises? For what? Something they're not even
liable for. The most that crooks can normally take from one account is a
couple of hundred dollars, and it's the bank's problem if it happens. So
my feeling is, why insult your customer?

[THE **CYBERTHIEF**]

Not long ago, I was faced with a real dilemma. One of my sons had a birthday coming up, and he wanted a guitar he'd seen on eBay. That particular guitar, and no other. I know that eBay is part of the pulse of daily life for many consumers, who regularly log onto the auction site to buy everything from car tires to knight's helmets. But it isn't part of my life. The Internet frightens me. I think it's a wondrous invention and there are many things I love about it, but it unnerves me because of all the possibilities for fraud. A firm rule of mine is never to buy anything over the Internet with a credit card, and I tell my wife and kids the same thing. I just don't trust the feeble amount of security that's been incorporated into most websites.

But now there was this guitar and my son's birthday. So I logged onto eBay and found the guitar. In order to purchase it, I had to go to a feature called Pay Pal. It required that I enter my credit card number. Given my convictions, I was very reluctant to do that, but I was even more reluctant to disappoint my son. So I went through the drill and typed in my

MasterCard number and expiration date. Just as I was about to complete the transaction, I got panicky and had a change of heart. I pressed cancel. I'm not going to do this, I told myself. It violates all my principles. I signed off, unaware of my impending fate.

Fortunately, eBay tells you how to contact the owner of any item offered on its website, and so I sent an e-mail to the guy who was selling the guitar and asked him to call me. When he did, I talked to him for a bit and felt comfortable that he was legitimate. I told him I'd like to buy the guitar, but I wasn't going to give out my credit card on the Internet. I said I'd send him a cashier's check for the amount, and give him my Federal Express number so he could ship it to me. He agreed, I got the guitar, and my son was delighted.

Soon after, I received my MasterCard bill in the mail, and there was a two hundred fifty dollar charge from Pay Pal. I called and said that I hadn't bought anything. They told me to write a letter contesting it and they'd remove the charge. Then a package arrived at my house addressed to me. I opened it up and it was some ski pants. I hadn't ordered any ski pants. I didn't even recognize the company.

I called them up and was told it was an Internet purchase made on my MasterCard. I explained that I would never buy anything over the Internet. Obviously, someone had gotten hold of my credit card number, and the only way he could have done it was through that Pay Pal entry. Okay, the guy said, just put the pants in the box and send them back and I'd get a credit. I asked him why someone would use my credit card to buy something and then ship it to me? What probably happened, he said, was it was someone in my area. Most people are at work when packages arrive, and they get left on the porch. Thieves will order them, find out when they're to be delivered, and then steal them off the porch. Another possibility was the thief tried to have it delivered to a different address, but as a precaution, this company only shipped merchandise to the billing address on the card. Not wanting to arouse suspicion, the thief probably allowed it to be sent anyway. What did he care? He wasn't paying for it.

Once I got off the phone with the ski pants company, I called MasterCard and alerted them to the shenanigans with my card. The representative checked my account activity. As of that moment, it showed purchases of $3,600, none of which I had made. They were all Internet purchases, since there was no need for a signature or anything. My card was canceled, and I had to send a notarized affidavit attesting that those were not my charges.

So here I was, one more victim of Internet fraud. The sole time in my life that I used the Internet to attempt to buy something, and just for a minute, I got scammed. I never even completed the transaction, and yet my card number was preserved on the site and someone got hold of it. If this happened to me, who's constantly on the alert for swindles, it shows you how vulnerable computers have made us.

THE PORTABLE THIEF

There's no question about it: the Internet is a criminal's dream come true. Forty million people use the Internet every day, and to a thief, that translates into the ability to cheat an immense number of people all at the same time. Estimates are that more than 5 percent of Internet trans-actions are fraudulent, compared to less than half of one percent for brick-and-mortar retailers. Every day, thieves are sitting before their terminals, trying to break into somebody's system, working on that way to bypass security.

With the Internet, a thief doesn't need to come to your business or your home to steal from you. He does it by computer. A con man nor-mally had only the ability to reach people through the medium of him-self, and so he could only cheat a limited amount of people in a small area. Back in my days pushing bad paper, I was constantly on the move, and I had to be. Part of the reason was to evade capture, but also I needed to find new victims I hadn't yet fleeced. A con man today never has to board a plane. Using the Internet, he can deceive people all over the world, without having to talk to them. He doesn't even have to get dressed.

When it comes to fraud, appearance used to matter. When I started doing check forging, I was sixteen, but I was over six-feet tall. I looked like an adult, and I was able to act the part. If I'd been a bashful, pimply-faced teenager, there would have been no way I could have gotten away with what I did. But with electronic fraud, you don't know who the criminal is. You can't see him or her, because the person is sheltered by the technology's anonymity. You have literally opened yourself up to millions of criminals, and not only domestic ones. When you're on the Internet, you don't know if you're dealing with someone from Nigeria, Syria, Hong Kong, Malaysia, or Buffalo. And have you ever tried to get a refund from another continent? You won't enjoy the experience.

Computer crime, or cybercrime as it's called, is one of the newer forms of fraud, but it's a tremendous growth industry. One of the frightening things about fraud with computers is the speed at which it happens. When people use the Internet, they talk of going on "Internet time," meaning that everything transpires at warp speed. Well, criminals like Internet time too. A well-executed bank robbery, the physical stealing of the money, is going to take a half-hour, easily. With an electronic heist, we're talking a couple of milliseconds.

So much about computers make me uncomfortable, because they're the doorway to limitless amounts of money. Money is continually transferred electronically between banks and financial institutions, trillions of dollars a day flying around the world as electronic pulses. If a hacker slips inside a bank's computer, he can commit bank robbery of unprecedented proportions, with a mouse rather than a gun. Here's a statistic that shocks even me: only 6 percent of all websites are considered secure by experts. That means that 94 percent aren't. The 6 percent are almost all big financial institutions, because they're the only ones willing and able to spend the money to do it. It can cost at least $50 million for a bank to secure a website. Every day, ten thousand new websites are added, 94 percent of which are not secure. Despite this, most of us fail to acknowledge the fact that the computer is like a weapon. For the purposes of robbing someone, it's the same as a gun. The only difference is semantics. With a gun, it's called armed robbery. With a computer, it's called white-collar crime.

THEY SHOULD FRISK FOR A MOUSE

Computers have become such a potent weapon that in 1999, the U.S. Parole Commission made some telling changes in its rules. High-risk parolees can now be restricted from using computers and the Internet without written approval. In other words, don't just keep guns out of the hands of repeat offenders; keep these guys away from the computers.

And for good reason. In 1994, Vladimir Levin, a thirty-year-old Russian payroll programmer with thick glasses, used a rather primitive computer to steal $10 million from Citicorp's wealthier customers. With the help of some confederates, he managed to transfer the money into accounts with phony names scattered among obscure banks in the Middle East, Europe, and elsewhere. Then accomplices would go in and withdraw the sums. A stool pigeon ultimately turned him in, or he might never have been caught. He was arrested when he left Russia to go to London for a computer exhibition. Levin was generally considered to be the first online bank robber, and his theft was the largest computer crime on record.

As Levin's crime illustrates, a big difference with electronic fraud is the quantities involved. With regular fraud, the amounts are often fairly small and only add up over time. With electronic fraud, we're often talking about losses of millions of dollars in each caper. The FBI says that total losses from computer-related crime exceeded $250 million in 2000, double what they were in 1999, and since so much of it is underreported, it could be in the billions.

Unfortunately, law enforcement has not kept pace in its training of agents in how to combat computer crime. One recent study of cybercrime found that only a tiny amount of the federal government's law enforcement budget is spent on computer-crime training and staffing. Many police officers don't even have e-mail.

Incidentally, outright theft of computers—the actual machines themselves—is itself a big problem. Security experts say computer theft is now second only to auto theft, and it's much easier getting your car back than your computer.

HACKERS AND CRACKERS

If you have any doubt about the seriousness of electronic theft, think about this: six out of ten American companies and government agencies have been hacked so far, including the FBI, the CIA, the Secret Service, and the White House.

A twenty-year-old computer hacker confessed to breaking into two computers of the National Aeronautics and Space Administration (NASA) that were normally used to design satellites and for e-mail and internal functions. The hacker installed a program onto the computers that allowed him to host a chat room. On his chat room, he advised people to visit a particular pornographic website, and he earned eighteen cents for each visit someone made to it. Before long, he was making three hundred dollars to four hundred dollars a week.

A sixteen-year-old Miami boy broke into computers of the Defense Department and NASA, downloaded software, intercepted messages, stole data, and caused some of the computers to be shut down for three weeks. He repeatedly penetrated computers that monitor threats to the United States from nuclear, biological, and chemical weapons, as well as traditional arms. Too bad they didn't monitor attacks from sixteen-year-old hackers. Fortunately, the government said none of the affected computers was related to the command and control system, so the kid wasn't on the brink of launching a rocket or knocking a satellite out of orbit, but I hear these things and have to wonder, what's next?

A few years ago, a band of German hackers wrote their own Microsoft ActiveX control. The control designed by the Germans made a slight adjustment in the popular personal-finance program Quicken. Whenever the user paid a bill online using Quicken, he would also make a small contribution to the account of the hackers. Stealing money a small slice at a time like this is known as a "salami" attack, and a computer can make a lot of salami.

There's so much invasion of computers that distinct subcultures have emerged. The term "hacker" is now most commonly used to refer to teenagers who break into computer systems for kicks, the way kids of earlier generations smashed eggs on windshields or did graffiti. It gets them bragging rights among their peers. To them, bringing down the computer network of the Joint Chiefs of Staff is the same as playing Donkey Kong. After a sixteen-year-old boy was caught prowling in government and business computer systems, he explained, "All the girls thought it was cool."

Full-fledged thieves who invade computers as a profession are referred to as "crackers." There's quite a robust underground market in cracking. Adept crackers can command ten thousand dollars and up for breaking into a corporate website, and just as baseball players arrange bonuses if they hit a certain number of home runs or pitch so many innings, they merit bonuses for stealing trade secrets or doing damage to a competitor's computer system.

THE PROGRAM THAT LAUNCHED
ONE THOUSAND SCAMS

We all learned how the Greeks won the Trojan War by concealing themselves inside a large hollow wooden horse that got them into the walled city of Troy. The simplest method crackers use today to invade a computer is a piece of software that operates by a similar deception—a Trojan Horse program.

Just like with the real Trojan Horse, a Trojan Horse program has two functions operating simultaneously, one that you see and one that you don't. It does something overtly innocent like demonstrate a game, show a greeting card, or offer an mp3 song. But while that benign activity is going on, something insidious is happening. Basically, the criminal dupes you into running something whose exclusive purpose is to burrow its way into your computer without you knowing about it.

Trojan Horse programs take different forms, and you can find dozens of them offered free right on the Internet. One common scam works like this. The criminal sends you an ordinary e-mail. It's easy enough to find out anyone's e-mail address through a routine Internet search. The e-mail says, "Hey, how you doing? Want to see something cool?" and contains an attachment. The key is the attachment. When you open it, there might be a game demo or some little piece of entertainment. You watch it and have a few chuckles. But invisibly embedded in that demo is a Trojan Horse program known as a keystroke recorder, whose subcommands instruct the computer to record everything the user types on the keyboard. That information then gets sent to the computer of the criminal. He now knows your passwords and account numbers, and your credit is at his disposal. These programs were originally designed so employers and parents could check on what their employees and kids were up to, but like so many legitimate ideas, they've been put to alternative, malicious purposes by thieves.

The Trojan Horse could also carry a more elaborate desktop monitoring program that functions almost exactly like a surveillance camera. Now when you're on line, the criminal views live on his computer everything that you type and see on your screen. He could be in Turkey, but it's as if he were sitting beside you. If you log on to your bank account, entering your account number and your PIN, the thief in Turkey sees precisely what you're doing. He can then log on to your account and have your bank send him a check that cleans out your savings. And you never even knew he was there.

A Trojan Horse can also deposit a remote access program that not only enables a crook to see what someone is doing, but also lets him get into that person's computer, fool with his files, and disrupt his system. The best known of these snooping devices is Back Orifice. It was devised by a hacker group called the Cult of the Dead Cow. The program's name spoofs Microsoft's Back Office software. Again, these programs have a legitimate purpose. The majority of companies have them so employees can work from home or while they're traveling. Well, thieves like to telecommute, too.

One of the more ingenious and remarkable Trojan Horse scams was pulled a few years ago by three men on Long Island. They set up several voyeuristic websites named beavisbutthead.com, sexygirls.com, and ladult.com that advertised free "adult" pictures. Internet users who happened upon the sites in their Web surfing were instructed to download a viewer program that would allow them to see the sexy pictures, and a lot of men did just that. What did they have to lose? The pictures were free, weren't they?

Unfortunately, however, the viewer that was to furnish the pornographic pictures turned out to be more than just a viewer. It also housed a Trojan Horse that commanded your computer to do a few other things. It shut down your volume control so you wouldn't hear anything coming out of your speakers. Then it hung up your modem line and dialed a phone number in Moldova, a tiny nation you probably rarely called that was one of the former Soviet republics. With the speakers shut off, you couldn't hear that scratchy telltale sound of a modem dialing a number. The call to Moldova was answered by a computer that reconnected you to the adult site and caused a photo of an unclothed girl to show up on your screen. While you were admiring her curves, you were paying big-time for a transatlantic call.

It got worse. There was only one photo, and it wasn't that great, so most people abandoned beavisbutthead pretty quickly. But leaving the site didn't disconnect the call to Moldova. Even when you signed off the Internet and went on to write some poetry in your word processing program, your modem was still talking to Moldova. The hijacking of your modem call didn't end until you shut off your computer, which could have been hours later. If you left it on all night, you were in for a really rude surprise. Some people found charges as high as three thousand dollars on their phone bill. In just six weeks, the scam attracted 800,000 phone minutes to Moldova. Never was the country so popular.

WHAT TO DO

There are plenty of tools designed to thwart Trojan Horses, but it's a constant battle against criminal ingenuity. Anti-Trojan Horse programs and anti-virus software are widely available, but they need to be updated regularly if they're going to succeed against the latest Trojan Horses and viruses. And you need to use some common sense. Don't download attachments from people you don't know, and don't download software off the Internet unless you're sure of the site that's offering it. If you download a program from a website you're unfamiliar with, that's about the same as ordering your prescription drugs from Nigeria. You need to know the source and content of every file you download. Even if the file says it comes from a friend, be doubly sure before you download an attachment.

THE HIDDEN AGENDA

Criminals think differently than most people. To avoid being scammed, you have to start thinking the way a criminal does. For instance, I visited a company while it was going through the frantic preparations for the

Y2K rollover, when everyone feared computers might misconstrue dates after January 1, 2000. Everywhere I looked, programmers were scooting around the premises, fixing computer code.

I asked the executives, "Who are you using to prepare your computers?"

"Oh, these guys from India," they said. "They're really sharp. And they're cheap."

"Really?" I'd said. "Did you check out their backgrounds? Did you have them bonded? How do you know you can trust them?"

They looked at me and their jaws dropped. They didn't know if they could trust them.

Their thinking was, these guys know computers and they're inexpensive, as were a lot of other off-shore firms from India, Russia, and Taiwan that were fixing Y2K problems.

But I was thinking, this is a golden opportunity for cyberthieves. When else have so many computers been opened up and touched by strange hands, with the blessings of their owners? I knew that any dishonest programmer could easily implant a so-called "back door" or "trap door," a hidden entryway for him to get into the system whenever he wanted and steal data or funds. I have no doubt that many trap doors were part of the Y2K packages that companies got such a great deal on. Whenever you allow programmers to work on your computer system, for whatever reason, look into their background so you know who they are. A bank doesn't allow just anyone to fix the locks to their vault. The same thinking should apply to your computer.

GOING, GOING, GONE

The number one source of crime on the Internet is online auctions, in large part because so many people use them and they're such perfect settings for deceit. The FBI gets hundreds of complaints a week about them. There are stories of fraudulent paintings and "rare" Barbie dolls that are not so rare, of nonexistent kidneys sold for transplants. There are auction sites that sell suspect dinosaur fossils and pieces of meteorites. Sometimes the con artists use established auction sites to run their cons.

Often, though, they set up their own auction sites and advertise expensive items like Cartier watches and personal computers that a lot of consumers would be interested in. They ask victims to send money for the goods and then deliver nothing, or a counterfeit version of what they wanted. And it may be months before consumers realize what they got was counterfeit. Once enough money comes in, the sites vanish.

One of the most common auction scams is when a con artist maintains he bought a nonrefundable but transferable airplane ticket. Unfortunately, something came up and he no longer can use it. It's always for a popular destination and a time of year when plenty of people would be interested. He's willing to sacrifice it at a loss; he just doesn't want to have to eat the entire amount. The winner gets rewarded with a counterfeit ticket or nothing at all. Frequent flier mileage also turns up a lot on auction sites. The con artist claims his miles are good for a ticket anywhere in the world. The bidder sends the money and gets a letter saying, "Unfortunately, I just learned that I can't transfer the miles. Don't worry, I'll send you a refund." People have been waiting years for their refunds.

Every Christmas sees a predictable surge in auction fraud. There's always a hot toy that every child must have, but there's insufficient supply. So, con artists advertise on auction sites that they've got the toy. The Sony Playstation2 was the toy of Christmas 2000. Many people ordered them from phony auction sites and got nothing but an encounter with fraud. The address for the business that operated one site offering Playstations was a derelict house in Canada. The toll-free number consumers were invited to call was in California. The fax number to which they were told to send copies of their credit calls to speed their order was in the state of Washington. The money the company collected was wired to a bank in Florida. Does that sound like any business you want to deal with?

If you're going to buy merchandise from online auctions, and many people swear by them, research the seller carefully. Look for the person on other websites. Some auctions allow members to furnish feedback on their experiences with different sellers. Even the feedback option is susceptible to fraud, however, as unsavory sellers will post glowing reports on themselves. Some auction sites like eBay provide limited insurance.

Probably the best type of auction to get involved in is one that offers an escrow service, where you pay a small fee and the money is held until your goods have been received.

THE MYTH OF SECURITY

Just about any type of scam gets a boost from the Internet, but the web has really opened up a new world of opportunity for credit card thieves. As I so rudely found out, whenever you use your card to buy something online, you're putting your account at risk. Crooks just love to log on to steal your card number.

One of their primary hacking tactics is "sniffing." When you type something on the Internet, it doesn't go straight to the website you're visiting. Rather, the data gets divided up into what are known as packets. These packets get routed from computer to computer, until they all co-alesce at the intended web destination. Criminals will plant "sniffers" on website computers, most commonly those hosting shopping sites, and the sniffers intercept the packets, copy down the information, and then allow the packets to proceed to the website. Packets destined for shopping sites naturally contain loads of credit card numbers, and they're the sweetest smell of all.

This data then gets relayed to the computer of the criminals, where they sort it out and use it for ill-gotten gains. The whole process is essentially the Internet version of wiretapping.

But the chief way credit cards are stolen with computers is by breaking into the storage computers of sizable e-commerce companies and copying the extensive inventory of credit card numbers housed in their data bases. In late 1999, in the weeks leading up to Christmas, a rather brazen intruder helped himself to an early present when he broke into the computers of CD Universe, an online music store, and swiped more than three hundred thousand customer credit card numbers on file. Identifying himself as Maxim—he told the reporters he communicated with that he was sixteen and from Russia—he e-mailed CD Universe and demanded one hundred thousand dollars. If the website didn't pay, he threatened to divulge the card numbers on the Internet. If he was paid, he said he would fix CD Universe's security bugs, destroy the stolen card files, and forget about their store forever.

Well, CD Universe officials refused to respond to blackmail. On Christmas Day, Maxim made good on his threat. He set up a website that he called Maxus Credit Card Pipeline and began listing some of the stolen credit card numbers, adding new numbers on a daily basis. With a click of one's mouse, anyone who logged onto the site could pick up a credit card number, name, and address.

The website operated for two weeks before some security experts found out about it, and alerted the Internet system that was carrying the site without its knowledge. It promptly shut it down. By that point, however, a traffic counter suggested that a few thousand visitors had downloaded more than 25,000 credit card numbers. Maxim also claimed that he had used some of the cards himself to raise some money.

The e-mail trail on the hacker suggested that he was indeed somewhere in Eastern Europe, making it difficult for American law enforcement to touch him.

Not long ago, someone broke into Western Union's website and accessed 23,000 credit card numbers and expiration dates. Western Union had to call all 23,000 customers and tell them to cancel their credit cards. These were people who, a week before, had innocently transferred money through Western Union using their cards. You'd think a company the magnitude of Western Union would have a secure website, but it didn't.

An editor at MSNBC, hearing about hackers wreaking havoc day after day, said that if it's so easy to break into websites, why can't my reporters do it? So he told two of his reporters to go home and get online and see if they could download credit card names, numbers, and expiration dates. He assumed it would take a couple of days. They were back within a few hours with 2500 credit card accounts.

The problem is, too many e-commerce companies don't care if credit cards get stolen over their site, because it's generally the credit card companies' problem, and it costs staggering amounts to ensure security. If you're Bank of America or Citicorp, it's worthwhile to spend $50 million or $100 million to secure your site. But if you and I are selling outdoor lightbulbs or cheese, we're not going to spend $50 million. Where would we get it?

WHAT'S BEING DONE

The Internet is so widely considered to be lacking in security, that companies have been forced to conceive of new ways to pay online. Late in 2000, American Express announced what it called a "private payments" service for credit card charges on the Internet. In effect, it's a disposable credit card. We've got disposable cameras and disposable contact lenses, so why not a disposable credit card? The way it works is that a customer registers on American Express's website, entering a name, password, and account number. Then the customer gets a private payment number that can be used once and only once. When you make a purchase online, you use that number rather than your regular credit card. As soon as the transaction clears, the number is worthless to anyone who gets hold of it. So if you want to send some flowers to Mom, you punch in the number, you've got the flowers, and the credit card number is immediately void.

American Express also offers a Blue card. If you order one, the company supplies you with a Smart-Card reader that gets attached to your home computer. It works pretty much the same way that a card reader does at the gas station or department store. The card has to be swiped through the reader, which authenticates purchases only after the correct PIN number is typed in.

Visa has been testing an online verification system of its own. One version goes like this: when you make a purchase over the Internet at a retailer's website, a tiny window appears on the screen that asks for a password. When you type it in, that password is transmitted not to the store's site, but to the bank that issued the card. This makes it harder for someone who has a stolen card to use it, because without that password being verified by the bank, the transaction won't be processed.

In my view, these one-time use cards for Internet buying are a good thing. We need them, because there's no faith in the security of online transactions.

If you're going to give your credit card number over the Internet, at least make sure that the site uses S.S.L., or secure sockets layer, encryption technology. The way to tell is if the screen shows either a closed lock or an unbroken key icon. Another sign is if the merchant's web address shifts from "http" to "https" when it processes a transaction. This is far from a secure site, but it's better than a site that doesn't have encryption technology.

WHAT TO DO

Computer crime can be so much harder to track down than traditional criminal activity, and I find that you need to approach it differently. As soon as fraud is suspected, it's important to call in an expert before the evidence can be hidden. That means don't let anyone touch the computer system. What the security experts will do is undertake a forensic investigation of a computer, using a technique known as imaging, where experts take a copy of the contents so they can be studied without disturbing the original.

Sophisticated crackers know how to shred electronic files and create self-destructing e-mail, but forensic experts have their own ways of finding data, no matter how many times it's been deleted. There are file undeleting programs that often will catch rookie thieves, more elaborate tools like hex editors that enable you to view even deleted data, and magnetic sensors and electron microscopes that seize on the fact that every file deposits magnetic traces on the disk. Measuring changes in magnetic fields allows experts to reconstruct deleted files or overwritten areas.

Security experts also use things like a "honey pot" or "goat file," which is a collection of phony files meant to lure a hacker. If he bites and tries to steal them, the system is alerted so he can be traced.

As I've mentioned, things you yourself can do to prevent electronic theft include using encryption tools, firewalls, virus scanners, Trojan Horse cleaners, and intrusion detection programs. There are e-mail filters to block messages from known spammers. You can also subscribe to an e-mail filtering service that will scan e-mail for spam because they're endlessly tricky—sometimes their ruse is even an invitation: "If you don't want future mailings from us, reply to this address." You think they're being considerate. They're not. If they get a reply, the scammers know you're a live address and they'll sell it to endless other scam artists. But spammers keep creating new addresses, so it's a constant battle. And there are so-called Tiger Teams, computer experts, some of them reformed hackers, who come in and try to penetrate your system and then suggest ways to secure it. Just keep in mind that there is no such thing as an invincible system.

The FBI says if it had one tip to share to help catch cyberthieves, it would be to make certain your computer's internal clock is synchronized to national standards, because that helps agents trace a thief's steps.

Employees also need to do a better job of protecting their passwords into their systems. A common scam is for hackers to call employees, identify themselves as part of the company's technology staff, and say they're doing a routine check of passwords. Needless to say, if you receive one of these calls, always check with your company before divulging information. You need to choose a difficult password, a mix of letters and numbers, and you ought to change it every six months. Hackers have their own password-cracking software that tests words from lists of commonly used passwords—ordinary names, cartoon characters, rock bands. You wouldn't believe how many people, for simplicity's sake, use "password" as their password. Many others unimaginatively use their first name, or actually use none at all but have the "enter" key be their password.

Above all, consumers have to be smarter. When you go online, blind faith doesn't work. Know who you're dealing with. Don't be deceived by some highly-professional looking website. That doesn't mean it's legitimate. And no matter how you pay for something, you need to keep records of purchases, because they're your best defense against fraud.

It's obvious to me that electronic theft will only get worse, and cyberthieves will become even craftier at stealing and covering their tracks. There's a familiar saying in the computer underground: if you're a good hacker, everyone knows your name, but if you're a great hacker, no one knows who you are. A lot of criminals haven't even moved online yet, and you can bet they will. Electronic commerce is still growing at a dizzying pace. So as criminals see more opportunity, they'll be logging on looking for their cut.

9

[WHEN THE
LABEL LIES]

I t's hard to know what you're getting when you buy something today. And I mean anything. Just ask men in India. Indians, particularly those with money, have a fondness for buying foreign goods. They figure the quality far exceeds domestic brands. And so it's no surprise that there's been good business in brand-name, supposedly high-quality prophylactics "imported" from the United States and Singapore. Wealthier Indians don't mind paying the substantial premiums they command.

The trouble is, many of the condoms are actually imported from no farther away than Calcutta and Bombay. They carry foreign labels and colorful packaging, but they're decidedly inferior counterfeits, far worse than the cheapest Indian brands. Laboratory tests have concluded that 90 percent of them leak or are of such poor quality that they give dubious protection. Thousands of men have bought the fraudulent condoms, possibly bringing on unwanted pregnancies and exposing themselves to HIV.

But don't think that counterfeit birth control products are an entirely male issue. Fakery is not a sexist industry. In Brazil, counterfeit Microvlar, the country's most popular birth control pill, has been actively marketed by thieves. The well-disguised fakes, made out of flour rather than active ingredients, have resulted in a number of women becoming pregnant and/or developing unusual bleeding.

IS IT REAL OR IS IT . . . ?

When you buy something at the mall, the supermarket, or the corner deli today, you really don't know if you're getting what you paid for. Is it real or is it fake? Often the experts themselves don't know. Fake products are hitting store shelves by the bushel, tripling in magnitude in the last decade and costing American companies on the order of $350 billion a year. It's become a sweet business for scam artists. Dozens of counterfeit wholesalers are said to work in New York alone, with some of them making as much as $3 million a year.

Estimates are that at least 5 percent of all products are phony, and in some industries, the percentage runs much higher. Something like 22 percent of all apparel and footwear is estimated to be counterfeit. No brand has been spared: Lacoste, Armani, Calvin Klein, Tommy Hilfiger, Polo, Donna Karan, Nautica, and so on. Counterfeit leather products have long been popular with tourists, who load up on fake Louis Vuitton, Gucci, and Charles Jourdan bags and wallets. The better the brand awareness, the greater the likelihood of counterfeiting. We all love Swiss watches, and so it's no wonder that an estimated ten million counterfeit Swiss watches are sold each year. More than a quarter of the computer software being run on computers in the United States is said to be fraudulent, and in some countries, 90 percent of it is fake. I've heard that the counterfeit golf equipment business is larger than the real golf equipment business. Hours after the Taylor Made Golf Company introduced a new $300 driver at the Professional Golfers' Merchandise Show in Orlando not long ago, counterfeiters were selling their own fake replicas for half the price—at the same trade show.

Pretty much anything that sells gets counterfeited these days. Counterfeiters deal in mundane items like ball-point pens, correction fluid, socks, perfume, adhesive tape, stereo speakers, as well as more esoteric products like cargo hold covers for ships. I've even heard of counterfeit butterscotch candy.

The problem is not merely a cosmetic one, or one of phony denim that doesn't fit or wear quite as well as the genuine label. Pharmaceuticals consistently lead the list of counterfeited products, because while medicine is expensive to develop, it's relatively cheap to reproduce. There is also widespread counterfeiting of automotive and aircraft parts—there are actually decent odds that when you board any commercial plane it contains a few counterfeit parts. These can result in lethal consequences. It's one thing to be stuck with counterfeit shampoo, deodorant, or talcum powder. It's quite another to be ingesting fake prescription drugs: fake anti-malarial tablets, fake decongestants, fake aspirin. It's one thing to be fooled into buying fake athletic socks. It's quite another to have counterfeit brake pads installed in your new car.

There's a lot of shoddy counterfeiting of products, and simple side-by-side comparisons generally will separate the genuine from the fraudulent. But, as with other areas of fraud, counterfeiting has improved enormously. Again, technology has been a tremendous boon to the scofflaw. With the work of the best counterfeiters, not only are the products perfect replicas, but so are the labels and the packaging. Even people who work in the industry can't tell that they're fakes.

A few years ago, Alfred Dunhill, the British luxury goods and tobacco company, was experiencing highly sophisticated counterfeiting of its purses and billfolds. A seizure of the products took place in Oregon, and a chain of counterfeiters was brought to trial. Naturally, the prosecution needed to demonstrate in court that the seized goods were in fact fake, or else there was no case. But the goods were so precisely counterfeited that prosecutors had to trot out an entire team of experts to testify. The fakes, which were being made in Asia, were so good that it took forensic analysis to identify them. Despite this, the result was a hung jury. The jury may have been sending any number of messages, including that it was utterly confused, but I suspect that one of them was that they weren't entirely convinced that the counterfeits were truly counterfeits.

These days, the counterfeiter often uses the same machinery that the genuine manufacturers do, as well as the same packaging. Unilever came across a group of thieves in Chicago who were counterfeiting brands of their liquid detergent. They were ordering bottles from the same place Unilever got them in Canada. Then they filled them with cheaper soap and sold them to bodegas. Counterfeiting liquid detergent hardly seems worth the effort, but they were doing it with gusto.

Allied Domecq, a big wine and spirits distributor, found that a large proportion of its Fundador Brandy sold in the Philippines was counterfeit. It had been going on for so long, in fact, that local residents had come to believe there was a Philippine version of the product. The counterfeit bottles were perfect imitations, and in fact, were often empty Fundador bottles that were refilled. The only way you could tell the difference was when you tasted the brandy. There were actually different levels of the counterfeit brandy, some better tasting than others. Counterfeiters pretty much put anything in the bottle, as long as it had the same color and general flavor of brandy, but a few were more artful. But none of it truly tasted like brandy, since the thieves used sugar cane and flavors like rum.

Determined to put a stop to the counterfeiting, Allied Domecq changed the look of its bottles. It designed a new, hard-to-counterfeit label and it added a plastic cap and a guala, which is a plastic ball inside the neck that prevents the bottle from being refilled. The counterfeiting declined significantly.

IT'S NOT JUST FAKE FUR

To a large extent, counterfeiting is ruled by organized crime syndicates. Like other forms of fraud, it is growing so rapidly because penalties are inadequate and rarely enforced. There are extremely high profits and low risk, a combination that will always attract criminals. A number of years ago, the former head of the Born to Kill gang in New York said he made $13 million a year selling counterfeit Rolex and Cartier watches. Think about it. Low-grade quartz watches were shipped in from Hong Kong that cost $3.00. Fake trade names and logos were slapped on for an additional 50 cents. Then the watches were sold on the street for thirty dollars.

Dunhill pens sell for one hundred twenty dollars or so. Counterfeiters sell them for half that. And they look great, pretty much indistinguishable from the real thing. How do they do it? Well, they're selling you virtually the real thing. Counterfeiters go to the same factory in Korea that makes the plastic barrel for Dunhill and buy the same barrel. Then the crooks go to the company that makes the cap for Dunhill and buy that. Well, then isn't it the same pen? Just about. Dunhill's clip that allows you to attach the pen to your pocket is 18-karat gold. The counterfeit pen has a gold-plated clip. And since the counterfeiters don't have anything like the overhead and marketing budget that Dunhill has, they can settle for much less markup.

With organized crime involved, there's enough money available that counterfeiters establish factories that rival those of legitimate manufacturers. I heard about a counterfeit coffee facility in Dagestan, a Russian republic, that can churn out 1.2 million units of coffee a month. An Asian facility making counterfeit athletic shoes is said to employ more than a thousand workers.

Counterfeiting often plays a significant role in money laundering, because laundering always works best when there's a product involved. Authorities believe that the reason inexpensive items like correction fluid and trash bags are counterfeited is to wash money from other criminal activities like weapons smuggling and loan-sharking. Police using trained drug dogs have found heroin stuffed inside counterfeit Chanel and Louis Vuitton handbags. Criminals were doubling up, importing counterfeit products and drugs all at once. You have to realize, crime syndicates are business operations, and their executives sit around and make strategic decisions just like executives in Fortune 500 companies. One day, at the weekly marketing meeting, some guy probably spoke up and said, "Look, we're bringing in these counterfeit purses and we're bringing in drugs, why not combine the two? It'll be more cost-effective." The idea probably got him employee of the month.

The money is so good in counterfeit products, that terrorists are believed to often fund their activities by trafficking in fake goods. Terrorists in Northern Ireland are thought to have supported their violence by selling counterfeit veterinary products, perfume, video games, and computer software. The FBI believes the bombing of the

World Trade Center was financed by the sale of counterfeit T-shirts and sportswear.

"MADE IN CHINA" MORE THAN YOU KNOW

Counterfeiters live all over, but a great deal of the merchandise originates in places like China, Korea, and Vietnam. China may well be the leading supplier of counterfeit products to the world, and just about anything the Chinese consumer buys is quite likely not real. You go to the store in China and there's fake Skippy peanut butter, fake Gillette razor blades, fake Knorr chicken soup, fake Hellmann's mayonnaise, fake Kellogg's Corn Flakes, fake Lux soap, fake Rejoice shampoo, fake Huggies diapers, fake fertilizer, fake liquor, fake motor oil, fake chewing gum, fake cell phone batteries, even fake toilet paper. The goods are probably rung up on a counterfeit cash register and packed in counterfeit grocery bags.

Procter & Gamble began selling its products in China in 1991, and that same year counterfeits were already on shelves. The soap company says counterfeiters make fraudulent copies of their shampoo bottles and fill them up with the cheapest blend of raw ingredients. Then they'll top off the product with a touch of the real shampoo to make it look and smell authentic. Each year, the problem worsens.

Royal Philips Electronics has said 40 percent of counterfeit Philips light bulbs in the Philippines come from China. Volkswagen said two-thirds of the car parts sold in China under its brand name are fakes. Hitachi has the same problem with counterfeit electronic products. The Chinese press wrote up some thieves who put together an entire car from used and counterfeit parts that they tried to sell as a new Audi.

China has begun cracking down on the problem, under pressure from foreign companies. But some pretty major cultural shifts have to take place. Local governments have been famous for protecting factories churning out counterfeit goods. Philips said that the prime counterfeiter in Zhangzhou in the Fujian province was even given an "outstanding youth" award by the local government.

All these cheap Asian fakes serve as fodder for all types of little scams. You know when you take transatlantic flights and the airline crews come around with little trolleys of duty-free items you can buy? Some dishonest crew members on British Airways figured out a way to augment their income. They bought counterfeit products like Raymond Weil watches, Chanel perfume, and Gucci sunglasses while on layovers in Hong Kong and Singapore. Then they substituted the fakes for the genuine products on the trolleys they wheeled around, and passengers unwittingly bought them. The crew members then sold the legitimate goods back in England to stores or on the black market. They would take watches to jewelers and tell them they had gotten them as unwanted gifts, and the jewelers would gladly buy them.

A big part of the problem is that most consumers don't care if something is fake, as long as it looks like the real thing and it costs less. And it's not just penny-pinchers who buy phony Gucci and Fendi bags. One counterfeiter said he had a steady client who was a neurosurgeon's wife. Some rich people, he said, buy fake handbags and luggage from him for trips, so they don't have to worry if they get stolen in hotels. Then they had the real thing for dinner parties and local use. The business has become very open. Counterfeit items are easily obtained on the streets of all large American cities. In Italy, they're sold by street peddlers known as *"Vu cumpra,"* which means "wanna buy." They even take out ads in the local papers. In Sweden, there was a mail order catalogue that sold all manner of counterfeit merchandise. It was called, "Fake."

SALTING TALES

In few areas of fraud have technological advances been more welcome than among counterfeiters. "Cyberfakes" is the name that the garment industry has given to computer-generated logos and designs. The counterfeiter scans a real logo into his computer. Then he transfers it to a computerized embroidery machine. Using the image as a master, it recreates the design on just about any garment he chooses. Counterfeiters can buy an embroidery machine small enough to fit inside a suitcase for just three thousand dollars. Label-making machinery can be acquired in the same way, but it is much more expensive. More commonly, counterfeiters will farm out the work of counterfeit labels to factories in developing countries.

As U.S. Customs has gotten sharper at detecting illegal apparel imports, counterfeiters have introduced new tricks. They import what they call "blanks," perfectly legal unlabeled apparel. The clothes will then be taken to factories, usually around New York or Los Angeles, and low-wage laborers will attach the counterfeit brand-name labels and logos to them.

Another nettlesome issue is what are known as "overmakes," "back-door," or "cabbage." A factory making legitimate clothing for a brand will deliberately make extra garments and then sell these "overmakes" to criminals.

A related concern is diversion and the gray market. For instance, products merchandised in the United States are also sold in Africa, but at a lower price to meet the local market. So, a legitimate company will ship goods to a wholesaler in Africa, who will divert them to someone in Milwaukee, where he can get a bigger return, because while there might be a 40 percent discount off the list price in Africa, there's only a 15 percent discount in the United States. This is often a fraud against the sales contract, but it's difficult to enforce because it's so hard to trace where shipments wind up. In the 1990s, for instance, Unilever sent a lot of soaps, shampoos, salves, and creams to Russia. Most of it ended up back in Brooklyn.

Like many other companies, Unilever has attacked the diversion problem by conducting a little contest. It's called "Lucky Bonus." When it sends out a pallet of goods, it will tuck three $25 coupons inside. When the pallet is unloaded and the product removed to put on store shelves, the handlers will find the coupons. The instructions tell them that if they fill them out with their name and address and return them to Unilever, they'll get a check for $25. The key is having that name and address. That tells Unilever whether the pallet got to its intended destination. The concept is known as "salting," and was developed by American Cyanamid for its Old Spice cologne, which was being diverted. It's neither a high-cost solution nor a high-tech solution, but it works.

BUYER BEWARE

I do occasional work for Microsoft, which, given its dominant market presence, has been a principal target of counterfeiters for years. It's gotten so bad that Microsoft can barely get a new piece of software out before counterfeit versions make their own debut. In some instances, counterfeit versions of Microsoft products have beaten the real thing to market. You can go to various Internet auction sites and bid on fraudulent Microsoft programs that sell for a fraction of their retail price.

In early 2000, a guy was busted in the state of Washington, Microsoft's home state, for making counterfeit Microsoft products, including Office 97, Office 2000 Professional, and Office 2000 Premium. He was turning out tens of thousands of copies in his apartment. When they raided it, the FBI found several computers, a sixteen-tray replicator, a color copier, a shrink-wrapping machine, and packaging materials.

A few years ago, an Asian ring was busted in South El Monte, California. The ring had two locations, one to manufacture fake Microsoft CD ROMs and disks, and another to make counterfeit manuals, certificates of authenticity, boxes, and even contest entry forms for free trips. Nothing was omitted. The products seized were estimated to have a market value of more than $10 million.

In Digital Park, a high-tech business center just outside Cambridge, England, a young Texan opened a company several years ago called PolyMould that made counterfeit versions of the most popular software products, including Microsoft Office and Windows NT. Down the road from the facility was one of Microsoft's own research and development centers.

An Asian gang took a different approach to scamming Microsoft. They established a fake school they called West Hill College. Then they ordered software from Microsoft at the education discount of one-third the retail price. They repackaged the CDs in counterfeit boxes, and sold them at full price through a phony computer wholesaler they created.

Microsoft puts a ton of security features in their products, everything from edge-to-edge holographic images to watermarked security paper with an embedded thread and a heat-sensitive strip that reveals "Genuine" when rubbed for a few seconds, but they face an ongoing struggle. I've worked on the Microsoft warranty that's contained in all of the company's software. It has to be changed every couple of years because it keeps getting counterfeited. For instance, within days of the Windows 98 OEM security manual cover being introduced, a counterfeit product was already identified and confiscated in several cities. The knock-offs imitated both the manual cover and the security devices.

The problem is that software counterfeiting keeps getting easier. CD recordable drives that allow anyone to make copies of software cost a few hundred dollars. With desktop publishing programs and document scanners, it's simple to duplicate manuals and warranties. But even though counterfeit software closely resembles the real thing, it doesn't always work as well. Often, counterfeiters sell untested software. It may have been copied hundreds or thousands of times from a real version and is defective. The result can be viruses that corrupt your hard drive or cause system failure.

KA-CHING!

I've always figured that security at casinos is as tight as it gets, and there was no reasonable hope of replicating the chips and tokens in casinos. That was before I spoke to a guy from Rhode Island, who had recently been released from prison for perpetuating a massive slot machine token fraud. He had scammed virtually every major casino in the country with counterfeit five-dollar to hundred-dollar slot machine tokens.

Originally, the man had been a tool and die maker who made custom jewelry for dealers, but he got tired of the business and retired at an early age. He had been a real workaholic, and had too much time on his hands. He broke up with his fiancée. He was at loose ends. The Foxwoods Resort Casino in Connecticut had recently opened, and a friend dragged him there to cheer him up. He wasn't really into gambling, but he was mesmerized by the hundred-dollar slot machine token. He admired the intricate detail of it. It reminded him of a piece of jewelry that he might manufacture. That set wheels turning in his head, and he found himself drawn to the challenge of making a counterfeit token.

He found out it was no simple project. Slot machines are equipped with sophisticated electronic coin comparators. These measure everything about any coin that gets deposited, to make sure it's a legitimate token. The comparators confirm the outside and inside diameter of the coin, the center of the coin, the magnetic image the coin throws, the number of serrations on the outside of the coin, the weight, and so on. A coin has something known as a "closed collar," the raised outside border of the coin. For a counterfeit coin to pass muster, it has to have a closed collar that is just the right height. Hence, a counterfeit coin has to be exact. There are a lot of difficult-to-duplicate features.

So this guy got to work, acquiring equipment, and then modifying it for his precise needs. He made coins, tested them at Foxwoods, found they wouldn't work, made changes, tested the new coins, and on and on. It took him more than a year before he had a counterfeit token that beat the machine. At that point, he became addicted. He made tens of thousands of tokens. To keep from arousing suspicion, he began playing at casinos in Atlantic City and Las Vegas. Different casinos had different tokens, and he had to replicate theirs. But he had become an expert. When he was caught at Caesar's in Atlantic City in late 1996, he had 750 pounds of coins in the trunk of his car, one of the biggest cases on record of gambling token counterfeiting.

To prevent further counterfeiting, token manufacturers have been offering security alloys, which are metals with very limited availability and unique properties. The latest protection is a code engraved in the token. Slot machines are programmed to read the code, and if it's not there, the token is rejected.

STICKER SHOCK

Underwriters Labs (UL) has faced one of the more unusual counterfeiting problems. UL, a non-profit organization founded in 1894, doesn't make any products, a fact which by itself, one would think, would make the company impervious to counterfeiting. What it does do is test and certify the safety of more than 14 billion electrical products a year, things like power supply cords, ceiling fans, night lights, transformers, switches, and surge suppressers. Its testing engineers simulate power surges. They bend wire to see if it breaks. They dunk products in water. If something survives a UL testing, it's good. Once a product has been certified by the organization, it is allowed to display the UL provided tag. It's often referred to as the "American Mark of Safety."

Starting in the early 1990s, UL became aware of untested products bearing counterfeit UL tags that were coming into the United States, primarily from China. It first learned of the counterfeiting when it caught phony seals of approval on Christmas lights. Then they began showing up on other electrical goods. The products were not only inferior, but also dangerous. There were lights, fans, electric surge protectors, and other products that were improperly grounded or wired with incorrect polarity. There were dummy surge protectors that would overload if you turned on a computer, printer, and TV simultaneously. Plugs were so inferior that chunks of them would fall off when you pulled them out of a socket. Extension cords were liable to give a user a shock. Fans were at risk of catching fire. In one tragic case, a young girl was electrocuted by sucking on an incorrectly wired and falsely labeled Christmas candle.

Disturbed by the implications of this counterfeiting, UL in 1994 began using silver, tamper-evident holographic labels for all of its certified Christmas products, and has since required them on an array of electrical products coming out of China. In addition, it's trained U.S. Customs inspectors to identify counterfeit labels and has put retailers on alert as well. One of the problems for U.S. Customs officials is that there is no legal requirement for electrical equipment to carry the UL labels, though if they do have the labels, it's a crime for them to be counterfeit. The new label has been doing a good job in controlling the threat, though it hasn't stopped altogether.

A DIFFERENT KIND OF DRUG PROBLEM

Remember that classic film *The Third Man* based on the haunting Graham Greene thriller? The movie is set in post-World War II Vienna, where Holly Martins, an American, goes in search of his old college buddy, Harry Lime. He discovers that Lime is dead, and hears disturbing stories of how he made a fortune trafficking in fraudulent drugs. One of his schemes was selling counterfeit penicillin. Martins has a hard time accepting some of the bad things he hears about him, until he visits a hospital and sees all the children whose health has been threatened by injections of Lime's penicillin.

That's fiction, but there's plenty of fact in it. It takes at least a decade and upward of $150 to $200 million to bring a new pharmaceutical to market. Counterfeiters, with the assistance of a chemist, can copy it in a matter of days, using equipment that costs a few thousand dollars. But they don't trouble themselves worrying too much about the safety of their product. Counterfeits that hurt and kill are the dark side of fraud, and it's the part that really disturbs me. Counterfeit drugs are a threat to public health. They're very difficult to detect and control, and they've led to illnesses and death. In 1997, the World Health Organization estimated that more than five hundred people had died from fake medicines.

In the United States, dozens of deaths and hundreds of adverse reactions have been connected to a counterfeit intravenous antibiotic from China that is used to treat serious blood infections. There were 3,000 deaths in Nigeria in 1995 attributed to fake meningitis vaccines. Counterfeit antibiotics made from talcum powder and counterfeit eye drops made from contaminated water were discovered in Africa. Brazil has suffered deaths from bogus antibiotics and cancer treatments. In southern Vietnam, police raided a gang and found a thousand fake Viagra tablets.

Some counterfeiters ply their trade without even making a product. Criminals regularly go to wholesalers and buy expired aspirin and other ordinary over-the-counter medications that were going to be junked. They pay twenty cents on the bottle, and the wholesalers are happy to get it. The criminals then change the dates on the boxes and resell them to drugstores.

Crooks root through Dumpsters outside of hospitals and look for syringe bottles that have been discarded in hazardous materials bags. The thieves take them, refill them with sugar water, and sell them as medicine. The only way to tell is to turn the bottle over and look for two pinholes. A fraudulent one has to have a second pinhole in it made by the criminal when he inserted a needle to refill it.

DIFFICULT TO DIGEST

It's not just drugs that can cause harm. So can foods and food supplements, drinks, vitamins, literally anything that you digest. A number of individuals were caught in 1999 for selling expired baby formula and nutritional products for invalids. They had obtained them under the false pretense that the products would be used for animal food. In 1995, two

California men intended to distribute a half million cans of counterfeit Similac baby formula. Fortunately, the illegal operation was busted before most of the products were distributed, and there were only a few reports of illnesses. But there have been other instances where counterfeit formula has caused rashes and seizures. In Mexico, fake Tequila and other alcoholic beverages have caused illness and some deaths. "Collectors" pay for empty bottles outside stadiums, and then refill them with other liquids and pass them off as the real thing.

Anything you apply to your skin, if it's counterfeit, puts you at risk. A phony version of a popular shampoo was found to contain bacteria that could cause infections. Another counterfeit brand has led to hair loss. Counterfeit cosmetics have been found to contain residue of industrial solvents and carcinogens. When you use them, you can suffer severe allergic reactions.

Counterfeit pesticides and fertilizers have decimated crops in developing countries, contributing to famine and death. A counterfeit chemical fungicide containing chalk was said to have been responsible for destroying two-thirds of the coffee crop in Kenya and Zaire. In Kenya, criminals were caught with counterfeit "Super Doom" insecticide. They diluted the weed product with kerosene and other ingredients and resold it, considerably diminishing its effectiveness.

NUTS AND BOLTS—AND EVERYTHING IN BETWEEN

Counterfeiters are without scruples. They'll put anyone at risk for profit (law enforcement agents once came across a shipment of counterfeit Cabbage Patch dolls that had been doused with kerosene to keep rats away while they were transported from overseas). Industrial valves have a long life cycle and are easy to recondition, and so they've been targets of counterfeiters for years. The FDA recalled $7 million of intra-aortic pumps used during open-heart surgery, after it discovered malfunctioning counterfeit parts in the devices. Sometimes, genuine used valves are improperly reconditioned so they can be resold as new. In one case, graphite seals that made the valves fire-safe were removed and not replaced.

Counterfeit nuts and bolts caused parts of a building to collapse during an earthquake. In the early 1980s, a contractor building a Saturn plant in Tennessee died because a counterfeit bolt snapped. It looked like the real thing but was made of cheap metal, not the specified high-quality carbon steel. In 1992, a fire erupted on a Navy destroyer, killing two sailors, after a counterfeit bolt connecting a steam line broke in the ship's engine room. One of the problems with small parts is that to determine if a bolt is inferior, you need to subject it to metallurgical tests, and analyzing a simple 40-cent bolt can cost two hundred dollars.

Every type of car and machine part is counterfeited—brakes, horns, oil filters, radiators, suspensions. Counterfeit brakes were found in Nigeria that were made from compressed grass that burst into flames when they were tested. In 1991, a woman and her child were killed in an auto accident in the United States that was precipitated by a counterfeit brake pad. The pad was made out of wood chips. The U.S. Department of Commerce estimates that 210,000 American workers could be added to the work rolls if the parts were made legally.

THE FRIGHTENING SKIES

Equally frightening is the number of counterfeit parts flooding the airline industry, a full 75 percent of which are used in critical applications. According to the Federal Aviation Authority (FAA), between 1973 and 1993 bogus parts played a role in at least 166 U.S.-based aircraft accidents or less serious incidents. The worst accident of all occurred in September 1989. The tail section of a turboprop plane tore loose, causing the plane to crash into the North Sea. All fifty-five people on board were killed. The cause was eventually traced to counterfeit bolts in the tail. It was never determined where they came from, because the repair station that installed them didn't have a parts and supplier registration system.

In 1990, Bruce Rice, the president of Rice Aircraft, a Long Island airplane parts distributor, was jailed for four years for stripping and replacing used parts and falsifying documents to suggest that they were new.

Between 1977 and 1988, Rice sold counterfeit rivets and fasteners to Grumman, Air France, the Israeli Government, United Airlines, and American Airlines, among others, posing a serious safety threat to thousands of aircraft. Fortunately, no accidents were known to have resulted from the phony parts.

A few years ago, a company in Southern California was caught selling counterfeit parts to McDonnell Douglas. They were small devices that keep an airplane's landing gear from shaking, and were used on Douglas's DC-9 commercial airplanes. In 1995, in a separate incident, six hundred light planes were grounded after a supply of parts for Textron's Lycoming engines were discovered to be fake.

But there have been crashes involving Bell Helicopters in which the only thing truly Bell about the craft was the nameplate. The rest of it was rebuilt with scrap or counterfeit parts. In 1987, a traffic reporter riding in a helicopter was killed when the helicopter crashed while he was broadcasting live. It was determined that the accident was caused by a clutch made of counterfeit parts.

Who's to blame? A lot of people. And it's not enough just to make sure there's good paperwork on a part. Forgers can forge the paperwork. One of the best safeguards is to know your supplier.

A few years ago, undercover Congressional investigators paid a visit to a Miami scrap yard. They came across some jet engine blades marked with a red tag saying they were "unserviceable." But when the dealer saw they were interested in the blades, he removed the tag. He told them: "I know some of you boys rework these things, but that's not my concern." The blades sell for around $1,500 new. The investigators bought them for $1.30.

WHAT'S BEING DONE

Because of the sophistication and growth of counterfeit products, far more attention is being paid to preventing them, but a lot more needs to be done. Packaging is an essential ingredient in deterring counterfeiters, particularly in the pharmaceutical industry, where bottles are reused by counterfeiters. I do a fair amount of work with drug companies, and I find that the best security is to combine overt with covert security features, features you can see with features you can't see.

The most common overt technique is the tamper seals common on over-the-counter medications. These days, that technology is being combined more and more with holograms. They're a very strong tool, and are widely used on closure seals and hang tags. They're even increasingly put on packaging to make a product more visibly vibrant. If you go to the toothpaste aisle at the supermarket, you'll notice that all the premium toothpastes have holographic packaging.

I like holograms, but the problem is that they're normally not registered. Anyone can go to a company in Taiwan and get a hologram duplicated. Often, they're silver foil with white screen printing on them. Counterfeit holograms are easy to slip through Customs. You can stuff enough fake holograms in a matchbox to put on ten thousand dollars or twenty thousand dollars worth of counterfeit packages.

So a hologram is fine if it's in conjunction with another feature that you can't see. For instance, you could use a hologram combined with a covert feature like machine-readable information encrypted on the hologram. Other covert features include putting a fluorescent dot on the label of the packaging that's invisible to the naked eye and which can't be removed even by washing—you use a reader light to pick it up. There are also special coatings like microthin metals that change when slit or punctured. There is reactive invisible ink or visible coloring-changing inks. There are reactive threads that are woven into fabrics and emit a fluorescent color when put under a hand-held ultraviolet reader. There are scratch and view labels that reveal the words "original." And there is chemical tagging, for fuels, drugs, and pesticides. There's even a "biocode technology" where marker chemicals can be added to capsules of drugs that can then be authenticated with test strips.

Another new technique is DNA (deoxyribonucleic acid) marking. Joe Barbera, the creator of "The Flintstones," and "The Jetsons," used to employ a DNA pen with ink that contained fragments of his own genetic code to authenticate his drawings. And now a company called DNA Technologies has come up with a means of mass-marking items with an ink containing DNA. The company marked millions of items of official merchandise at the Sydney Olympics, using an ink that contained DNA strands from an Australian athlete and a chemical that can be identified with an optical scanner. The company gets the DNA either from a blood sample or a swab of the mouth, and then makes copies of it that it mixes into the ink. The ink was put right on the souvenirs or on a tag attached to them. Among other things, DNA Technologies put a DNA tag on Mark McGuire's seventieth homerun ball.

Holograms can be copied, but DNA is pretty much counterfeit-proof. The company estimates that there's about one chance in a trillion that a counterfeiter could duplicate the DNA sample. Those aren't the kind of odds that any sane criminal would take.

One shortcoming is there's no hand-held device that can test for the DNA. Vendors can scan a shirt and pick up the chemical in the ink, but not the DNA. If something seems fishy, the product has to be sent to the company for further testing.

EVERYONE HAS TO GET INVOLVED

Fighting counterfeit goods is going to take a lot more dedication, and I don't mean simply on the part of manufacturers. Stores have to do a better job of training their employees to discriminate the real from the fake. Packaging with blurry lettering or misspellings—"certifidate" instead of "certificate" of authenticity—is a giveaway. Sometimes, counterfeiters will try to protect themselves by slightly altering a product name—for instance, "Yeal" locks that resemble and are packaged to look like "Yale" locks.

If the problem is ever going to be contained, the general public has to start to care. You can't perpetuate a scam unless there's an honest person willing to go along. Years ago, I was visiting New York with my family. My boys were young then. We had eaten lunch at Wolf's Delicatessen, and while I was paying the check, my kids asked if they could wait outside. I said, fine, as long as they were close enough so I could see them through the windows. Almost immediately, some guy came up to them with a satchel. He swung it open and it was filled with watches. By the time I hurried out to them, they were already picking out famous designer watches at ludicrously low prices. I shooed the guy away, and I had to explain to my kids that the watches were counterfeit and the guy was a crook.

Adults know better, and ought to behave better. Do you really want to keep buying those fakes on the street corner and putting money in the pockets of criminals, or do you want to support legitimate business?

10

[EMPTY **PROMISES**]

niprime Capital Acceptance was a small automobile dealer based in Las Vegas. Its shares were publicly traded, but it hadn't made much earth-shattering news in awhile, and its stock price reflected that. You could buy a share for less than a buck, and normal volume was a meager 20,000 shares a day. Then one day in the summer of 1999, it made a stunning announcement for any company, but particularly for a car dealer: it had come up with a cure for AIDS.

Not surprisingly, the news was the talk of Internet stock chat rooms. There was, of course, patter about the considerable medical and humanistic ramifications of this development, but the chat room talk was more focused on monetary impact. One message called Uniprime "the greatest stock ever." Another spoke of it as "a once in a lifetime opportunity!!!" and was like "buying Microsoft now at a nickel."

The day of the announcement, Uniprime's stock rocketed from $1.75 to $5.00, and 5 million shares changed hands. Just like that, the company had a market value of $100 million. One bulletin board message said:

"Hallah! Hallah! Hallah! Shout it from the rooftops of the banks." Thousands of messages were posted about the stock.

The AIDS cure was reported as the work of a new Uniprime subsidiary, New Technologies and Concepts, which was headed by a man named Alfred Flores, who described himself as a doctor. According to the news the company put out, New Technologies had developed an intravenous treatment called Plasma Plus that Flores had been testing for fifteen years at General Hospital in Madrid. It said the treatment reversed infections from HIV in five patients treated at the hospital.

It seemed too amazing to be true—and it was. The Securities and Exchange Commission (SEC) determined there was no cure for AIDS. It said Alfred Flores was a con man. In fact, during much of the time he was supposedly testing the AIDS treatment, he was in a Colorado prison serving time for a conviction for conspiracy to commit murder. But he had been in the vicinity of the medical profession. He had apparently spent some time as a janitor in a nursing home.

Alfred Flores was arrested and trading in Uniprime stock was halted. When trading resumed, the stock settled down at a quarter a share. Investors who bought in the heat of the frenzy collectively lost millions of dollars.

Unfortunately, securities and investment opportunities are a particularly ripe focus for crooks, because there have been so many real rags-to-riches tales brought about by the stock market. And, as we've seen again and again, there's a slender line between what's real and what isn't. A band of criminals posted an actual SEC warning about online scams on a website of theirs that was itself promoting an online securities scam.

The money funneled into investment scams is breathtaking, even to me. One well-executed scheme can attract $100 million in ill-gotten gains. And if you're one of the hapless victims, the chances of getting your money back are abysmal, even if the swindler is caught. *USA Today* did an analysis of how well the SEC has performed in recovering illegal gains that convicted financial scam artists have been ordered to hand over. The newspaper found that between 1995 and 2000, the agency collected less than 17 percent. A decade earlier, the recovery rate was more like 50 percent. In a number of large cases, the SEC had recovered nothing.

PUMP AND DUMP

One easy way callous con artists make money in the market is with "pump and dump" cons. Popular as far back as the 1920s, they are now going stronger than ever. These days, stocks are hyped with fictitious positive news on Internet message boards and in chat rooms by scam artists posing as experts. But all they know is how to take your money. Then the scam artists dump their shares, sending the price down before investors can get out.

A man who worked for a company called PairGain Technologies set up a website to resemble the Bloomberg business news site that many investors turn to for the latest business and financial news. He then posted an article on the site saying that PairGain was about to be bought by an Israeli company. To create further buzz, he wrote messages on bulletin boards with links to the fake Bloomberg site. The day he concocted the fraudulent story, PairGain stock rose about 30 percent before the company put out a release disavowing the report.

In another case, several criminals bought a hundred and thirty thousand shares in NEI Webworld, a bankrupt company whose assets had been liquidated several months before. Then they posted fake e-mail messages on hundreds of Internet bulletin boards, suggesting that NEI Webworld was going to be acquired by a wireless telecommunications company. Before the postings, the stock was trading at between nine and thirteen cents a share. On the morning of the postings, the stock rocketed to $15 5/16, before plunging back to a quarter a share. The criminals realized a gain of $362,625.

A twenty-three-year-old California man sent out a fake news release to Internet Wire, a company that distributes business news releases, saying that the chief executive officer of Emulex Corporation had resigned. He hadn't, but within an hour of the release's posting, the stock of the communications equipment maker plunged from $113 to $45. The actual value of the company declined by a staggering $2.5 billion. The hoax was quickly revealed, and the stock recovered. But investors who sold during the selling spree lost more than $100 million. In this case, the scam artist had sold shares short, betting on their decrease in price, and thus profited from the sharp fall.

The explosion in online trading has allowed mere kids, between their math and social studies classes, to dabble in securities fraud. We saw that when a fifteen-year-old New Jersey boy was caught by securities regulators in 2000, after he racked up profits of hundreds of thousands of dollars in a pump and dump scheme. The kid, who became the envy of a lot of other teenagers for his prowess, bought shares of lightly traded companies and then promoted them with hundreds of messages on Internet bulletin boards. When they soared, he bailed out. He was the youngest stock swindler the government has ever come across, but I fear he won't be the last. When asked why he did it, he said, "Everybody does it."

Part of the problem is that greed obscures judgment. Even though it makes no sense to risk your savings on unknown people who call you up or post messages on online bulletin boards, otherwise intelligent people seem to do just that with outright fervor. Here's my favorite illustration of how ridiculous it can get. In 1994, the Motley Fool, a popular personal finance website, concocted a fictitious stock as an April Fool's joke. They mentioned a company, Zeigletics, in their newsletter, and said it developed technology that connected sewage disposal systems in Chad and traded on the Halifax Exchange. Almost at once, messages turned up on financial bulletin boards discussing the merits of the company, and people actually tried to buy shares in it.

CAPER CRUSADERS

It's astounding how far a con artist can take a securities scam. No matter how outlandish the pitch, there are investors who swallow it. Two New Jersey scam artists collected nearly $2 million by promising safe, high yields investing in wishing wells that solicited money for charity. In another case, a bunch of people saw no reason not to invest in an eel farm. If this seems far-fetched, it isn't. The animal kingdom is actually quite well represented in the scam world. There are schemes centered on snail ranches and ostrich stud farms. There was an ostrich farm in Australia where the ads claimed, "The birds just won't stop laying." A coconut production business in Costa Rica was promoted on a website. The promoter said he had agreements with A&P for coconut chips.

A popular fraud has to do with selling "U.S. Dollar Bonds." Scamsters who market them spin colorful tales of how they were issued in the 1930s and 1940s by the Central Intelligence Agency (CIA) to assist Chiang Kai-shek in fighting the communists. The way they tell it, the bonds were buried in caves by his generals and their descendants, and then lay there untouched until they were recently discovered; now you can buy them for just a fraction of their face value. The con artists print up official-looking Treasury bonds that they sell, and people do buy them, often clients in China, Taiwan, and Singapore.

No such Treasury securities were ever issued, and they don't even look like anything the Treasury ever issued, as they often list the Ministry of Finance of the United States and the Washington Bank of America as their place of origin. Neither ever existed. Confront the con artists with this information, and they'll say, "Well that's the CIA for you, you know how they are."

There are many instances of criminals essentially creating a shell company simply to attract investors. One of the most ambitious was the infamous ZZZZ Best carpet-cleaner caper. This was the one where a teenage swindler named Barry Minkow truly constructed a house of cards. In 1982, when he was sixteen and living in Reseda, California, he began a rug-cleaning business in the garage of his parents' house. He called it ZZZZ Best. Friends admired his drive and lofty aspirations. The business always seemed prosperous, although in fact it lost money. But Minkow had thievery in his blood, and he raised capital to fund the business in ways that most corporations rarely consider. He orchestrated burglaries to collect insurance money. He forged money orders from a local liquor store. When customers paid with credit cards, he would add fraudulent charges to the accounts.

Feeling the need for a bigger arena, he created a fake appraisal company that purportedly arranged restoration work for insurance companies. A bizarre friend of his became the company's head. The fake appraisal company created fictitious paperwork indicating that Minkow's company had received contracts from insurers to restore fire-damaged buildings. Minkow used this fictitious business, confirmed by the appraisal company, to persuade bankers and investors to give him money. Out of thin air, he concocted endless contracts from insurance companies to tackle office buildings that had been devastated by fire and water. He had an associate draw up forged documents representing the contracts, but there were no actual carpets to restore. Investors looking into the business would be referred to the fake appraisal company, which confirmed the deals. One time, when an auditor wanted to look at a restoration, the company hurriedly leased a building and dressed it up to look like a work site. It fooled the auditor.

In 1986, Minkow took his ruse of a carpet-cleaning company public, and the market capitalization swelled to more than $200 million. His young age captivated the press, and he gained wide publicity, which served to further stimulate investor interest. The fraud began to unravel when word got out about Minkow's credit card overcharges. Once investigators began probing the company, the end was near. In 1988, Minkow was convicted of fifty-seven counts of fraud and sentenced to twenty-five years in jail. Investors lost more than $100 million.

THE FORECAST? STORMY

Many of the most successful investment scams work their prey slowly, reeling them in like a trout. That's how the forecaster scam works. A man who identifies himself as a broker calls or writes you and, insisting no obligation on your part, offers you an investment tip. He tells you about a stock to watch that he thinks is going to do very well in the near term. "I don't want you to buy the stock, or even think of investing any money with me," he insists. "After all, you don't even know me. Just keep an eye on this stock and see how it does." Ostensibly, his point is to demonstrate his market savvy, and the sort of market intelligence he's privy to. His real point is to set a trap.

So, out of curiosity, you watch the stock and, sure enough, it goes up. A couple of weeks later, he contacts you again and offers a second tip, a stock he dislikes that he predicts will take a beating. "I don't want you to short it or anything," he says. "Just notice how it does." Sure enough, that stock goes down. Now you're hooked. He calls again, and this time he has an investment opportunity for you, a sure-thing stock that he strongly urges you to buy. You've been mightily impressed by his uncanny feel for the market, so not only are you willing to invest, but also invest heavily. You send him $10,000 or $25,000 to buy the stock he suggests. He doesn't buy it. He vanishes with your money.

How was he so insightful about those two predictions? He really wasn't. He starts with a base of potential dupes. Say he identifies a hundred people. With his first call, he tells half of them that the stock he chooses will rise, and the other half that it will fall. It has to do one of the two, and so fifty people are going to be impressed with his prediction. Those are the fifty he calls back with his second prediction; again, he tells half a stock will go up and half that it will decline. He's left with twenty-five who have seen him be right two out of two times, more than enough to fleece.

PONZI SCHEMES—TRIED AND TRUE

One of the oldest investment tricks of scam artists is the notorious Ponzi scheme, a persistent type of securities fraud where money is never invested in anything, but instead the cash that comes in from new recruits is used to pay obligations to earlier investors. And the scam artist, of course, always keeps a healthy apportionment for himself. The fraud is named for Charles Ponzi, who defrauded Italian-Americans in Boston in 1920 with a scheme purportedly involving postal reply coupons, which were prepaid return postage used in foreign correspondence.

Ponzi schemes come in every imaginable variety. You read about a new one almost every week, and they always promise enormous returns for short periods of time. I have to laugh at how absurd the pitches are. Some years ago, a group of companies in Kansas touted a get-rich-quick investment involving fungus. They sold investors "Activator Kits" that would grow fungus cultures. Most people wouldn't imagine that much of a market for fungus exists, but these promoters convinced people that these cultures would be bought by a cosmetic manufacturer they were connected to for a hefty profit. To remove any worries, the promoters "guaranteed" the profit. Something like twelve thousand people in thirty states sent in their money. As in any Ponzi scheme, the promoter strung investors along by paying early ones with money from subsequent recruits, always keeping some for himself. Eventually, the pool of investors is exhausted and most people end up getting nothing back from their investment.

In another case, a young busboy in Ohio offered what seemed like an enterprising idea. He advertised for investors to pool their money with him so he could buy rock concert tickets in bulk. Then, as he explained it, he would scalp the tickets at substantial markups. Everyone had read about rock concerts selling out in one hour and people camping out in line for days, so why not? He rounded up more than $7 million from almost three thousand people. But he never bought any tickets. His Ponzi bubble burst like all the others, when he ran out of new investors to pay off the earlier ones.

A ONE-WAY TICKET TO MELCHIZEDEK

If there were a country where only scam artists lived, it would have to be the Dominion of Melchizedek. It's a gorgeous, postcard-perfect tropical island in the South Seas. It's got a heavenly climate. There are no taxes. There's little banking legislation. The government is very much hands-off. Dozens of banks operate on the island, and you can open your own for a few thousand dollars. Or that's how it's billed.

Only don't go looking for Melchizedek on a map. It doesn't exist. It's a fictitious country created for the purpose of perpetuating investment scams. A convicted con artist apparently thought it up in 1990, naming it after the "righteous king of peace" in the Old Testament, and it's been at the center of a web of conspiracy for scam artists and their swindles ever since.

Law enforcement authorities have warned of innumerable scams connected to Melchizedek. In one typical scheme, investors were told that they would get a return of more than 300 percent in a matter of months, by investing in financial certificates arranged by a Melchizedek bank. Hundreds of investors in the United States contributed more than $1 million. But it was nothing more than a Ponzi scheme. So were other scams involving Melchizedek government bonds, Melchizedek certificates of deposit, and bonds of St. Charles University, a fictitious college that supposedly existed in the fictitious country. Frauds involving the mythical country have sprouted up in cities throughout the United States, as well as England, Australia, Hong Kong, and China.

The men behind the scams are often ex-convicts, including a guy who went to jail for trying to fix a horse race in Australia by dyeing a horse.

After his release from jail, he was appointed "governor" of Melchizedek territories in the Pacific.

PYRAMIDS OF DENIAL

One of the oldest forms of securities fraud is the pyramid scheme, an overture laced with promise that is never fulfilled. It's been around so long, I would think that everyone is aware of it and no one would dare fall for one. Nonetheless, people do every day. Pyramid schemes are similar to Ponzi schemes, but they are hierarchical and promise profits based on investors recruiting others to join the program, not from any product or investment. The variations are endless, but the principle is identical. They typically start with a chain letter or e-mail inviting you to make a small investment in order to reap immense rewards. Chain letters themselves aren't illegal, but they're a nuisance and I wouldn't advise anyone to bother with one. When a chain letter asks you to send money, it crosses the border of illegality and becomes a pyramid scheme.

Many conventional pyramid scams ask you to send a small amount of money, five dollars or ten dollars, to five other people who have already signed on. You're provided with a list of participants, and instructed to eliminate the top person and add your name to the bottom. Everyone in between moves up a spot. Then you're advised to send copies of the letter to everyone you can think of. When new people join, each of them will send you money. Since the chain grows at an exponential rate, the money coming to you should grow to a staggering level.

"Gifting clubs" or "giving" programs seem to be the pyramid scam of choice in recent years. Here, the money you're asked to send is termed a "gift". And it's often strongly pointed out by promoters of these gifting clubs that whatever money you subsequently receive is tax-free, because the Internal Revenue Service (IRS) doesn't tax gifts under $10,000. In actuality, the IRS defines a gift as something given without expectation of getting anything in return, which is not the hook in these scams.

The way many gifting clubs work, participants, typically women, are invited to join a club of some sort. One club was called "Ya Ya Sisterhood" and another was the "Businesswoman's Networking Club." Some of them promote a charitable connection, and they usually claim they have the approval of the state Attorney General. To join, you have to make a cash gift to the highest-ranking members, those at the top of the pyramid.

In one gifting scam, participants gave cash gifts of $100 in order to move up through levels named freshman, sophomore, junior, and senior. There were ultimately six steps to the program, and the required investment ranged from $100 to $4,000. Once you completed the six levels, you needed to make a gift of $7,850 and you would receive a tax-free payment of $62,800.

Another gifting tree went by the name, "The Dinner Club." This group was organized according to the four courses of a dinner party. Eight people known as appetizers filled the bottom row of the tree. They had to pay five thousand dollars apiece to the dessert person at the top of the tree, in order to be seated at the dinner party. As new people joined, the bottom rung advanced to the "soup and salad" level and on to the "entrée" rung before themselves becoming a "dessert". If you became a "dessert", meaning if enough people were suckered in to elevate you to that level, you were expected to receive $5,000 apiece from the latest crop of eight participants: $40,000. That's a $35,000 profit on their original gift. Most people, though, never get to the top and lose all their money. The crooks, though, always arrange themselves in the tree so they ensure that they get their gifts.

When you examine the mathematics, a pyramid scheme looks awfully tantalizing. If you're asked to send $10 to ten people, that's $100 you're out. But you add your name to the list of participants and get ten new people to join. They each send you $10, and you're back to even. If each of those ten recruits ten additional people, then the next level of the pyramid has a hundred people. You collect $1,000. Another round produces a level of a thousand people. You get paid $10,000. The next level grows to ten thousand people. You collect $100,000. One more round brings you $1 million.

The trouble is that in order to perpetuate these pyramids, more and more people must be recruited to feed those at the upper levels. Once the supply runs out, the pyramid collapses and the people at the bottom are out their money.

And that's why pyramids have to fail. The supply of people is not infinite. By the time one pyramid scheme reaches its eleventh level, assuming each new participant recruits ten new people, it will have exhausted the entire population of the planet. Plus, no new wealth is being created. Any money that one participant earns, another participant loses.

HANDICAPPING DEATH

The way a criminal thinks is, whenever something becomes popular as a legitimate investment is when it becomes a perfect candidate for an illegitimate investment. A case in point is what are known as viatical investments. The word viatical comes from the Latin *viaticum*, referring to the money and supplies given as traveling expenses to a Roman official when he departs on a journey. Viatical investments are, in essence, death futures.

A couple of decades ago, the idea was hatched of allowing terminally ill people a way to get money from their life insurance policies while they were still alive, to pay for needed medical expenses or to take one final vacation with loved ones. The way they work is that brokers arrange for investors to buy a certain percentage of the death benefits of the policies of the terminally ill, always leaving 20 percent or so for the estate. Someone given a year or two to live might have a $200,000 policy. For an investment of $100,000, investors might buy $150,000 of the face value. The ill person would get immediate cash and if he died soon, the investors would get a handsome return. How good a return, of course, depended on how well they managed to handicap death.

Policies that get viaticated are generally those of people diagnosed with AIDS, fatal cancers, and other catastrophic illnesses. It's something of a ghoulish business, but investors look on it as helping a sick person. And, of course, there's money to be made.

As recently as 1990, this was a small, arcane business, amounting to less than $100 million of viaticated policies. But it has grown to more than $1 billion. Consequently, criminals have taken notice and moved in, so much so that law enforcement authorities say viatical investment scams have become rampant, and rank among the top-ten investment frauds being perpetuated.

Viatical scams take different forms. Some are as blatant and straightforward as selling policies to investors on fictitious patients, or else selling legitimate policies over and over again. One viatical investment firm collected $115 million in investor money, but only $6 million was used to buy life insurance policies. The promoters found various other uses for the balance of the money. They bought twenty-five homes, thirty-four luxury cars, two helicopters, three motorcycles, and several boats.

Other viatical scams are more elaborate and cheat both the insurers and the investors. In these cases, scam artists recruit terminally ill people and help them obtain life insurance by lying on the applications about their condition. This process is known as "clean sheeting." It doesn't work with large policies, because medical exams and blood tests are required, but insurance companies skip those details with small policies.

These clean-sheeted policies are then immediately sold to investors. They're also called "wet ink policies," because the ink on the contract is barely dry when the policy is sold. Once the policyholders die, these policies are often contested as being fraudulently obtained, then canceled. Crooks in California obtained clean-sheeted policies amounting to more than $11 million before being caught.

Investors have been snapping up these policies. Thieves pitch them as a safe, high-return investment. And they add that the investor is engaging in a humanitarian act, providing desperately-needed funds to the terminally ill.

The truth of the matter is, even legitimate viatical investments are risky. Chronically ill people may live a lot longer than was estimated, cutting down on the yield to investors. New AIDS drugs and other medical breakthroughs work against your investment. In addition, many of these policies are term policies, and if the person outlives the term, there is no death benefit at all. An eighty-four-year-old California woman invested $85,000 in the hope of receiving $139,000 when a policyholder died. The expectation was that he would die within a year. Years later, he was still alive. He might outlive the woman.

WHAT TO CHECK

Given that you can lose money on these investments if they're legitimate, imagine what it's like to invest in a scam. There are some telltale signs to

be aware of, though none are guarantees. Many legitimate viatical investments are themselves insured, but no viatical scam is, at least not with
any real insurer. A legitimate investment will allow you to pay your
money to a reputable escrow agent; a scam artist won't. If it's on the up
and up, the purchase agreement should state that the insurance policy
you're investing in is past the period of contestability, generally two
years from when it was issued. The best protection of all, though, is only
to deal with a reputable and large viatical broker. And realize that you're
making a speculative investment no matter what.

THE MYTH OF THE INNER CIRCLE

There's a natural inclination by people who don't have a lot of money, to
think that people who do have a lot are privy to investment opportunities
that are closed to them. It wouldn't surprise them to learn about clan-
destine securities peddled only to the rich, for suspicions about the government and financial institutions are widespread. Criminals are well
aware of such suspicions, and exploit them with appalling consequences
for investors.

In the little town of Mattoon, Illinois, population 18,500, a sixty-six-
year-old retired electrician started an investment fund called the Omega
Trust and Trading, which promised a fifty-to-one return. According to
the fund's literature, its head was an international banker who had
worked for Fortune 500 companies (when investigators interviewed
him, he couldn't quite remember their names) and was one of a handful
of people in the world who had the know-all and ability to conduct secret
multimillion-dollar trades.

It was not an original thought. Many investment schemes tell people
there's a secret banking system in which "prime banks" and the wealthy
participate. The returns are well beyond what ordinary people can realize, as much as 70 percent a week. Ordinary people can share in the
bounty if they pool their money and allow someone connected to this
system to invest it for them.

A common pitch is, you're asked to put money into a trust account
backed by a guarantee (often fake) from a "prime bank," "top-100 world
bank," or "top-25 European bank." You're told that your money will be

leveraged to buy prime bank instruments, which can generate enormous returns. In fact, your money goes offshore, never to return. Another pitch: You pay the promoter a fee in return for a promise that you will be "leased" a much larger sum of money to invest in prime bank instruments at great interest rates.

In the Omega trust, investors were told their capital would be invested in foreign bank debentures. Money was invested from all over the country, as well as from Australia and China. The mastermind of the scheme laundered the money by handing out interest-free loans to local residents and by starting businesses.

There is no such thing as bank debentures. No secret banking system exists, at least not on this planet.

One of the giveaways in Mattoon was when residents began buying new trucks and cars and opening businesses, even though some of them had jobs that paid minimum wage. In the fall of 2000, law enforcement authorities charged a group of Mattoon residents and others with perpetrating an investment scheme that duped more than ten thousand people throughout the world of more than $12.5 million.

RED FLAGS

Obviously, you just can't be too careful with your money. Before you part with it, look at all investments on the SEC database to be sure they're registered. All American companies with more than five hundred investors and $10 million in assets must be registered with the SEC. Smaller companies have to file information with the SEC, or with the state securities regulators where they're based. To check if a broker is licensed, go to the website of the National Association of Securities Dealers Regulation. One thing the Internet has done is made it easier to do research on a company, so go to reliable sites and check analyst reports. There's no need to rush into something.

I would never invest in anything described as "risk-free" or "guaranteed," particularly offshore investments. It's an automatic red flag if the promoters say the state Attorney General has approved it. Check with the Attorney General's office and find out for yourself. Take note of how you're asked to pay. If a broker wants your bank account number to speed things along, forget it. If you're told to send money to a P.O. Box or some-place offshore, forget that, too.

The bigger the promised return on an investment, the higher the likelihood that it's a scam. But just because a return is reasonable, don't assume the investment is real. One of the biggest scams in recent years is fraudulent promissory notes sold to the elderly. Promissory notes are a short-term debt companies use to borrow cash. Con artists exploit a loophole in securities laws that exempt some nine-month promissory notes from regulatory scrutiny. The con artist starts a marketing firm and recruits unwitting insurance agents to sell the notes. Unlike so many investment schemes with their 100-percent-plus returns, these typically promise 9 to 12 percent interest, enough to attract a conservative in-vestor without arousing suspicion. They're touted as risk free and bonded by foreign insurance companies, which usually are fake. The local agents are often known and trusted by the investors, and are fooled as well by the con artists. Eventually, investors get notices that the com-pany behind the notes has gone bankrupt and that's the end of their in-vestment.

A good rule of thumb is, the more exclusive something is positioned to be, the more likely it's trouble. Once-in-a-lifetime opportunities are usually once-in-a-lifetime chances to lose all your savings. If something is billed as getting "imminent" regulatory approval, that means it will never get regulatory approval. When I see ads on television promoting some new elixir or wonderful product, the words that always tell me it's a scam are "not sold in stores." Think about it, if someone has a great product, why wouldn't he sell it in stores? The reason is because there's something fishy about it.

It's the same with investments. When I hear about an investment op-portunity and am told it's not available through brokerage houses, then that's criminal-speak for "only available through con artists." If you really could make 100 percent on your money in a week, you wouldn't need to find out about it in an e-mail from a total stranger. You can bet Merrill Lynch and Paine Webber would be selling it, too.

[STEALING **YOUR SOUL**]

or Michelle Brown, there was life before identity theft and then there was life after identity theft. Life after was a torment.

Brown, the young California woman I began this book with, couldn't understand why someone had stolen her identity. Why her, of all people? And how did it happen? One day she told her property manager about how someone was going around using her name and her credit, and that the police and credit bureaus had mentioned that identity thieves are sometimes a relative or someone you know. Did she have sisters who might have something against her, a close friend with a grudge? She had been offended. She had two sisters, but she knew neither of them was the one, and no friend was that malevolent.

Her property manager listened to her carefully, and then he said, "I know who's doing it."

Or he thought he did. A woman he knew vaguely, Heddi Ille, had a history of committing credit fraud. He figured it might well be she.

The police looked into it, and they concluded that it was indeed she. Heddi Ille was a woman in her early thirties, about five-foot-seven and weighing 200 pounds. She looked nothing like Michelle Brown. And she was mixed up with drugs. For months, the police pursued her, but it wasn't until more than a year after she had stolen Michelle Brown's identity that she was caught, and then it was only because someone had turned her in. To add to the insult, Ille was arrested under the name Michelle Brown. On her record, that name was listed as an alias.

Heddi Ille had never met Michelle Brown, and knew virtually nothing about her. Like most crooks, she had wanted one thing: a vehicle that allowed her to steal. One day, she had happened to sneak a look at the rental applications at the apartment complex where Michelle Brown was living, and had chosen her information to work with. She was a similar age, and that may have been all that mattered. That one document was all it took.

In their arrogance, thieves rarely consider the consequences for the victim. They're in it strictly for the money. For a long time, Michelle Brown wondered if she would ever become whole again. It required a massive effort for her to get her credit straightened out. "Identity theft leaves a very dark and filthy cloud around the victim," she said. Even now, she is extremely circumspect. She has eliminated all but one credit card. She refuses to write checks when she buys something in a store. She worries that her name will be on a list of delinquents and she'll be hustled off by security guards. Her mail comes to a private mailbox. For her birthday, a friend gave her a shredder, and she now shreds all credit card solicitations and any other material containing personal information.

She carries around official papers that confirm who she is, though she's afraid to travel overseas, particularly to any third-world country, out of fear she'll be mistaken for the jailed Ille and be imprisoned. Even in this country, she shudders every time she sees a police car. She drives safely under the speed limit and never forgets to signal if she's making a turn. The last thing she wants is to be stopped and somehow mistaken for the other Michelle Brown, the one who ought to be in prison.

Two years after she started, Heddi Ille was convicted of perjury, grand theft, and possession of stolen property, though, as so often happens, not of identity theft. Not only was she initially booked as Michelle Brown, but also when she sent letters to friends from federal prison she wrote that name on the return address, until the real Michelle Brown objected. She felt Heddi Ille had stolen quite enough from her for long enough.

THE CRIME OF THE FUTURE

I've saved identity theft for last, because I'm convinced it's the crime we have the most to fear going forward. To my mind, identity theft is the crime of the future. And I think of it as the mother of all scams, because it steals everything, a person's very being.

In so many ways, it's the scariest and most seductive white-collar crime of all, and we've barely scratched the surface. It'll probably be ten years from now before identity theft is in full swing, but we've already seen its striking escalation. At the beginning, someone stole your identity because he wanted to get a credit card in your name. These days, he'll say, wait a minute, I'll get a car loan in your name, wait a minute, I'll get a mortgage in your name, wait a minute, I'll assume your entire identity and get a job in your name and you'll have to pay the taxes.

Physical attributes like DNA are unassailable and unique to you. No criminal can steal them. But we have become the various numbers that have been assigned us, and, with modern technology, that makes us increasingly vulnerable. All a thief has to do is get hold of a single set of digits—your bank account, your credit card number, or especially your Social Security number—and he can take up residence in your life. If you have great credit, he suddenly has great credit.

Anyone with a Social Security number can become a victim—even a newborn baby or someone who's dead. Some identity thieves can pick your pocket for months and even years before they're detected. They know just how to keep a victim's suspicions at bay.

A Virginia couple was puzzled when a friend said he couldn't reach them because their number was unlisted. They knew they were in the book, but figured it was a lame excuse for not inviting them to a party. When they heard the same thing from another friend, they checked with the phone company. It said the husband had asked that the number be unlisted. They shrugged that off as some mix-up, until they got a call to verify that they wanted their new Visa card mailed to a different address.

They had ordered no card and had no new address. They quickly got a credit report and found that someone had already obtained another card in their name and a cash advance against it. Then they got it. The identity thief had requested that their number be unlisted so creditors couldn't reach the couple.

Back in my criminal days, I engaged in identity theft of sorts. To be precise, I guess you could say that I engaged in profession theft. Although I never took on the identity of a living person—I never believed in crimes against the individual—I became a generic copilot and a lawyer and a doctor, among my guises. To pull this off took cleverness and perhaps a bit of a diabolical mind. You needed to be able to turn on the sweet grease and charm. I had to learn about airplanes and pilot lingo. I had to learn the law. I had to learn a suitable amount of medicine. I had to create believable IDs and acquire uniforms. I had to be able to stay cool under pressure.

Today, the identity thief can do what I did, and so much more, hiding behind numbers. No one tests his knowledge.

Identity theft is so new that it wasn't even formally recognized as a specific federal offense until 1998, when, prompted by growing evidence of the crime, Congress passed a law, the Identity Theft and Assumption Deterrence Act. And though I speak of it as the crime of the future, because of its potential, it already is an enormous problem. I've heard estimates that half a million Americans a year are victims.

Identity theft is a chilling crime because the perpetrator is innocent until proven guilty, while the victim is guilty until he proves himself innocent. Until you've been caught up in this crime, you can't imagine how hard it is to prove that innocence. It can be a nightmare of unimaginable proportions to get your credit and your identity back, if you ever fully do.

A HORSE OF MANY COLORS

The approaches taken by identity thieves vary a great deal. Most often, the thief is a total stranger, someone you've never seen and who has never seen you. But not always. A woman living alone in her own house took on a roommate for some added income and companionship. The roommate lived with her for nine months. She was amiable enough, and always paid her rent on time. One day she told the woman she had gotten a job offer out West, and so she would be moving. The woman was happy for her, and thought nothing of it.

A few weeks after the roommate left, the woman got a call from a bank officer. The officer said the bank had received her most recent mortgage payment, the same as always, but it hadn't received the payment for her second mortgage. "Second mortgage?" the woman said. "What second mortgage?" It seems that the roommate, by rummaging through the woman's utility bills and other mail, had acquired enough information to pose as her and take out a second mortgage, the money that got her out West.

One identity thief managed to accumulate more than one hundred thousand dollars in credit card debt, take out a federal home loan, buy several homes, motorcycles, and handguns, all in the victim's name. But that still wasn't enough for him. He would also call the victim and hector him, taunting him that he could buy all he wanted for as long as he wanted, and he would never be caught. Finally, the thief filed for bankruptcy—naturally in the victim's name. At the time, identity theft wasn't a federal crime, so when he was finally caught the criminal served a brief sentence for making a false statement to purchase a gun. There were no other repercussions. He made no restitution to the victim. Meanwhile, it took the victim and his wife four years and fifteen thousand dollars to restore their credit and reputation.

A Milwaukee man used a stolen Social Security number to obtain additional identity documents and set up an array of fraudulent accounts. Under his new identity, he got a job at the Wisconsin Supreme Court then stole eighty thousand dollars of computer equipment from the court. While he worked there, he also collected Social Security benefits because he claimed he was disabled and unemployed.

Con artists will steal the identities of the prominent as well as the unknown. The FBI came across two Memphis thieves that said they stole the identities of six leading executives, including the chief executive officers of Lehman Brothers, Coca-Cola Enterprises, and Hilton Hotels. Two of the impersonated executives had recently died.

Before they were caught, the hucksters managed to order $730,000 worth of diamonds and Rolex watches over the Internet. They did this by having the credit card companies and banks change the billing addresses of the executives to hotels in the Memphis area, then ordering the merchandise to be shipped to the hotels. The attraction of using the names of wealthy executives was their credit was so good. When the jewelers that sold the goods contacted American Express about putting purchases of $40,000 on cards purportedly belonging to the executives, there was no hesitation. They got immediate approval.

IT'S AS EASY AS . . .

How does someone steal your identity? With the sharp erosion of privacy, the variants are endless. A thief doesn't have to break into your home or hold you up. It all gets done on the sly.

One straightforward method is "shoulder surfing," which I told you about earlier with ATM fraud. A thief watches you as you punch in your credit card or calling card number at a pay phone. Or he eavesdrops on your conversation as you give your number to a hotel or merchant. From that one number, he gathers other information about you and is on his way.

Another popular approach is "Dumpster diving." Crooks root through your garbage cans, trash bins outside stores, or on street corners, or communal Dumpsters. They toss away the chicken bones and old newspapers, and collect credit card statements, bank statements, phone bills, copies of checks, or anything that shows your name and address. These records are gold to an identity thief.

How many times have you gotten a stack of "preapproved" credit cards in the mail and, already being flush with cards, simply tossed the envelopes in the garbage without ripping them up? The identity thief thanks you very much. He goes ahead and attempts to activate the cards, often with success. Some credit card companies require that you activate a new card only from your home phone number, but this precaution hasn't been universally adopted. A few years ago, federal authorities broke up the Trash Ring, a group that stole more than $10 million in dozens of states, largely by recovering cards and account information from Dumpsters and trash cans.

If you've been divorced, the transcript of your case, bulging with financial and credit information that you had to reveal, as well as your Social Security number, is public record. A thief need only stop in at the courthouse and scribble down what he needs.

One recently-arrested identity thief, a low-level employee at a drug company, happened to come across a box of personnel records for three dozen former employees. The box was lying in a storage closet of the company. When you've got a criminal mind, a box like that is a bonanza. The thief, along with several accomplices, used the records to get credit cards, buy more than one hundred thousand dollars of goods, and rent three apartments in other people's names. For a time, they lived a joyous life that was way beyond their own means.

Employees at a New Jersey car dealer used the company access to the three leading credit bureaus—Equifax, TransUnion, and Experian—to find strangers with good credit histories, some of them living as far away as Alaska, and then opened up credit card accounts in their names.

A group of Nigerians established themselves in the industrial cleaning business. They had trucks. They had uniforms. They had cleaning supplies. In due course, they had customers. They would come into the company offices at night and clean the place. And they did a beautiful job. But they cleaned the offices of more than grime. They knew how to get at personnel records and would copy Social Security numbers and whatever other useful information they found and steal identities.

And there are endless come-ons that thieves use to sucker people into unwittingly divulging personal information. Not long ago, some fairly provocative flyers suddenly popped up in scores of black communities throughout the South and Midwest. They were stacked on tables in churches, stuck in windshield wipers of parked cars, and tacked to the bulletin boards of senior citizen centers and nursing homes. The headline on them read: "Apply for Newly Approved Slave Reparations! Claim $5,000 in Social Security Reimbursements!" The body of the flyers said that blacks born before 1928 could be eligible for slave reparations under the "Slave Reparation Act." Those born between 1917 and 1926 could apply for Social Security disbursements because of a "fix" made in the Social Security system.

Obviously, a burst of good fortune like this was something that would pique a person's interest, and it seemed plausible. There had been a lot of talk and press about proposed legislation that would pay reparations to black people. But the whole thing was nothing more than a trap set by a ring of identity thieves.

In the Atlanta metropolitan area, a man posing as a jury administrator from the local court system would call people, mostly the wealthy and business owners, and say, "You've forgotten to respond to a summons for jury duty and face a penalty. I can straighten it out right now for you, if you just give me some basic information." Assuming they had overlooked the summons, or it had gotten lost in the mail, the victims would unquestioningly provide their birth dates, mother's maiden name, and Social Security numbers.

Thieves are not at all squeamish about stealing the identity of someone that recently died and resurrecting him for the purpose of spending money. This works because credit bureaus usually don't learn about someone's death for six to twelve months. A common place to locate the personal information necessary here is an obituary. People fail to realize the abundance of material contained in an obituary, particularly that all-important mother's maiden name so universally used for identification means.

One pair of identity thieves stole hundreds of thousands of dollars from some two-dozen victims in seven states. Most of them were selected out of *"Who's Who in America,"* which in its biographies of prominent Americans gives birth date, place of birth, mother's maiden name, and home address, sufficient information for them to request birth certificates and establish credit.

Recently, there was a run of identity thefts involving admirals of the U.S. Navy. One admiral complained that he had been a victim, then another admiral and another—ultimately seven in all. It happens that the thieves were digging out personal information on them from the Congressional Record. It routinely lists all the data a criminal needs to become a military officer.

One woman had her identity stolen by her boss. She was hired by the owner of a magazine publisher, and, in filling out her employment application, divulged the usual supply of personal information. Little did she know that her employer had ruined her own credit in the past and couldn't even get a credit card. Within months of the woman being hired, her boss took out a card in her name and began using it. Who would suspect their boss? But literally anyone can be after your identity.

Years ago, I predicted that once there was a shake-out among all the dot-com startups, criminals would step in and offer to buy up the assets of failed e-commerce companies. Why would they? To get their databases, rich with personal information on customers, including credit card numbers. I bet it's already happened. When it was functioning, the retailer Toysmart.com assured its customers that their personal information would never be shared with anyone. When it went bankrupt in May 2000, that promise went out the window. It took out ads offering to sell its database. Fortunately, a subsidiary of Walt Disney agreed to pay it fifty-thousand dollars to destroy the information before it got into the wrong hands.

NUMBERS FOR SALE

The Internet has become the equivalent of an electronic shopping mall for identity thieves. Endless websites have sprung up that sell personal information. One site, docusearch.com, will retrieve a person's Social Security number for a mere forty-nine dollars. How long will it take? One day.

It's all perfectly legal. They buy this information from the nineteen states that use the Social Security number for the driver's license number. They'll go to a driver's license bureau and ask, how many Social Security numbers do you have? They're told, 1.3 million. Okay, can we buy them for $8 a number? They'll approach one of the major health insurers, with millions of numbers, and again buy them for $8 apiece. They buy numbers from collection agencies and credit bureaus, and they resell the information for $49 a number. The only thing you have to type in is the person's name and the last-known state you believe he or she lived in, and within seconds, up comes the Social Security number. I've gone online a number of times to test it out and they've never not had the number. Try it yourself.

Another website, netdetective2000, brags that it will find out "everything you ever wanted to know about your friends, family, neighbors, employees, and even your boss!" All you do is take your mouse and click on the information you want. It's a complete dossier: the person's name, date of birth, Social Security number, address, bank, bank account number, what stocks he owns, who his stock broker is, where he works, what he does at his job, what he makes, if he has children, his children's names, their ages, and their Social Security numbers.

If you're wondering who's telling them all this information, you are. When you bought a camera, there was a warranty card, and attached to that warranty card was a consumer questionnaire. Are you married, divorced, single, separated? Are you a doctor, a lawyer, a professional, a technician, or other? Do you earn between $20,000 and $50,000, $50,000 and $100,000? Do you bank at a bank, credit union, savings bank, or mutual fund house? You went right down the list answering all their questions and all of that information went into a data base. Then they turned around and sold it, and the next thing you know, it was being used against you.

There's another website that advertises on TV called 1-800–SEARCH. They say they can find out if someone has a criminal record. Then, in a lower tone of voice, they say, "or fifty other things." And the fifty other things are just about anything you would want to know about someone. It's unbelievable what they know about people—practically everything down to their favorite doughnut and how they did in third-grade social studies—and I'm talking about ordinary people who think they live a private life.

Everything is for sale. A Social Security number is $49. A birth certificate is $79. A driver's license is $90. Or if you want an entire package of documents just for the purpose of assuming someone's identity, it goes for $2,000.

I went to the doctor the other day. It wasn't my regular doctor, but an oral surgeon I hadn't seen before. The receptionist had me fill out a new patient questionnaire, then she needed my Blue Cross card, which contains my Social Security number, and my driver's license. She made copies of both, and all this was deposited in the doctor's file. That receptionist, or the next receptionist, could easily sell that information.

In a number of instances, low-paid hospital orderlies have stolen and sold patient information. Medical records are especially attractive to identity thieves, as they contain your Social Security number, date of birth, and even a physical description. Some criminals, to help their fraud, have actually undergone plastic surgery to look more like their victim. Imagine that—someone who not only says he's you but looks like your twin!

A twenty-three-year-old New Jersey man was surfing the Internet at the public library one day, when he happened across the site of the Securities and Exchange Commission (SEC). There, he discovered a database of disclosure forms that public companies must file with the regulatory body. These forms contained the names of company officials and their Social Security numbers. Using the name of an official of a company who was thirty-four years older than he, he managed to gain approval for a $44,000 car loan from a major bank. He got a quote for car insurance from an online broker, then used a fraudulent MasterCard to pay for the policy. To actually buy the car, he needed proof he was the executive, so hc picked up a fake birth certificate and W-2 form from a website that sold fake credentials. Then he went and bought a new Prelude. Because the executive had such excellent credit, the thief actually negotiated better financing from the car dealer than he had from the bank.

SHADOW OF YOURSELF

Once your identity has been stolen, everything doesn't just return to normal. You'll find yourself inconvenienced long after the culprit is caught. After she had been victimized, one woman put an alert with the credit agencies that if anyone applied for credit in her name, she had to be called and told about it. Months afterward, she was shopping for Christmas gifts and decided to buy her son a TV at an electronics store. Since you got a discount if you opened a credit account with the store, she tried to do so. The salesperson went to process it, only to come back and tell her, he was sorry, he couldn't extend her credit because there was nobody at her home when he called. Of course not, she said, I'm here talking to you. Well, he said, your credit bureau says I have to speak to you at your home before I can issue credit. So she had to drive home, take his call, then drive back.

A highly placed corporate executive had his identity stolen by a major drug dealer. These days, when the executive travels overseas, he has to carry an official letter with him that states that he is not the drug dealer. He'll always have to carry that letter with him. His life has been irrevocably changed.

I read about a woman writer who had her Social Security number stolen while she was living overseas. Using her name and number, the thief ordered telephone service in California, ran up thousands of dollars in bills, and then vanished without paying them. When the writer returned to the United States and applied to rent an apartment in New York, the landlord found she had a negative credit rating and wouldn't rent her the apartment. She had to take a sublet while she tried to get to the bottom of things.

She filed a police report. The cop who handled the case said he got an average of four complaints of identity theft a day. Not until she threatened to sue the collection agency charged with her case, did the agency relent and agree to correct her rating. It told her, however, that it might take as many as ninety days before her credit was restored at the national credit agencies. Four years later, the unpaid bills remained on her rating. She was still unable to rent an apartment.

An elderly woman went into the hospital for cancer surgery. While she was there, her daughter hired some cleaners because she wanted her mother to come home to a perfectly clean house. Not long afterward, the mother got a succession of calls from collection agencies. The cleaners had found enough personal information in the house to steal her identity. During the long ordeal of trying to straighten the mess out, the woman lost her house.

There was a man who worked as a salesman in a department store in California. One day he had his wallet stolen, which contained his driver's license, Social Security card, and military ID. Seven months after his wallet was stolen, he was called into the firm's main security office and told he had been caught shoplifting at one of the chain's other stores. He had done no such thing. In fact, he had been working in his usual store at the time. He even produced a letter from his boss confirming that. Still, he was fired. The man who had stolen his wallet had assumed his identity and done the shoplifting.

He got other jobs, but was dogged by the crimes of the thief. He'd apply for a job, a check would be done on him, and he'd be told, sorry, his services weren't needed. He later found out from the police that the rap sheet in his name included arrests for shoplifting, burglary, and arson. He went bankrupt. He lost his home. Finally, he legally changed his name to distance himself from the identity theft, but his life is only a shadow of what it once was.

As you can see, the financial losses are only part of what the victim suffers. Often, it's the emotional toll that's most debilitating. For even if the thief is caught and prosecuted, it can take months and even years of painstaking effort to recover the good credit standing that was so quickly destroyed. At a Congressional hearing on identity theft, one victim recounted her ordeal after being victimized for $110,000: "We had to submit handwriting samples to twenty different merchants; we had to submit notarized documents and affidavits. It was like filling out our tax return twenty times with twenty different sets of instructions."

AN IDENTITY THEFT QUIZ

As with all fraud, prevention is the most valuable step you can take against identity theft. Police are not sufficiently trained to investigate this crime and jurisdiction is often a problem, since you may live in Maine and the person who stole your identity may be in Idaho. I understand the FBI has been speaking to local police departments and asking them what they want from the FBI. The police tell them that they can handle local drug problems really well. What they can't handle is if someone walks in and says he or she is a victim of identity theft. So they want the FBI to get more involved in white-collar crime, and I think you'll see that start to happen in the years to come. Right now, though, it's hard to get the attention of the FBI, because it usually requires a threshold of $250,000 before it tackles a fraud case. There are 13,500 FBI agents in the world, and only 3,000 are assigned to financial crimes.

The best thing you can do is to count on yourself. I devised a little identity theft quiz to give yourself to determine how susceptible you are.

Each of the following statements represents a possible avenue for ID theft. If any of them describes you, add the points to your score.

☐ You receive several offers of pre-approved credit every week (5 points). Add five more if you don't shred them before putting them in the trash.

☐ You carry your Social Security card in your wallet (10 points).

☐ You don't have a post office box or a locked, secured mailbox (5 points).

☐ You drop off your outgoing mail at an open, unlocked box or basket (10 points).

☐ You carry your military ID in your wallet at all times (10 points).

☐ You don't shred or tear banking and credit information when you throw it in the trash (10 points).

☐ You provide your Social Security number whenever asked (10 points). Add five points if you provide it orally without checking to see who might be listening.

☐ You're required to use your SSN as an employee or student ID number (5 points).

☐ Your SSN is printed on an employee badge that you wear (10 points).

☐ Your SSN or driver's license number is printed on your personal checks (20 points).

☐ You are listed in a *Who's Who* guide (5 points).

☐ You carry your insurance card in your wallet and it contains your SSN or your spouse's SSN (20 points).

☐ You haven't ordered a copy of your credit report for at least two years (10 points).

☐ You don't believe that people root around in your trash looking for credit or financial information (10 points).

If you scored more than 100 points, you're at high risk. You should purchase a paper shredder, become more security aware in document handling, and start to question why people need your personal data. If you scored 50–100 points, your odds of being victimized are about average, though higher if you have good credit. If you scored 0–50 points, my congratulations. You've got a high security IQ. Keep up the good work and don't let your guard down now.

A NEED TO KNOW BASIS

As you can see from that test, to steer clear of identity thieves you really need to adopt a "need to know" approach to all of your personal data. In the future, someone had better prove to you why he must have any of your information before you give it to him.

You have to memorize key numbers like PIN numbers and Social Security numbers, rather than carry cards around with you. If you're making a phone call that requires you to convey personal information, don't do it at an open booth where someone can overhear you. Ever more popular cell phones are even more susceptible to eavesdropping, so be especially wary of passing along personal information on a phone.

It makes sense to keep a minimum number of credit cards, so that it's easier to keep track of them. But no matter how many or few you have, make sure you check all of your financial statements carefully. So often we take a quick look at our credit card statements, and if the total seems about right, we just pay the bill and toss the statement aside.

If you don't receive a monthly statement for any account, that could be a tip-off; call immediately and ask about it. If you're notified that your statements are being mailed to another address that you haven't authorized, tell the financial institution what has happened and that someone may have accessed your account. And maintain your own records of your spending. Then if you need to dispute a transaction, your records will support you.

When you order checks, refrain from putting any additional information about yourself—your address, middle name or initial—on them, since checks can be lost or stolen. I'm amazed at how many people put their Social Security number on their checks. You ask them why and they say they do it because they're always asked for the number when they cash a check in the store, so they want to make it easy. Sure, for crooks.

Have your personal information deleted or kept private in listings such as phone books, driver and motor vehicle records, direct marketing solicitation lists, and listings by the major credit reporting bureaus.

When you're traveling, even for brief periods, you should have your mail held at the post office or ask a friend or relative to collect it for you. Mail letters with checks and personal information in them from an office mailbox rather than from your home mailbox. My feeling is the post office ought to ask for ID before granting change of address requests, and they should at least send a card to the current address to confirm the request. Meanwhile, you should write your credit card companies and advise them not to accept any notification of an address change without verifying the change with you.

Don't ever enter unfamiliar contests or sweepstakes, and I'm not crazy about entering even familiar ones. Any information you give to contests or charities may be sold or reproduced in ways you can't imagine. If you get an unsolicited call offering you a credit card or prize but wants personal data like your Social Security number, ask for a written application. If they say they can't do that, hang up. If they do send you an application, look it over carefully and make sure that it's from a recognizable organization.

I recommend that everyone get a shredder. I have one in my house and one in my office, and I shred everything that goes into the wastebasket, no matter how innocuous it seems, but especially everything that contains any personal information about me. I assume what appears unimportant to me could be very important to a criminal. You should assume the same.

And you really have to stay on top of credit agencies, because for the most part, they take what's fed to them and don't verify it. And it's all one-sided. Anyone who's a client can send in something bad about you. But you never get asked about it. That's the biggest problem I have with how they work. They don't get anything from you; they get it all from who you buy stuff from. In addition, my impression is the error rate of these agencies is horrible. My name is Abagnale. That's hard to mess up. But what if your name is Smith or Jones? A problem Joe Smith has may end up on Jim Smith's credit report. And it'll take a Dream Team of lawyers to get it off.

You ought to get your credit report several times a year and thoroughly check it. Michelle Brown told me she gets hers every month. There are services like Credentials Services International and Inquiry Notification

Service that cost about $25 a year, that send you a collated credit report from the principal agencies—Equifax, Experian, and TransUnion—three times a year. Also, when anyone applies for credit in your name, they send you a letter notifying you. I belong to two of these services, so in case one misses something I'm hoping the other one will catch it.

Unfortunately, it's almost impossible to get a fraudulent entry removed from your credit report. Even if you prove something is wrong, they don't delete it. They put an asterisk next to it, and a note at the bottom that says the customer disputes this entry. How helpful.

In 2000, the government approved a bill that allows consumers and businesses to sign contracts online and know that their e-signature is just as binding as one in ink. This gives electronic signatures the legal weight of paper signatures, and makes a contract binding immediately. The law took effect on October 1, 2000, and already we have completely electronic mortgages available. I'm against the whole idea. I fear this will lead to still more identity theft. It's too easy to steal or duplicate a e-signature. Who is going to have the signature? Who is going to store it? How will they protect it?

Under the law, a digital signature could take any of a number of forms—a string of numeric code that is encrypted or thumbprints or irises read by special devices. Because of identity theft, many Florida banks currently require non-customers to leave a thumbprint when cashing a check, and some large banks in the Orlando area are taking thumbprints from all new customers. California, Texas, and Georgia are among states that require drivers to give a thumbprint or fingerprint when they come in to get or renew a license. But if you give your thumbprint to an organization and they put it in a database, and someone breaks into that database, as they will, and steals that thumbprint, are you going to go out and get another thumbprint?

Additionally, there are ways to get around fingerprints. Impostors will coat their fingers with airplane glue, which, when it dries, covers the skin's ridges and makes for useless fingerprints. Or they'll spray their fingers with clear lacquer or hair spray, which congeal in the grooves and spaces of your prints.

Maybe a system that scans your iris sounds impenetrable. But what if someone knocks you unconscious and then holds your eye in front of the scanner? What if someone points a gun at you and forces you to sit in front of the iris device?

The idea of giving thumbprints or copies of your iris raises the hackles of many people, myself included, because of the privacy issues involved. We could end up with a national identity system that tracks and monitors people, and that gets me to wondering if the cure is worse than the disease. The Internet has already irrevocably altered the nature of privacy and turned us into a culture of transparency. Why make it worse?

You have to decide at what point is your personal security coming at the expense of your privacy. E-signatures mean that you're giving out more of your identity. You have to ask why? Why do you have to surrender something else just for convenience? Why can't you wait to overnight something? Why does everything have to be instant? Instant breakfast. Instant camera. Instant mortgage. You can't wait a day? It has to happen in ten seconds?

WHAT THE GOVERNMENT CAN DO

If we're serious about combating identity theft, it's going to take a federal solution, beginning with changes in the way the Social Security number is used and the free and easy access businesses have to people's credit reports. At the moment, the Social Security number has been ruined. When I was growing up, no one knew your Social Security number. Now it's everywhere, and so it's worthless for identification purposes. But it's still being used that way.

There are steps everyone can take to safeguard their own number. Whenever someone asks for your Social Security number, you ought to make sure you know who you're dealing with and that they absolutely need the number. If a business requests it to confirm your identity, ask if there's an alternative number that can be used.

But these steps aren't enough. The government needs to pass a law that will clamp down on the use of the Society Security number as a uniform identifier. A measure that would do just that has been introduced in Congress and defeated several times. It won't help me or anyone my age or older, but it will ensure that the number will be more secure for my kids and grandchildren.

We also have to force credit-granting agencies to require more identification and buttress their credit card policies. We need to restrict the
selling of personal information by credit bureaus, state and federal
agencies, and marketing firms. The federal government has to take this
issue up—and soon. If it doesn't do something, so many people are going
to be running around claiming to be the same person that we won't know
who anyone is.

WHERE THERE'S A WILL

In a world of wolves and sheep, I look on myself as a sheep dog. I try to
make people think about things. Fraud, as it continues to grow, will really
test our society. It will challenge us to decide, what is enough? We've
come to tolerate fake luggage and an occasional fraudulent purchase assigned to our credit card, but now, with our very selves being stolen, it's
getting to crunch time.

Twenty years from now, there will be entire categories of frauds that
the best science fiction writer couldn't even imagine, just as decades ago
no one would have imagined Internet fraud because no one imagined the
Internet. As more and more gets done electronically, I think you're going
to see an explosion in crimes where there's no human face you can identify. There won't be any line-ups; who are you going to line up—e-mail
addresses?

There is an undeniable appeal of scams. I understand that better than
anymore. When you discover the way they work, it's like being taken
backstage at a magic show. But scams aren't entertainment. They gnaw at
the fabric of society and ruin lives. We have to look at white-collar crime
as being every bit as dangerous as armed robbery.

Every day, I hear of a new fraud. I recently learned of a famous soccer
star who never uses his real signature to sign checks or business documents, because so many people know his autograph that thieves are continually forging his signature. So he signs checks by printing his initials.
He's lost his signature to crooks.

I was talking to a highway patrol officer in Tennessee who specializes
in automobile fraud, and he told me there are roughly twelve million
classified ads run each year in the United States for used cars. About

three-quarters of them are believed to have been placed by "curb-stoners." Curbstoners are con artists who buy wrecked cars and cosmetically repair them and sell them as if they're new, or else buy leased vehicles that are only a couple of years old, but have maybe a hundred thousand miles on them. They roll back the odometers to 29,000 miles and sell them for much more than they paid. They're called curbstoners, because if you reply to their ad, they make a point to come to you and sell you the car at the curb outside your house or office. The curbstoners are slick. They always have a story: "I just had my first kid, so I've got to sell this Honda so I can get a station wagon." It's become an enormous problem, because the titles are forged and it's nearly impossible to trace these crooks. And when I hear that three-quarters of the classified ads for cars are frauds, that tells me there's no way I'd ever respond to one.

I read about con artists who scan newspapers for pleas for lost dogs. They call up the distraught owners and tell them they found their pet while they were traveling and took it home with them before learning of its true home. They offer to ship the dog to them as soon as they wire the airfare. People are so ecstatic to hear that their dog has been found, they send the money.

On and on it goes, but we don't take it seriously. Once, as a TV demonstration, I went up to a cashier at the express lane of a Kroger's store and used the store manager's driver's license to cash a check. The store manager obviously had a different name. I'm white. He was black. Why bother to ask for an ID if you're not going to take it seriously?

We sorely need stiffer penalties and real jail time for white-collar criminals. I think it's ridiculous that if I have drugs on me I'll get five or ten years in prison, but if I rip off $20 million I'll probably get probation. I'll give you another solution that I've been propagating without success for years. Companies don't care enough about losses from fraud, because in most cases they can deduct a hundred percent of their losses from their income taxes. By lowering their taxes, that write-off cuts their losses significantly. Well, if Congress passed a law that said from now on businesses can deduct only half of their losses from fraud, companies would wake up and get much more proactive and fraud would decline. But who's going to introduce such a bill, and who would vote for it?

One thing we can do without any legislation is teach our kids better ethics. I was talking with a top executive of a big company, and he told me something his teenage son confided to him. After school lets out, his son gathers with his friends in the parking lot and they take out their homework sheets. They look at the math assignment and divvy it up: "You do problems 1–5, you do 6–10, I'll do 11–15. And then we can e-mail each other the answers." It was a sobering discovery. The executive told his son, "You get an A for creativity and a D for not learning anything."

I heard about high school students at another school who were counterfeiting tickets to the annual school musical and selling them. There's hardly any money involved—but it's the thrill of the scam. Otherwise decent kids are being corrupted, because it all seems so harmless. It's not about lawbreaking as much as beating the system. Everyone wants to get from point A to point B as quickly as they can.

I'm not trying to overly scare you. I don't like habitually skeptical people, and it's not my desire to breed a country of paranoid citizens. But in this land of milk and money, I've seen too many cons, come across too many phony products, watched too many slick pitches. Once you become a victim of a major fraud, your whole life changes. It takes the average person two years to clear his or her credit once it's been corrupted. And it may take a lifetime to recover from the emotional anguish.

You need to start looking at the world the way I do, with eyes wide open. Ask me when fraud will stop and the answer is never. Fraud has become one of the constants of life. To bet against its continued inroads without action being taken is a sucker's bet. We have to decide: Do we take control of fraud, or does fraud take control of us? We have the might to reduce fraud. The question is, do we have the will?

[FRAUD **RESOURCES**]

Abagnale & Associates
(800) 237–7443
www.abagnale.com
Secure document consultants.

American Association of Retired Persons (AARP)
(800) 424-3410
www.aarp.org

A national organization of people fifty years or older, it offers tips on fraud prevention, especially crimes against the elderly.

Association of Certified Fraud Examiners
(800) 245-3321
www.cfenet.com

An international organization dedicated to fighting fraud and white-collar crime through prevention and education.

Authentication News— Reconnaissance International
www.reconnaissance-intl.com
(303) 779-1096—U. S.
44 (0) 1784-497008—England

A trade publication that covers counterfeiting of all manner of products and news of the latest techniques to combat counterfeiting.

Boise Cascade
(503) 224-7250
www.bc.com

A leading manufacturer of secure check stock. Although individuals or companies can't buy checks from them, printers can purchase their paper.

Consumer Federation of America
(202) 387-6121
www.consumerfed.org

A national organization of consumer groups, it dispenses information on fraud and acts as an advocate for consumers.

Council of Better Business Bureaus
(703) 276-0100
www.bbb.org

An organization of local Better Business Bureaus, it provides consumer assistance and tries to arbitrate consumer complaints. It can direct you to your local Better Business Bureau.

Council of Foundations
(202) 466-6512
www.cof.org

A nonprofit association of grantmaking foundations, this is a good resource to check on the legitimacy of a charity or foundation.

Department of Justice—Identity theft:
www.usdoj.gov/criminal/fraud/idtheft.html

This government website offers tips on how to prevent identity theft and lists recent cases.

Equifax
Credit Bureau
(800) 525-6285 (report fraud)
www.equifax.com

One of the three major credit reporting agencies. It furnishes information and tips about preventing fraud.

Experian
Credit Bureau
(888) 397-3742
www.experian.com

Another of the major credit reporting agencies that also offers suggestions on guarding against fraud.

Federal Bureau of Investigation (FBI)
(202) 324-3000
www.fbi.gov

The Justice Department's law enforcement arm, the FBI investigates federal crimes and offers tips on fraud prevention and lists of the most common frauds.

Federal Deposit Insurance Corporation (FDIC)
(800) 934-FDIC
www.fdic.gov

The entity that insures bank deposits and promotes sound banking practices. It provides consumer assistance in dealing with banking matters under federal consumer protection laws.

Federal Trade Commission (FTC)
(202) 326-2222
www.ftc.gov

The government agency that enforces many federal antitrust and consumer protection laws. The place to go for information, or to file a complaint for things like loan scams, telemarketing fraud, charity scams, phone swindles, lottery scams, and identity theft.

Immigration and Naturalization Services
(202) 514-1900
www.usdoj.gov

The government agency that deals with immigration matters, and the place to go for information about passport fraud and scams involving fraudulent immigration documents.

InterGov
(317) 823-0377
www.intergov.org

An international organization devoted to safe use of the Internet, it offers on-line scam prevention services.

Internal Revenue Service (IRS)
(800) 829-1040
www.irs.ustreas.gov

The IRS provides information on tax frauds and investigates tax crimes and related financial crimes. Companies can report embezzlers to the IRS and consumers can file complaints about fraudulent or deceptive charities with the agency.

The Nilson Report
(805) 983-0448
www.nilsonreport.com

The leading trade publication covering consumer payment systems.

Office of the Comptroller of the Currency
(800) 613-6742
www.occ.treas.gov

The agency of the Department of Treasury that regulates national banks and deals with fraud involving these banks.

Privacy Rights Clearinghouse
(619) 298-3396
www.privacyrights.org

A nonprofit consumer information, research, and advocacy program that offers tips on how to safeguard your personal privacy. It deals with issues like Internet privacy, identity theft, telemarketing, medical records, workplace privacy, among others.

Product & Image Security Magazine
(847) 318-1524
www.eci-internationa.com/ pismain.html

The official journal of the Label and Tag Security International Association, it covers the problems of counterfeiting, retail theft, and product tampering, along with solutions to these threats.

Securities and Exchange Commission (SEC)
(202) 942-8088
www.sec.gov

The agency that regulates sales of securities and public offerings, it can answer questions about security transactions and verify the registration of securities dealers and firms.

Social Security Administration
(800) 772-1213
www.ssa.gov

The government agency that administers the Social Security program, it offers a hot line to report fraud involving your Social Security number and furnishes information on identity theft.

Standard Register Company
(800) 755-6405
www.standardregister.com

An industry leader in providing secure documents. It offers a wide array of security features that will protect your documents against fraud. It services many of the leading Fortune 500 companies.

TeleCheck
(800) 835-3243
www.telecheck.com

The leading check acceptance company, it offers electronic check conversion, check guarantee, and check verification services to businesses and merchants.

TransUnion
Credit Bureau
(800) 680-7289
www.transunion.com

One of the three major credit reporting agencies. It disseminates an array of fraud prevention information.

United States Federal Reserve Bank
(202) 452-3946
www.federalreserve.gov

The body that regulates state banks that are members of the Federal Reserve System.

United States Secret Service
(202) 406-5708
www.treas.gov/usss

The government agency charged with investigating counterfeiting of U.S. currency and safeguarding the payment and financial systems of the United States. It also investigates financial institution fraud, computer fraud, and cases involving false identity documents, among other crimes.

ACKNOWLEDGMENTS

More people helped in the preparation of this book than I could name, but I would like to express my thanks to all those who shared their stories of fraud with me, especially Michelle Brown, Jim Fowler, the director of security at Unilever, E. King Rogers, the vice president of loss prevention at Target, and Lewis Kontnik, the publisher of *Authentication News.*

I would also like to express my appreciation to the three thousand companies and associations that have given me the opportunity to work with them over the years, most notably the Standard Register Company, Profit Recovery Group, Morgan Stanley Dean Witter, Citibank, Bank of America, U.S. Bank, Key Bank, Union Bank of California, First Data Corporation, Data Business Forms-Canada, and Leigh-Mardon-Australia.

I owe a debt of gratitude to all of the outstanding and truly dedicated men and women of the Federal Bureau of Investigation, who have supported me over the last twenty-five years and have afforded me the great privilege of being able to teach at the FBI Academy and assist with programs in the field offices of the bureau throughout the United States.

For their editorial wisdom, my thanks to Charles Conrad of Broadway Books, as well as to his assistant, Becky Cole. I could not have written this book without the help of Sonny Kleinfield, and I thank him for all his assistance and encouragement.

Most important of all, a special acknowledgment to my wonderful and loving wife, Kelly, who has supported me and loved me for more than twenty-five years.

ABOUT THE AUTHOR

The author of *Catch Me If You Can,* **Frank W. Abagnale** is now one of the world's most respected authorities on counterfeiting and secure documents. For more than twenty-five years he has worked with the FBI's Financial Crimes Unit. Today he teaches at the FBI Academy and for the FBI's National Academy, a program that instructs local, state, and federal law enforcement agencies nationwide. The founder of a secure-document corporation based in Washington, D.C., he lectures regularly worldwide. He lives in the Midwest with his wife and three sons.